GREAT LIVES OBSERVED

Gerald Emanuel Stearn, *General Editor*

EACH VOLUME IN THE SERIES VIEWS THE CHARACTER AND ACHIEVEMENT OF A GREAT WORLD FIGURE IN THREE PERSPECTIVES—THROUGH HIS OWN WORDS, THROUGH THE OPINIONS OF HIS CONTEMPORARIES, AND THROUGH RETROSPECTIVE JUDGMENTS—THUS COMBINING THE INTIMACY OF AUTOBIOGRAPHY, THE IMMEDIACY OF EYEWITNESS OBSERVATION, AND THE OBJECTIVITY OF MODERN SCHOLARSHIP.

L. JAY OLIVA, *editor of this volume in the Great Lives Observed series, is Professor of History and Vice-Dean, University College of Arts and Science, New York University. His publications include* Russia in the Era of Peter the Great, Peter the Great, *and* Misalliance: A Study of French Foreign Policy in Russia During the Seven Years War.

GREAT LIVES OBSERVED

Catherine the Great

Edited by L. JAY OLIVA

*I have authority to demand silence
of this generation of Russians,
but what will posterity say?*

—NICHOLAS KARAMZIN

A SPECTRUM BOOK

PRENTICE-HALL, INC., ENGLEWOOD CLIFFS, N. J.

To my parents, with love and gratitude

Contents

v

4

Catherine's Government 61

Catherine's Accession Manifesto, *61* Catherine's Decree on the Deportation of Serfs to Hard Labor, *62* Catherine's Manifesto against Pugachev, *62* The Charter of the Gentry, *64*

PART TWO
CATHERINE THE GREAT VIEWED BY HER CONTEMPORARIES

5

Dashkova: Her Majesty's Inventive Spirit 69

6

Countess Golovine: Maternal Solicitude 79

7

Radishchev: The Groans of Thy Subject People 87

8

Buckinghamshire: The Remains of a Fine Woman 95

9

Shcherbatov: Arbitrary Worldly Principles 101

10

The French Embassy: Paternity of Grand Duke Paul 111

18

Introduction

Catherine the Great is one of the most fascinating and intriguing women in history. Her reputation as lover and conqueror, and her well-carved image as a luminary of the cultural enlightenment of the eighteenth century are the main parts of this image. But there is something even more spectacular about the achievements of this extraordinary woman—it is seldom remembered that she was not a Russian; that even after she had come to Russia, it was very unlikely that she would rule; and that even after she won power, it was predicted that her reign would be short and disastrous. That Catherine the Great was born a minor German princess and was able to raise herself to the imperial throne of Russia is itself a stupendous achievement, even in the century of stupendous achievements in which she lived. As a story of political planning and personal success, then, the life of Catherine the Great is well worth the study.

Catherine was an amazing woman as well as a successful politician. She harbored high passions, great talents, a deep capacity for self-deception, a sex life of astonishing activity, a sophisticated understanding of foreign affairs, a love of military adventure, an ability to command and overawe those whom she led, and a wide interest in the cultural and intellectual affairs of her century.

It has been charged against Catherine that she was a dilettante in almost everything that she undertook: that her interest in the cultural affairs of Europe was merely a disguise to convince Europe's leading intellectuals to become propagandists for her Imperial policy of expansion into Poland and Turkey; that her politics were always the politics of expediency, and that the true problems of Russia languished under her administration; that the conquests of Poland and of Turkish territory that glorified her name in her own day were really useless conquests that distracted Russia from the main business of internal development; and that her own mind was so steeped in deceit that no tinge of sincerity ever colored any of her actions. There is a great deal of truth to many of these charges, but these truths only highlight the fascination of her character. After all, in a century replete with coups d'état, she ruled the Russian empire for thirty-four years; and, during one of the longest reigns in the history of the Russian throne, she effected its most substantial territorial conquests. Perhaps the greatest testimonial to her political genius is the popular image that she has left behind. She identified herself so completely with Russian interests that few, if any, Russians bothered to remember that she was a German

1

by birth, a Protestant by upbringing, and a European cosmopolitan by preference. She left Russia far different than she found it; Pushkin said that Peter gave Russia a body but that Catherine gave Russia a soul. The imperial boundaries and the cultural life of Russia were substantially expanded during her reign and, regardless of the amount of credit scholars assign to her personally, popular history has already made its judgment.

Catherine was born Sophia-Augusta in the port of Stettin on the Baltic, into a minor princely family of Prussia that made its living in service to the King. The primary business of the house of Anhalt-Zerbst, and the specific pursuit of her mother, was the proper marriage of the children; the family into which Sophia-Augusta was born prided itself on the marriage of its offspring into the royal houses of Europe.

Russia had such an opening in the person of its heir to the throne, Grand Duke Peter of Holstein, the nephew of the reigning Empress Elizabeth of Russia. This boy, himself a convert to Russian Orthodoxy, had been taken into Russia from his native German duchy and put under the protection of the Empress in order that she might have an heir. In 1743, when Grand Duke Peter was sixteen, Empress Elizabeth went in search of a wife for him. Catherine's mother, the Princess Joanna, did her best to convince King Frederick of Prussia that her daughter would make an excellent match and would provide a possibility of cementing Prussian influence at the Russian court. In 1743, the Empress Elizabeth decided upon Sophia-Augusta, then fifteen years old, and she undertook her journey into Russia.

When Catherine met her future husband, she was entirely unimpressed by him. He was weak, egotistical, unbalanced, ineffective, alienated from the Russian court, dedicated to his former duchy in Holstein, and entirely Lutheran and German, both in attitude and in preferences. Catherine was converted to Russian Orthodoxy and received the name by which she is known to history. After a year of instruction and education at the Russian court, she was married to Grand Duke Peter, in 1745, and became Grand Duchess Catherine of Russia.

Catherine's life as Grand Duchess from 1745 to 1762 was an extraordinarily difficult one. She was never on good terms with the Grand Duke Peter; he was deficient as a husband, and peculiar as a person. She was, in every way, alone, and it was clear to her that she would have to make her own way and find her own place at the Russian court. She immediately began to learn the Russian language, to convince the court of her good will, to be inoffensive, and to cultivate Russian manners. She studied the rituals of Orthodoxy and was careful always to reflect respect for her new religion. In these activities, she contrasted sharply with her husband, who made no attempts to adjust himself to the traditions, the environment, or the religion of the Russian court.

The years as Grand Duchess also provided one of the most intriguing personal mysteries surrounding the Grand Duchess Catherine and the Romanov Dynasty. The reader will have an opportunity to judge the evidence for this mystery himself. Catherine, in her memoirs, indicated that her years as Grand Duchess included a number of extramarital affairs; the first, with a member of a noble Russian family, Serge Saltykov, immediately preceded her first pregnancy. Catherine's memoirs imply that Saltykov was the father of the Grand Duke Paul. If this were true, the implications for the future were clear; the Romanov Dynasty had come to an end and a German Princess and a minor Russian nobleman had produced a new line of rulers for Russia. (This was an extremely important fact for the nineteenth century, when revolutionaries questioned the validity of the Russian autocracy and wished to attack its roots among the populace.) Since that time, historians have indicated that, in looks and behavior, the Grand Duke Paul very closely resembled the Grand Duke Peter, his legal father. On this basis, some historians have discounted the evidence of the memoirs and have insisted that the Grand Duke Paul was, in reality, the son of the Romanov house. The reader himself may wish to sift the evidence.

Whatever the truth of the paternity of the Grand Duke Paul, there is no doubt that Catherine began her series of liaisons with men of the court during her tenure as Grand Duchess, and that Serge Saltykov was one of these liaisons. Catherine also had an affair with the secretary to the British Ambassador, a Pole named Stanislas Poniatowsky, who is presumed to be the father of her daughter, Anne, and who, in 1764, was installed as King of Poland by Catherine's troops.

Despite her careful planning, Catherine became involved, several times during the 1750s, in court cabals that jeopardized her status in Russia, and confirmed her own devious nature. Her alienation from her husband and the frequent and increasingly more serious illnesses of the Empress Elizabeth forcefully reminded her of the precarious condition in which she lived. It was clear to Catherine that if the Empress should die and her husband should ascend the throne, the duration of her stay as Empress-Consort might be short. Catherine would not have liked the convent life that was the usual fate of disgraced Russian royalty. It was her purpose, then, to find allies and to convince them that some other alternative was preferable to the future rule of Tsar Peter III. During the 1750s, she found allies in the Grand Chancellor of Russia, Alexei Bestuzhev-Riumin, and in the British Ambassador to Russia, Sir Charles Hanbury-Williams. The most consistent scheme that echoed through Catherine's secret planning was the idea of substituting Catherine's son, Grand Duke Paul, for Grand Duke Peter on the throne, and the placement of Grand Duchess Catherine as Regent; in this way, Catherine could insure that not only would she survive, but also that her power would be greatly increased.

The Empress Elizabeth of Russia died in 1762. Much to the surprise of the Russian court and foreign ambassadors, Grand Duke Peter ascended the Russian throne as Tsar Peter III with no difficulty; the standard coups d'état of the eighteenth century were not repeated, and Peter, with all the confidence that his German upbringing and his lack of political awareness could provide, became Emperor. He remained Emperor for six months.

Historians know very little of the real details of Catherine's seizure of power in 1762. Her own account, in a letter to Stanislas Poniatowsky, and the accounts of observers, such as the British Ambassador and her friend Princess Dashkova, provide some information. What we do know is that the Grand Duke Peter undertook a program that was bound to alienate influential people at the Russian court. Historians formerly assumed that Peter's difficulties stemmed from programs that were unpopular with the Russian populace: his alienation from the Russian Orthodox Church, his Prussian behavior, his diplomatic and military reversal of alliances. It seems clear now that the alienation of the population had very little to do with the troubles of any of the Russian emperors and empresses in the eighteenth century; more important was the attitude of the Guards Regiments and the bureaucracy in St. Petersburg toward the programs of the ruler. Peter's mistakes were primarily in reasserting the power of the crown, of contesting the power of the bureaucracy and the gentry over state policy and over local government, and especially in pursuing a war that was to his own dynastic interest but not to the interests of the Russian civil service or officer corps. Peter, who was more interested in his German holdings in Holstein than in Russian foreign policy, was intent on waging war against Denmark for the recovery of Holstein's lost lands. The idea of Russian troops being sent from the capital to a far distant war, in which the officers and the Russian bureaucracy had no interest, was unpopular with the Russian court, and it was no accident that the coup d'état against Peter III took place the day before the Guards Regiments were due to leave for a Danish war. The Guards Regiments strongly suspected, probably justly, that Peter III was trying to destroy the effectiveness of the guards as a political instrument in the Russian capital, while, at the same time, pursuing his own German dynastic ambitions.

Catherine certainly took advantage of the unpopularity of Peter III's programs during 1762. The events and results of her coup d'état indicate that she carefully organized support among the officers of the Guards Regiments surrounding the capital, and that she won the support of significant bureaucrats in the Russian government who feared the emergence of a government program alien to the developments since Peter the Great. In June 1762, while Peter III was saying farewell to his mistress at his summer palace in the country, Catherine, roused by her supporters, made a tour of the Guards Regiments collecting assistance, marched into St. Petersburg, and was hailed at the Church of Our Lady of Kazan and at the Winter Palace as the new Empress.

Careful planning was evidenced by the gathering of the higher clergy to give her their blessing at the Cathedral, and by the assembly of representatives of the bureaucracy and the members of Senate at the Winter Palace who conferred the imperial power upon her. It is also important to note that the idea of a regency for the Grand Duke Paul, Catherine's son, was set aside in the midst of the coup d'état and that Catherine herself came to power in her own right. Emperor Peter III surrendered to Catherine, was interned at a summer palace at Ropsha, and died in a "drunken scuffle" that everyone in Europe accepted as an assassination. Historians need to know a great deal more about this most adventurous phase of Catherine's life.

The early period of Catherine's reign was essentially a time of testing. The prevailing characteristics of this period were insecurity, ignorance, and enlightenment. Catherine suffered from a sense of insecurity on the throne; she worried over those who had helped her to the throne, especially the Guards Regiments, and was always on guard against a counter coup and against attempts to limit her authority. In fact, many of the reforms that were introduced in this period were simply designed to pacify opposition, to allay a fear of despotism, and to provide a period of time in which Catherine could secure the throne against those who might plan to use her instability against her.

At the same time, Catherine came to the throne with scant information about the empire over which she ruled. She knew little of the administrative mechanisms or financial conditions of her empire, so she began to take an active role in government. She also undertook a series of tours: in 1763 she visited Rostov and Yaroslavl, in 1764 the Baltic Provinces, and in 1767 she traveled along the Volga River.

Yet while Catherine worried about the security of her throne and about her lack of knowledge of her own empire, she also began to govern with the only intellectual tools she had available—the principles of her own eighteenth-century education. It was Catherine's intent to begin the reorganization of her empire with the reform of the law code. Catherine followed the tradition of eighteenth-century thinkers who believed that if the proper and natural laws of a society could be uncovered and promulgated, then ultimately the citizens of the society forced to live in conformity with those laws would themselves be perfected. Catherine began to write an "Instruction" to those whom she would charge with the reform of the law. "Two years did I read and write," she later recalled, and the contents of the "Instruction" testified to Catherine's scope of reading. She began with an assertion that Russia was a European state, in order that the teachings of the *philosophes* would have application there. She felt that Russia needed an autocracy because government by one was better than government by many, and because Russia was too vast for any other form of government. The heaviest influence in the "Instruction" was that of Montesquieu, followed by Beccaria's *Crime and Punishment*.

Catherine created a Legislative Commission to consider her "Instruction" and to recodify the laws of Russia. The Commission met from 1767 to 1768. She invited representatives from the chief institutions of the state, from the cities and towns, the gentry, the state peasants, the non-Slavic peoples, and the Cossacks. Although this was a most representative assembly for its time, it still ignored the bulk of the enserfed Russian peasantry and the parish clergy. There was a total of 565 representatives in the Legislative Commission, who each came armed with lists of grievances and instructions. This Legislative Commission, which opened in 1767, held 203 plenary sessions before it was prorogued at the beginning of the Turkish War, late in 1768. Several subcommittees continued to function as late as 1774. The Commission failed to draft a new law code but it did leave an historically useful record of the primary grievances and concerns of Russian social groups. The "Instruction" and the Commission were doubly important; first, as evidence of Catherine's own state of mind, and second, as lessons that served to identify for Catherine the very narrow extent to which implementation of enlightenment ideals was practical in her society. The early experiments and experiences of her reign indicated that the guiding principles of her education might face substantial difficulty in their application to the government of a vast and intricate empire.

The second decade of Catherine's reign produced several practical problems of some magnitude. In 1774, the Turkish War reached its peak and Catherine's empire was struck by the Pugachev Revolt. The needs of war and a popular rebellion against the structure of the Empire tended to confirm Catherine in her reliance on the traditional forces of the society to preserve internal order and to maintain the strength of both her foreign policy and her vast armies. The importance of war and of revolt tended to push into the background her vague attempts to incorporate general European principles and, at the same time, convinced Catherine that domestic order was a high priority.

In 1774, Catherine, therefore, turned to a reform of provincial institutions. Provincial administration after Peter the Great had fallen into chaos, and the aristocracy demanded a voice in the management of provincial affairs since large numbers of the nobility were returning to their lands after 1762. This was especially evident in 1767, in the demands of the nobility at the Legislative Commission, and grew in intensity after the struggles of the Pugachev Revolt in 1773-74.

Catherine issued the Guberniia Reform in 1775, creating new institutions for the government of the provinces. She replaced Peter's large provinces by fifty smaller ones and divided and rationalized the operations of provincial administration. Aside from these institutional rearrangements, the Guberniia Reform also made provisions for aristocratic influence in local affairs. This direction was continued in the Charter of the Gentry in 1785, a charter designed to guarantee the privileges accumulated by the aristocracy during the eighteenth century, and to provide an incorporation of their interests for the defense of their privileges. The Charter of the Gentry recognized the nobles as absolute owners of both their lands and their serfs, it exempted them from the personal payment of taxes, it provided them judgment only by their peers, it exempted them from all punishment except by formal court sentence, it exempted them from corporal punishment, and it confirmed their right to own industrial concerns and operate fairs and to exploit their own mineral and forest resources. The gentry in each province were further entitled to form a Corporation of the Nobility with special rights to petition the crown, to nominate governors and members of the governing board, and, in general, to meet, discuss, and defend the rights of the gentry in the provinces.

There has been extensive debate as to the real impact of the Charter of the Gentry. Older historians have insisted that the document was simply the culmination of Catherine's surrender of local authority to the gentry rather than a contesting of their power, which might endanger her throne. In that view, the Charter was the last chapter in the history of a century-long rise of the Russian nobility, a sign of Catherine's failure to rule over all the citizens of her empire, which makes a mockery of her claims to "enlightenment." More recently, however, historians such as Professor Leo Gershoy, have emphasized the cementing of absolutism: "Exactly like the Prussian Junkers, the Russian gentry had become unpaid civil agents of the crown on the manorial estate, rich in prerogatives and privileges and devoid of power to challenge the monarchy."[1] Professor R. R. Palmer has provided an even more progressive view of this development: "What this amounted to was an attempt, in an enormous agrarian empire that rested on unfree labor and on military force, to map out an area of personal status, liberty, and security for those persons without whom the empire could not carry on. . . . For some to have a sphere of rights due to special birth or rank was doubtless better than for no one to have any assured rights at all."[2] From this perspective, the roots of Russia's nineteenth-century intelligentsia were planted in the Charter.

[1] Leo Gershoy, *From Despotism to Revolution: 1763–1789* (New York, 1944), pp. 116–17.
[2] R. R. Palmer, *The Age of the Democratic Revolution: The Challenge* (Princeton, N.J.: Princeton University Press, 1959), pp. 403–404.

Catherine acquired her title of "The Great" largely in terms of her accomplishments in foreign affairs. She was operating within the value system of her century, which judged the achievement of monarchs largely in terms of the expansion of their frontiers and the magnitude of their military victories. Judged in these terms, Catherine was a great success. When compared with the great monarchs of her century, none of her royal colleagues even approached the territorial acquisitions and the military conquests that Catherine the Great was able to boast. The most successful areas of Catherine's concern were in Poland and Turkey. In these areas, Catherine followed in the footsteps of her predecessors on the Russian throne, and proceeded to settle two of the great problems of Russia's political inheritance: the position of Poland, and the acquisition of the Black Sea coast.

The problem of Russia and Poland was an ancient one. In the time since Peter the Great (1682–1725), Russia had more and more effectively interfered in the affairs of the Polish commonwealth, and it was Catherine's intent that Poland be established as a satellite state on the Russian frontier over which Russia would exercise predominant control. The commonwealth of Poland was one of the largest in Europe, comprising twelve million people in almost three hundred thousand square miles of territory, but the Polish monarchy was in the waning days of its power. The Kingship was bounded by limitations of geography, politics, religious division, and constitutional checks. It was Catherine's plan, and the plan of her advisors, to establish Russian influence in Poland in order that the Russian border might be secured, that Russia might insure its participation in European affairs, and that the constant drain of peasants who fled to Polish territories might be ended. It is a popular historical view that Catherine's Polish policy was an unqualified success, that in the years between 1764—when she established a Polish nobleman as her candidate for the Polish throne—and 1795, the last partition of Poland, that Catherine absorbed almost half the territory of Poland under the administration of the Russian empire. In fairness, however, it must be noted that Catherine's policy of maintaining sole influence in Poland was not a success; her victories, especially against the Turks, tended to provoke European powers into believing that Russia's influence was expanding too far too fast, and that she could not be allowed to dominate the affairs of Europe. As a result, Catherine was ultimately forced to partition Poland and to share Polish territories with her Prussian and Austrian neighbors. In 1764, Catherine held sole influence in Poland, but by 1795 Polish territory had been divided among three great European powers and Russia had lost her autonomous buffer state. Still, in the eyes of history, the partitions of Poland were the great territorial aggrandizements of the century, and the bulk of the territory belonged to Catherine the Great.

Against her Turkish neighbors in the south, Catherine was even more successful. Since the seventeenth century, rulers in Moscow had aimed at the Black Sea coast and the fertile lands that lay along it; in the days of Peter the Great, expeditions were made down the rivers toward the Black Sea, but no real success was achieved. It was only in the reign of Catherine the Great that Russian armies successfully drove the Turks from the southern lands of Russia and opened the vast territories to Russian colonization. It was, therefore, not simply a political victory of Russia over the Turks, but an economic and social victory as well; these lands provided areas of expansion for the Russian gentry and the accompanying institution of serfdom. As a result of the conquest of the northern littoral of the Black Sea, Russian pressure on Turkey inevitably grew; access to Europe from the southern lands for the productive grain crops that would grow there necessarily involved Russia in passage of the straits. Therefore, Catherine's military conquests helped to determine the future of Russian-Turkish relations and to establish the outlines of the "Eastern Question" of the nineteenth century.

Catherine was not content to base her claims to glory on military conquests and political success alone. She emerged as one of the great patrons of the European Enlightenment. Her own education and disposition made her a prime figure of the cultural environment of the eighteenth century. She was a correspondent of Voltaire, of Frederick the Great, of Grimm, and of Diderot, and Catherine's letters are revealing evidence of her character; her exchanges with the great figures of her day reveal her natural belief in autocracy, her innate conviction of the correctness of her decisions, a tremendous need for recognition of her wisdom and her virtue, a consistently manipulated pressure on the great minds of Europe to provide her with a good press, and a very forceful and rather serviceable French style. It should be no surprise, therefore, that Catherine was the editor of a series of satirical journals and the author of several plays written in the French classical style. She was interested in education, and there was a notion prevalent in the eighteenth century that character was the primary aim of education, and that the control of environment could produce a new breed of men. It was the judgment of her advisors, therefore, that boarding schools were best, and that it might be possible to take elements from the lower orders of society and produce an enlightened "middling order of persons." Education, in this sense, was Catherine's answer to Russia's need for a middle class; elements of the lower classes were to be educated, away from their environment, and a new breed of Russian bourgeoisie was to be produced. Catherine ultimately effected a school reform in 1786, but, in competition with war needs, the money provided for these schools was never enough.

Catherine was the patron of the arts and sciences at her court. She developed the Academy of Sciences under her close friend, Princess Dashkova, and the Academy of Arts under her advisor and friend, Ivan Betskoi. While writers were patronized at the court, the most exciting literary surge in the reign of Catherine came not from those whom she patronized, but from those whom she opposed. Alexander Radishchev (1749–1802), a student of Voltaire and of Rousseau and an admirer of the American and the French Revolutions, wrote his *Journey From St. Petersburg to Moscow* in which the prevailing evils of Russian society, notably autocracy and serfdom, were clearly unveiled. The *Journey* was published in 1790, and Alexander Radischev was arrested; his death sentence was commuted to ten years exile in eastern Siberia. More opposition emerged in the figure of Nikolai Novikov (1744–1818) who issued a series of satirical journals between 1769 and 1774, and who was very active in the organization of charitable work inside the Russian empire, Novikov's work made him suspect to Catherine who considered him guilty of vile crimes. His publications were suspended in 1791, and he was condemned, without trial, to fifteen years in prison in 1792. Catherine's attitude toward dissent within her own empire contrasted sharply with the liberal face she presented to western Europe.

It was not the unrest of the intellectuals, however, that had the strongest effect on Catherine's attitude and on her policies—it was the unrest of the peasantry. The physical burdens on the Russian peasant in the eighteenth century were immense: taxes and special payments, army recruitment and labor service, forcible transfer of state peasants to gentry ownership in the conquered lands of the south, and assignment of peasants to horribly burdensome factory work. At the same time, the peasants were aware of a break in the logic of the institution of serfdom; after 1762, rumors everywhere indicated that the freedom of the gentry from state service would be followed by the abolition of serfdom. There had always been a very strong tradition of peasant revolt, and an equally strong tradition of imposters claiming the throne. Even more disruptive of peasant life was a serious plague that ravaged the Russian empire between 1770 and 1773. Finally, there was rising discontent among factory workers, especially those in the Urals, and among the minorities recently subjugated and being disciplined by the expanding Russian empire, especially the Yaik Cossacks, the Bashkirs, and the Kazakhs.

The focus of all these discontents was a Don Cossack named Emilian Pugachev, who had served in a Cossack detachment during the Seven Years' War and who had fought against the Turks in 1769. Pugachev raised the banner of revolt among the Yaik Cossacks in 1773, and Cossacks, Old Believers, minorities, factory workers, fugitive serfs, and elements of the peasantry rose with him in large numbers. Posing as Peter

III, Catherine's former husband, Pugachev expanded his forces from eighty men until the Volga Valley between Perm and Tsaritsyn was being ravaged by his scattered bands. At first, the government reaction was slight; Pugachev's early successes were not known at St. Petersburg until October 1773. When Catherine did discover the extent of the uprising, she was extremely concerned that news of such a revolt, showing discontent in her empire, should not reach western Europe. The city of Kazan fell briefly to Pugachev in 1774. Catherine was forced to assign General Peter Panin, one of the heroes of the Russian campaigns against the Turks, to lead regular troops against Pugachev. In September 1774, Pugachev was betrayed to the Russian army by some followers and was executed in January 1775. The death of Pugachev did not end the uprisings, however, and the revolt was followed by a decade of smoldering outbreaks and bloody repression.

The Pugachev Revolt was an important event in Catherine's reign. It signified to her the great difficulties of maintaining the order and security of her empire, and convinced her that, while her troops were fighting great battles at the front, she could not allow the empire to fall into anarchy behind them. Consequently, the Pugachev Revolt reinforced the drift of Russian policy in the century, and of Catherine's own views on social reforms. Thus, she continued to seek the allegiance and the services of Russian nobles as custodians of the Russian peasantry—at the price of reform for the Russian peasant. Enlightened ideas in her reign, therefore, were largely restricted to the areas of upper class cultural life.

The personal life of the Empress Catherine the Great has always contributed the most lurid chapters of her biography. Her attachments to men of the court, that began during her years as Grand Duchess, were continued and expanded during her reign. As Empress, however, it was no longer necessary for her to hide the existence of these men, and Catherine created the role of public favorite at the Russian court. There were, in the course of her reign, ten official favorites or "pupils," who enjoyed the attentions, affection, and beneficence of the Empress Catherine. These included Orlov (1772), Vasilchikov (1772–74), Potemkin (1774–76), Zavadovsky (1776–77), Zorich (1777–78), Rimsky-Korsakov (1778–80), Lanskoi (1780–84), Ermolov (1785–86), Dmitriev-Mamanov (1786–89), and Zubov (1789–96).

Several of these favorites played a significant role in Russian history. Gregory Orlov, the first of the official favorites, was one of five brothers who led the Guards Regiments in support of Catherine during the coup d'état of 1762. Gregory Potemkin, who lasted as a court favorite for only two years, was, nevertheless, a close friend of Catherine and an influential adviser until his death in 1791. He played an important role in the development of Catherine's Turkish policy, and had visions of his own role as a ruler of new territories to be conquered from the Turks and recreated as a personal kingdom. Potemkin remained one of the richest and most influential men in the empire, and he played a major role in the selection of the favorites who followed him. The last of the favorites, Platon Zubov, was in his early twenties when Catherine was in her sixties; he remained a favorite for the longest period of all—until Catherine's death in 1796.

There are several points to be made about Catherine's personal propensities: most of the favorites who enjoyed her attention suffered no vindictive reprisals from the Empress after removal from their post; and very few of the favorites were able to utilize their position to gain significant influence over the development of policy. Many favorites, such as Potemkin, were able to make contributions to decisions of the empire, but few, until the last years of Catherine's life, could have been described as evil influences. Catherine was able to distinguish rather clearly, until the last years of her life with Platon Zubov, between public policy and private life.

The greatest tragedy of Catherine's private life was her relationship with her son, Grand Duke Paul. Paul was born in 1754, while Catherine was Grand Duchess, and was raised by the Empress Elizabeth. The pattern of relationship between mother and son was established in these years: separation and animosity. Catherine treated Paul as if he were incompetent, and Paul's assassination in 1801 has lent credence to the idea that he was unbalanced. Actually, Paul's education was the best of any ruler in the century and his tutors were excellent. Paul married Wilhelmina of Hesse-Darmstadt in 1773, but she died in childbirth three years later. Within the year, Paul married Sophia of Württemburg, later the Empress Maria Fedorovna, and had a happy twenty-year marriage that produced four sons and six daughters. Paul was an inveterate traveler, and was attached to Prussia as his model and to the army as his way of life.

Paul's relationship with his mother was very poor. Catherine had the right to name her own heir, but heavy tradition favored the son following the mother or father to the throne. Catherine was never secure on her own throne, and always feared Paul as the focus of plots to replace her. As a consequence, she kept Paul far from any participation in state affairs and he learned little of domestic or foreign policy. In 1783, Catherine established Paul at Gatchina, a country palace, and, for the next thirteen years, he lived in virtual exile, appearing only occasionally at court. In Gatchina, Paul established a model community where he and his wife busied themselves with cultural work and charitable groups. The Empress Catherine also took Paul's children, the Grand Dukes Alexander and Constantine, and raised them as her own.

When Catherine died on November 6, 1796, the Grand Duke Paul became Emperor at the age of forty-three. Bright, very well educated, and well versed in the ideas of his century, he was, nevertheless, inexperienced, suspicious, and untrained for the task ahead. If Catherine had a serious drawback as an administrator, it was most certainly her unwillingness to overcome the serious difficulties between herself and her son, and to prepare a successor for the Russian throne.

Chronology of the Life of Catherine the Great

1729	Born Sophia-Augusta at Stettin, Prussia; daughter of Prince Christian August of Anhalt-Zerbst and Princess Joanna Elizabeth of Holstein-Gottorp
1744	Journey to Russia and engagement to Grand Duke Peter, nephew of Empress Elizabeth of Russia and heir to the Russian throne
1745	Conversion to Russian Orthodoxy, change of name to Catherine; marriage to Grand Duke Peter
1752–54	Relationship with Serge Saltykov, and birth of Catherine's son, the Grand Duke Paul
1755	Relationship with Stanislas Poniatowsky
1755–62	Increased involvement with the intrigues of court politics; friendship with Chancellor Bestuzhev and English Ambassador Hanbury-Williams
1762	(January) Death of Empress Elizabeth, and accession of Emperor Peter III and Empress Catherine
1762	(June) Coup d'état brought Catherine to the throne
1764	Installed Stanislas Poniatowsky, King of Poland
1765	Founding of the Free Economic Society
1764–66	Wrote *Nakaz*, or Instruction on the Codification of the Law, to the Imperial Council
1767–68	Meeting of the Legislative Commission to Codify the Law
1768–74	First Turkish War ended by Treaty of Kuchuk Kainardji
1773	The First Partition of Poland
1773	Visit of Diderot to Russia
1773–74	The Pugachev Revolt
1774–76	Ascendancy of Gregory Potemkin
1775	The First Provincial Reform
1783	Founding of Academy of Fine Arts under Princess Dashkova
1783	Russian Annexation of the Crimea
1785	The Charter of the Gentry issued
1787–92	Second Turkish War ended by Treaty of Jassy
1790	Radishchev published *Journey From St. Petersburg to Moscow*
1792	Nikolai Novikov, publisher and satirist, arrested
1793	Second Partition of Poland
1795	Polish Revolt and Third Partition of Poland
1796	Death of Catherine II

CATHERINE THE GREAT
LOOKS AT THE WORLD

*Catherine's life was an incredibly varied one. To pene-
trate her private life, we have available one of the most intriguing
documents of any age in her* Memoirs, *as well as her letters to
two best-known lovers. Revealing of her cultural interests, is her
correspondence with Voltaire, Diderot, and Falconet, as well as
sections of the* Instruction *that she composed for the reorganization of Russian laws. Her governmental interests are reflected in
the edicts and proclamations on her accession, her treatment of
the serf problem and of peasant revolt, and the historic Charter
of the Gentry of 1785.*

1

The Memoirs[1]

*Looking back from her Imperial heights, Catherine
composed the memoirs that covered her life as Grand Duchess in
Russia up to the year 1759. The* Memoirs *is a fascinating document, replete with the mysteries of Catherine's own personality,
obliging the reader constantly to estimate Catherine's sincerity
and her powers of self-deception. In these pages, Catherine is
seen as the ambitious schemer, the hypochondriac, the* philosophe,
*the lover. Through her eyes, the forces that surrounded her can
also be seen. Few historical personages have left such intriguing
evidence of their own formation and psychology. These memoirs,
calling into question the paternity of Catherine's son and, thus,
the legitimacy of the Romanov dynasty, were concealed from public view by the Tsars; the first edition was discovered and pub-*

---

[1] From *Memoirs of Catherine the Great*, edited by Alexander Herzen (New York:
D. Appleton and Co., 1859), pp. 24–28, 45–47, 54–60, 60–61, 81–82, 93–94, 102–103,
109–10, 115–16, 154–59, 165–70, 187–92, 197–98, 205–207, 208–209.

*lished in the nineteenth century by a Russian revolutionary,
Alexander Herzen, in hopes of discrediting the dynasty.*

ENGAGEMENT TO THE GRAND DUKE PETER: 1744

The arrival of my mother and myself seemed to give the Grand
Duke much pleasure. I was then in my fifteenth year. During the first
few days he showed me great attention. Even then, and in that short
time, I could see that he cared but little for the nation over which he
was destined to rule; that he leaned to Lutheranism; that he had no
affection for those about him; and that he was very childish. I was
silent, and listened, and this gained me his confidence. I remember his
telling me, among other things, that what most pleased him in me was,
that I was his cousin, as he could therefore, from our near relationship,
open his heart to me with entire confidence; and hereupon he went on
to inform me that he was in love with one of the maids of honour to
the Empress, who had been dismissed from court in consequence of the
misfortune of her mother, a Madame Lapoukine, who had been exiled
to Siberia; that he would have been very glad to have married her, but
that he was resigned to marry me instead, as his aunt wished it. I listened with a blush to these family disclosures, thanking him for his
premature confidence; but, in reality, I was astounded at his imprudence and utter want of judgment in a variety of matters.

The tenth day after my arrival in Moscow, it was Saturday, the Empress went to the convent of Troïtza. The Grand Duke remained with
us at Moscow. Three masters had already been assigned me: Simon
Theodorsky, to instruct me in the Greek faith; Basil Adadouroff, for
the Russian language; and the ballet-master, Laudé, for dancing. In
order to make greater progress in Russian, I used to sit up in bed when
every one else was asleep, and learned by heart the lessons which Adadouroff had left me. As my room was warm, and I had no experience
of the climate, I neglected to put on my shoes or stockings, but studied
just as I left my bed. The consequence was, that from the fifteenth day
I was seized with a pleurisy which threatened to kill me. It commenced
with a shivering, which seized me on the Tuesday after the departure
of the Empress for the convent of Troïtza, just as I had dressed for
dinner. My mother and myself were to dine that day with the Grand
Duke, and I had much difficulty in getting her to allow me to go to
bed. On her return from dinner, she found me almost without consciousness, in a burning fever, and with an excruciating pain in the
side. She fancied I was going to have the small-pox; sent for the physicians, and wished me to be treated in consequence. The medical men
insisted on my being bled, but she would not listen to the proposal,
saying that it was from being bled that her brother had died of the

small-pox in Russia, and that she did not wish me to share the same fate. The physicians, and the attendants of the Grand Duke, who had not had the disease, sent to the Empress an exact report of the state of matters, and in the meantime, while my mother and the doctors were disputing, I lay in my bed, unconscious, in a burning fever, and with a pain in the side which occasioned intense suffering, and forced from me continual moanings, for which my mother scolded me, telling me that I ought to bear my sufferings patiently.

Finally, on the Saturday evening, at seven o'clock, that is, on the fifth day of my disease, the Empress returned from the convent of Troïtza, and, on alighting from her carriage, proceeded to my room, and found me without consciousness. She had with her Count Lestocq and a surgeon, and having heard the opinion of the physicians, she sat down at the head of my bed, and ordered me to be bled. The moment of blood came, I recovered my consciousness, and, opening my eyes, found myself in the arms of the Empress, who had lifted me up. For twenty-seven days I lay between life and death, and during that period I was bled sixteen times, on some occasions as often as four times in the day. My mother was scarcely ever allowed to enter my room. She continued opposed to these frequent bleedings, and loudly asserted that the doctors were killing me. She began, however, to believe that I should not have the small-pox. The Empress had placed the Countess Roumianzoff and several other ladies in attendance on me, and it seemed that my mother's judgment was distrusted. At last, under the care of the physician Sanches, a Portuguese, the abscess which had formed in my right side burst. I vomited it, and from that moment I began to recover. I soon perceived that my mother's conduct during my illness had lowered her in every one's estimation. When she saw me very bad, she wished a Lutheran clergyman to be brought to me. I have been told that they brought me to myself, or took advantage of a moment of returning consciousness, to propose this to me and that I replied, "What is the good? I would rather have Simon Theodorsky; I will speak to him with pleasure." He was brought, and addressed me in a manner that gave general satisfaction. This occurrence did me great service in the opinion of the Empress and of the entire court. There was also another circumstance which injured my mother. One day, towards Easter, she took it into her head to send me word by a maid-servant that she wished me to give up to her a piece of blue and silver stuff, which my father's brother had presented to me on my departure for Russia, seeing that I had taken a great fancy for it. I replied that she could, of course, take it, though I certainly prized it very much, as my uncle had given it to me because I liked it so much. The persons about me perceiving that I parted with it unwillingly, and considering how long I had hovered between life and death, having only got a little better within the last two or three days, began to

complain of my mother's imprudence in giving any annoyance to a
dying child, saying, that so far from depriving me of my dress, she
ought not even to have mentioned the matter. The circumstance was
related to the Empress, who instantly sent me several superb pieces of
stuff, and among them one of blue and silver, but the circumstance
injured my mother in the estimation of the Empress. She was accused
of having no affection for me, nor any discretion either. I had accustomed myself during my illness to lie with my eyes closed. I was supposed to be asleep, and then the Countess Roumianzoff, and the ladies
who were with her, spoke their minds freely, and I thus learned a
great many things.

As I began to get better, the Grand Duke often came to spend the
evening in my mother's apartment, which was also mine. He and every
one else seemed to take the greatest interest in my condition. The
Empress had often shed tears about me. At last, on the 21st of April,
1744, my birthday, whence commenced my fifteenth year, I was able to
appear in public for the first time after this severe illness.

I fancy that people were not much edified with the apparition. I
was wasted away to a skeleton. I had grown; but my face and features
had lengthened, my hair had fallen off, and I was deadly pale. To
myself I looked frightfully ugly; I could not recognize myself. The
Empress sent me, on the occasion, a pot of rouge, and ordered me to
use it.

With the return of spring and fine weather, the assiduities of the
Grand Duke ceased. He preferred walking and shooting in the environs
of Moscow. Sometimes, however, he came to dine or sup with us, and
then he continued his childish confidences to me, while his attendants
conversed with my mother, who received much company, and with
whom many conferences took place, which did not fail to displease
those who were not present at them, especially Count Bestoujeff, all
whose enemies were in the habit of assembling with us, and particularly the Marquis de la Chétardie, who had not yet put forth any character from the court of France, though he carried in his pocket his
credentials as ambassador.

GETTING ALONG AT COURT: 1745

Now the Grand Duke had about as much discretion as a cannon
ball, and, when his mind was full of any thing, he could not rest until
he had unburdened it to the persons he was in the habit of talking
with, never for a moment considering to whom it was he spoke. Consequently he used to tell me all these things, with the utmost frankness,
the first time he saw me afterwards. He always fancied that every one
was of his opinion, and that nothing could be more reasonable than
all this. I took good care not to speak of these things to any one; but

they made me reflect very seriously upon the fate which awaited me. I determined to husband carefully the confidence of the Grand Duke, in order that he might at least consider me as a person of whom he felt sure, and to whom he could confide every thing without the least inconvenience to himself; and in this I succeeded for a long time. Besides, I treated every one in the best way I could, and studied to gain the friendship, or at least to lessen the enmity of those whom I in any way suspected of being badly disposed to me. I showed no leaning to any side, nor meddled with any thing; always maintained a serene air, treated every one with great attention, affability, and politeness, and, as I was naturally very gay, I saw with pleasure that from day to day I advanced in the general esteem, and was looked upon as an interesting child, and one by no means wanting in mind. I showed great respect for my mother, a boundless obedience for the Empress, and the most profound deference for the Grand Duke; and I sought with the most anxious care to gain the affection of the public.

From the period of our visit to Moscow, the Empress had assigned me some ladies and gentlemen who formed my court. A short time after my arrival at St. Petersburg she gave me some Russian maids, in order, as she said, to aid me in acquiring increased facility in the use of the language. This arrangement pleased me very much; for these persons were all young, the oldest of them being only about twenty; all, too, were very lively, so that from that time I did nothing but sing, dance, and play in my room, from the moment I awoke in the morning till I went to sleep again at night. In the evening, after supper, I brought into my bed-room my three maids, the two Princesses Gagarine and Mademoiselle Koucheleff, and we played at blind-man's buff and all sorts of games suited to our age. All these ladies mortally feared the Countess Roumianzoff; but as she played at cards from morning till night, either in the ante-chamber or in her own room, never leaving her chair, except from necessity, she rarely came near us.

MARRIAGE: 1745

At last the Empress fixed the 21st of August for the ceremony. As the day came nearer, I became more and more melancholy. My heart predicted but little happiness; ambition alone sustained me. In my inmost soul there was a something which never allowed me to doubt for a single moment that sooner or later I should become the sovereign Empress of Russia in my own right.

The marriage was celebrated with much pomp and magnificence. In the evening I found in my room Madame Krause, sister of the head lady's-maid to the Empress, who had placed her with me as my head lady's maid. From the very next day I found that this person had thrown all my other women into consternation, for on approaching one of them to speak to her, as usual, she said to me, "In God's name, do not come near me; we have been forbidden to whisper to you." On the other hand, my beloved spouse did not trouble himself in the slightest degree about me, but was constantly with his valets, playing at soldiers, exercising them in his room, or changing his uniform twenty times a-day. I yawned, and grew weary, having no one to speak to; or I endeavoured to keep up appearances. On the third day after my marriage, the Countess Roumianzoff sent me word that the Empress had dispensed with her attendance on me, and that she was going to return home to her husband and children. This did not grieve me much, for she had been the cause of a great deal of scandal.

The marriage festivities lasted ten days, at the end of which the Grand Duke and myself took up our residence in the Summer Palace, where the Empress was living; and the departure of my mother was beginning to be talked of. Since my marriage I did not see her every day; but she had very much softened towards me. About the latter end of September she took her departure, the Grand Duke and I accompanying her as far as Krasnoe-Selo. I was sincerely afflicted, and wept a great deal. . . .

At the Winter Palace, the Grand Duke and I occupied the apartments which we had previously used; those of the Duke were separated from mine by an immense staircase, which also led to the apartments of the Empress. In going to him, or in his coming to me, it was necessary to cross the landing of this staircase—not the pleasantest thing in the world, especially in winter. Nevertheless, we made the passage several times a-day. In the evening, I went to play at billiards in his ante-chamber with the Chamberlain Berkholz, while he romped with his gentlemen in the other room. My party at billiards was interrupted by the retirement of Brummer and Berkholz, whom the Empress dismissed from attendance on the Grand Duke, at the end of the winter of 1746. This winter was passed in masquerades given at the principal houses in the city, which were then very small. The court and the whole town assisted at them regularly.

The last of them was given by the Master-General of the Police, Tatizcheff, in a house called Smolnoy Dvoretz, belonging to the Empress. The centre portion of this wooden house had been destroyed by a fire; nothing remained but the wings, which were of two stories. One of these wings was set apart for dancing; but in order to go to supper, which was laid out in the other, it was necessary to pass, and this in the month of January, through the court-yard and the snow. After supper this journey had to be repeated. The Grand Duke returned home, and went to bed, but the next morning he awoke with a violent headache, which prevented him from rising. I sent for the doctors, who pronounced him in a burning fever of the most violent kind. He was carried in the evening from my bed to the audience-chamber, where, after being bled, he was placed in a bed arranged there for him. They bled him several times; he was very ill. The Empress visited him frequently during the day, and seeing me in tears, she was pleased with me. One evening, while reading the night-prayers in a small oratory adjoining my dressing-room, Madame Ismailoff came in. She was a person of whom the Empress was very fond, and she informed me that her Majesty, knowing I was much afflicted by the illness of the Duke, had sent her to tell me not to be cast down, but to put my trust in God, and that whatever happened she would not forsake me. She then asked me what I was reading; I told her the prayers for night, and she said I should hurt my eyes by reading such small print by candlelight. I then begged her to thank her Imperial Majesty for her goodness towards me, and we parted very affectionately, she to give an account of her mission, I to go to bed. Next day the Empress sent me a prayer-book printed in large type, in order to preserve my eyes, she said.

Although the room in which the Grand Duke was placed adjoined mine, I never entered it except when I felt that I should not be in the way, for I saw that he did not much care to have me there, but preferred being with his attendants, who, on the other hand, did not much suit me. Besides, I was not accustomed to pass my time alone among a set of men. Meanwhile, Lent came round. I went to my duty (fis mes devotions) the first week. Generally speaking, I was inclined to devotion at that period. I saw plainly that the Grand Duke cared little about me. A fortnight after our marriage he confessed to me again that he was in love with Mademoiselle Carr, Maid of Honour to her Imperial Majesty, since married to a Prince Galitzine, Equery to the Empress. He told Count Devier, his Chamberlain, that there was no comparison between that lady and me. Devier maintained the contrary, and the Duke got angry with him. The scene took place almost in my presence, and I witnessed their contest. Surely, I said to myself, it would be impossible for me not to be unhappy with such a man as this, were I to give way to sentiments of tenderness thus requited. I might die of jealousy without benefit to any one. I endeavoured therefore to master my feelings, so as not to be jealous of a man who did not love me. Had he wished to be loved, I should have found no difficulty in loving him. I was naturally well disposed, and accustomed to fulfil my duties; but then, too, I should have required a husband who had common sense, which this one had not.

I had abstained (fait maigre) during the first week of Lent. On the Saturday, the Empress sent me word that it would give her pleasure if I abstained during the second week also. I replied that I begged her Majesty would permit me to abstain during the entire Lent. Sievers, Marshal of the Court to the Empress, a son-in-law to Madame Krause, who was the bearer of this message, told me that the Empress was greatly pleased with my request, and that she granted it. When the

Grand Duke learned that I continued to abstain, he scolded me a good deal; but I told him I could not do otherwise. After he had got well, he still feigned illness in order not to leave his room, where he found more congenial amusement than in the formal life of the court. He did not quit it till the last week of Lent, when he went to his duty.

LIFE WITH THE GRAND DUKE PETER: 1745

After Easter, he had a marionette theatre set up in his room, and invited company to see it, and even ladies. This show was the most insipid thing imaginable. The room in which it was set up had a door which was fastened up, in consequence of its leading into one of the Empress' apartments. In this apartment there was a mechanical table, which could be lowered and raised so as to admit of dining without servants. One day, while the Grand Duke was in his room preparing his so-called theatricals, he heard people talking in this room beyond, and, with his usual inconsiderate vivacity, he took up from his theatre one of those carpenters' tools used for making holes in boards, and set to work boring holes in this condemned door, so that he could see all that passed within, and among other things, the dinner which the Empress was then taking there. The Master of the Hounds, Count Razoumowsky, in a brocaded dressing-gown, dined with her—he had taken medicine that day—and there were, besides, some dozen persons of those most in the confidence of the Empress. The Grand Duke, not content with enjoying the fruit of his skilful labour himself, must needs call all who were about him to share in the pleasure of looking through the holes which he had bored with so much diligence. When all were fully satisfied with this indiscreet pleasure, he came and invited Madame Krause, myself, and my maids, to go to his room and see something which we had never seen before. He did not tell us what it was, doubtless to give us an agreeable surprise. As I did not hurry myself sufficiently to gratify his impatience, he led away Madame Krause and my women. I arrived last, and found them stationed in front of this door, where he had placed benches, chairs, and stools, for the accommodation of the spectators, as he said. On entering, I asked what all this was about. He ran to meet me, and told me what the case was. I was terrified and indignant at his rashness, and told him I would neither look nor have anything to do with this impropriety, which would certainly bring him into trouble if his aunt should come to hear of it, and this she could not well help doing, seeing that there were at least twenty persons in his secret. All who had allowed themselves to look through the door, finding that I would not do the same, began to file off one after the other. The Duke himself became ashamed of what he had done, and recommenced working on his theatre. I returned to my room.

LIFE IN THE COUNTRY

In the country, the Grand Duke formed a pack of hounds, and began to train dogs himself. When tired of tormenting these, he set to work scraping on the violin. He did not know a note, but he had a good ear, and made the beauty of music consist in the force and violence with which he drew forth the tones of his instrument. Those who had to listen to him, however, would often have been glad to stop their ears had they dared, for his music grated on them dreadfully. This course of life continued not only in the country, but also in town. On returning to the Winter Palace, Madame Krause—who had all along been an Argus—moderated so far as often even to aid in deceiving the Tchoglokoffs, who were hated by every one. She did more: she procured for the Grand Duke playthings—puppets, and such like childish toys, of which he was passionately fond. During the day, they were concealed within, or under my bed; the Grand Duke retired immediately after supper, and as soon as we were in bed Madame Krause locked the door, and then the Grand Duke played with his puppets till one or two o'clock in the morning. Willing or unwilling, I was obliged to share in this interesting amusement; and so was Madame Krause. I often laughed, but more frequently felt annoyed, and even inconvenienced; the whole bed was covered and filled with playthings, some of which were rather heavy. I do not know whether Madame Tchoglokoff came to hear of these nocturnal amusements, but one night, about twelve o'clock, she knocked at the door of our bedroom. We did not open it immediately, as the Grand Duke, myself, and Madame Krause were scrambling with all our might to gather up and conceal the toys: for this purpose the coverlid of the bed answered very well, as we crammed them all in under it. This done, we opened the door. She complained dreadfully of having been kept waiting, and told us that the Empress would be very angry when she learnt that we were not asleep at that hour. She then sulkily departed, without having made any further discovery. As soon as she was gone, the Duke resumed his amusements until he became sleepy. . . .

This is the kind of life I led at Oranienbaum: I rose at three o'clock in the morning, and dressed myself alone from head to foot in male attire; an old huntsman whom I had was already waiting for me with the guns; a fisherman's skiff was ready on the sea-shore; we traversed the garden on foot, with our guns upon our shoulders; entered the boat together with the fisherman and a pointer, and I shot ducks in the reeds which bordered on both sides the canal of Oranienbaum, which extends two verstes into the sea. We often doubled this canal, and consequently were occasionally, for a considerable time, in the open sea in this skiff. The Grand Duke came an hour or two after us; for he must needs always have a breakfast and God knows what be- sides, which he dragged after him. If we met we went together, if not each shot and hunted alone. At ten o'clock, and often later, I returned and dressed for dinner. After dinner we rested; and in the evening the Grand Duke had music, or we rode out on horseback. Having led this sort of life for about a week, I felt myself very much heated and my head confused. I saw that I required repose and dieting; so for four- and-twenty hours I ate nothing, drank only cold water, and for two nights slept as long as I could. After this I recommenced the same course of life, and found myself quite well. I remember reading at that time the Memoirs of Brantôme, which greatly amused me. Before that I had read the Life of Henri IV by Périfix.

THE EDUCATION OF AN EMPRESS: 1750

Shortly after my arrival in Moscow, I began, for want of other amusement, to read the History of Germany, by le Père Barre, canon of Ste. Geneviève, in nine volumes quarto. Every week I finished one, after which I read the works of Plato. My rooms faced the street; the corresponding ones were occupied by the Duke, whose windows opened upon a small yard. When reading in my room, one of my maids usually came in, and remained there standing as long as she wished; she then retired, and another took her place when she thought it suitable. I made Madame Vladislava see that this routine could serve no useful purpose, but was merely an inconvenience; that, besides, I already had much to suffer from the proximity of my apartments to those of the Grand Duke, by which she, too, was equally incommoded, as she occupied a small cabinet at the end of my rooms. She consented, there- fore, to relieve my maids from this species of etiquette. This is the kind of annoyance we had to put up with, morning, noon, and night, even to a late hour: The Grand Duke, with rare perseverance, trained a pack of dogs, and with heavy blows of his whip, and cries like those of the huntsmen, made them fly from one end to the other of his two rooms, which were all he had. Such of the dogs as became tired, or got out of rank, were severely punished, which made them howl still more. When he got tired of this detestable exercise, so painful to the ears and destructive to the repose of his neighbours, he seized his violin, on which he rasped away with extraordinary violence, and very badly, all the time walking up and down his rooms. Then he recommenced the education and punishment of his dogs, which to me seemed very cruel. On one occasion, hearing one of these animals howl piteously and for a long time, I opened the door of my bed-room, where I was seated, and which adjoined the apartment in which this scene was enacted, and saw him holding this dog by the collar, suspended in the air, while a boy who was in his service, a Kalmuck by birth, held the animal by the tail. It was a poor little King Charles's dog of English breed, and the Duke was beating him with all his might with the heavy handle of a whip. I interceded for the poor beast, but this only made him redouble his blows. Unable to bear so cruel a scene, I returned to my room with tears in my eyes. In general, tears and cries, instead of moving the Duke to pity, put him in a passion. Pity was a feeling that was painful, and even insupportable in his mind.

A SERIES OF MALADIES

His Imperial Highness was to have gone hunting in the afternoon with Count Razoumowsky, but he remained at Taininskoe, while I returned to Rajova. On the way I was seized with a violent toothache. The weather began to be cold and wet, and we were but badly sheltered at Rajova. The brother of Madame Tchoglokoff, Count Hendrikoff, who was the chamberlain on duty with me, proposed to his sister to cure me instantly. She spoke to me on the subject, and I consented to try his remedy, which seemed to be nothing at all, or rather a mere charlatanism. He went immediately into the other room, and brought out a very small roll of paper, which he desired me to chew with the aching tooth. Hardly had I done so when the pain became so extremely violent that I was obliged to go to bed. I got into such a burning fever, that I began to be delirious. Madame Tchoglokoff, terrified at my condition, and attributing it to her brother's remedy, got very angry, and abused him. She remained at my bedside all the night, sent word to the Empress that her house at Rajova was in no way fit for a person so seriously ill as I appeared to be, and in fact made such a stir, that the next day I was removed to Moscow very ill. I was ten or twelve days in bed, and the toothache returned every afternoon at the same hour.

At the beginning of September, the Empress went to the convent of Voskressensky, whither we were ordered to go for the feast of her name. On that day M. Ivan Ivanovitch Schouvaloff was declared a Gentleman of the Bedchamber. This was an event at court. Every one whispered that a new favourite had appeared. I was rejoiced at his promotion, for, while he was a page, I had marked him out as a person of promise, on account of his studiousness; he was always to be seen with a book in his hand.

Having returned from this excursion, I was seized with a sore throat accompanied with much fever. The Empress came to see me during this illness. When barely convalescent, and while still very weak, her Majesty ordered me, through Madame Tchoglokoff, to assist at the wedding and dress the hair of the niece of the Countess Roumianzoff, who was about to be married to M. Alexander Narichkine, subsequently created chief cupbearer. Madame Tchoglokoff, who saw that I was scarcely convalescent, was a little pained in announcing to me this compliment, a compliment which gave me but little pleasure, as it plainly showed how little was cared for my health, perhaps even for my life. I spoke in this view to Madame Vladislava, who seemed, like myself, but little pleased with this order, an order evidently given without care or consideration. I exerted myself, however, and on the day fixed, the bride was led to my room. I adorned her head with my diamonds, and she was then conducted to the court church to be married. As for me, I had to go to Narichkine House, accompanied by Madame Tchoglokoff and my own court. Now, we were living at Moscow, in the palace at the end of the German Sloboda.

A DENTAL AFFAIR

On the 15th of December we left Moscow for St. Petersburg, travelling night and day in an open sledge. About midway I was again seized with a violent toothache. Notwithstanding this, the Grand Duke would not consent to close the sledge: scarcely would he allow me to draw the curtain a little, so as to shelter me from a cold and damp wind, blowing right into my face. At last we reached Zarskoe-Selo, where the Empress had already arrived, having passed us on the road, according to her usual custom. As soon as I stepped out of the sledge I entered the apartment destined for us, and sent for her Majesty's physician Boërhave, the nephew of the celebrated Boërhave, requesting him to have the tooth which had tormented me so much for the last four or five months extracted. He consented with great reluctance, and only because I absolutely insisted on it. At last he sent for Gyon, my surgeon: I sat on the ground, Boërhave on one side, Tchoglokoff on the other, and Gyon drew the tooth; but the moment he did so, my eyes, nose, and mouth became fountains, whence poured out—from my mouth, blood, from my eyes and nose, water. Boërhave, who was a man of clear and sound judgment, instantly exclaimed, "Clumsy!" and calling for the tooth, he added, "I feared it would be so, and that was why I did not wish it to be drawn." Gyon, in extracting the tooth, had carried away with it a portion of the lower jaw, to which it was attached. At this moment the Empress came to the door of my room, and I was afterwards told that she was moved even to tears. I was put to bed, and suffered a great deal during four weeks, even in the city, whither we went next day, notwithstanding all this, and still in open sleighs. I did not leave my room till the middle of January, 1750, for the lower part of my cheek still bore, in blue and yellow stains, the impression of the five fingers of M. Gyon. On new-year's day this year, wishing to have my hair dressed, I noticed that the young man who was to do it, a Kalmuck whom I had trained for this purpose, was excessively red, and his eyes very piercing. I asked what was the matter, and learned that he had a very bad headache and great heat. I sent him away, desiring him to go to bed, for indeed he was not fit to do anything. He retired, and in the evening I was informed that the small-pox had broken out upon him. I escaped with nothing worse than the fright which this gave me, for I did not catch the disease, although he had combed my hair.

THE AFFAIR WITH SERGE SOLTIKOFF: 1752

During one of these concerts, Serge Soltikoff gave me to understand what was the object of his assiduous attentions. I did not reply to him at first. When he again returned to the subject, I asked him what it was he wanted of me? Hereupon he drew a charming and passionate picture of the happiness which he promised himself. I said to him, "But your wife, whom you married for love only two years ago, and of whom you were supposed to be passionately fond—and she, too, of you—what will she say to this?" He replied that all was not gold that glitters, and that he was paying dearly for a moment of infatuation. I did all I could to make him change his mind—I really expected to succeed in this—I pitied him. Unfortunately, I listened also. He was very handsome, and certainly had not his equal at the Imperial court, still less at ours. He was not wanting in mind, nor in that finish of accomplishments, manner, and style which the great world gives, and especially a court. He was twenty-six years old. Take him all in all, he was by birth, and by many other qualities, a distinguished gentleman. As for his faults, he managed to hide them. The greatest of all was a love of intrigue and a want of principle. These were not unfolded to my eyes. I held out all the spring, and a part of the autumn. I saw him almost every day, and made no change in my conduct towards him. I was the same to him as I was to all others, and never saw him but in the presence of the court, or of a part of it. One day, to get rid of him, I made up my mind to tell him that he was misdirecting his attentions. I added, "How do you know that my heart is not engaged elsewhere?" This, however, instead of discouraging him, only made his pursuit all the more ardent. In all this there was no thought of the dear husband, for it was a known and admitted fact, that he was not at all amiable, even to the objects with whom he was in love; and he was always in love; in fact, he might be said to pay court to every woman, except the one who bore the name of his wife: she alone was excluded from all share of his attentions.

In the midst of all this, Tchoglokoff invited us to a hunting party on his island, whither we went in a skiff, our horses being sent on before. Immediately on our arrival I mounted my horse, and we went to find the dogs. Soltikoff seized the moment when the rest were in pursuit of the hares, to approach me and speak of his favourite subject. I

listened more attentively than usual. He described to me the plan
which he had arranged for enshrouding, as he said, in profound mystery, the happiness which might be enjoyed in such a case. I did not say
a word. He took advantage of my silence to persuade me that he loved
me passionately, and he begged that I would allow him to hope, at
least, that he was not wholly indifferent to me. I told him he might
amuse himself with hoping what he pleased, as I could not prevent his
thoughts. Finally he drew comparisons between himself and others at
the court, and made me confess that he was preferable to them. From
that he concluded that he was preferred. I laughed at all this, but I
admitted that he was agreeable to me. At the end of an hour and
a-half's conversation, I desired him to leave me, since so long a conversation might give rise to suspicion. He said he would not go unless
I told him that I consented. I answered, "Yes, yes; but go away." He
said, "Then it is settled," and put spurs to his horse. I cried after him,
"No, no;" but he repeated, "Yes, yes." And thus we separated. On our
return to the house, which was on the island, we had supper, during
which there sprung up such a heavy gale from the sea, that the waves
rose so high that they even reached the steps of the house. In fact, the
whole island was under water to the depth of several feet. We were
obliged to remain until the storm had abated, and the waters retreated,
which was not until between two and three in the morning. During
this time, Soltikoff told me that heaven itself had favoured him that
day, by enabling him to enjoy my presence for a longer time, with
many other things to the same effect. He thought himself already quite
happy. As for me, I was not at all so. A thousand apprehensions troubled me, and I was unusually dull, and very much out of conceit with
myself. I had persuaded myself that I could easily govern both his
passions and my own, and I found that both tasks were difficult, if not
impossible.

Two days after this, Soltikoff informed me that one of the Grand
Duke's valets de chambre, Bressan, a Frenchman, had told him that
his Imperial Highness had said in his room, "Sergius Soltikoff and my
wife deceive Tchoglokoff, make him believe whatever they like, and
then laugh at him." To tell the truth, there was something of this kind,
and the Grand Duke had perceived it. I answered, by advising him to
be more circumspect for the future. Some days afterwards I caught a
very bad sore throat, which lasted more than three weeks, with a violent
fever, during which the Empress sent to me the Princess Kourakine,
who was about to be married to Prince Lobanoff. I was to dress her
hair. For this purpose she had to sit on my bed, in her court-dress and
hooped petticoats. I did my best; but Madame Tchoglokoff, seeing that
it was impossible for me to manage it, made her get off my bed, and
finished dressing her herself. I had never seen the lady since then.

The Grand Duke was at this period making love to Mademoiselle

Martha Isaevna Schafiroff, whom the Empress had recently placed with me, as also her elder sister, Anne Isaevna. Serge Soltikoff, who was a devil for intrigue, insinuated himself into the favour of these girls, in order to learn anything the Grand Duke might say to them relative to him. These young ladies were poor, rather silly, and very selfish, and, in fact, they became wonderfully confidential in a very short time.

In the midst of all this we went to Oranienbaum, where again I was every day on horseback, and wore no other than a man's dress, except on Sundays. Tchoglokoff and his wife had become as gentle as lambs. In the eyes of Madame Tchoglokoff I possessed a new merit; I fondled and caressed a great deal one of her children, who was with her. I made clothes for him, and gave him all sorts of playthings and dresses. Now the mother was dotingly fond of this child, who subsequently became such a scapegrace that, for his pranks, he was sentenced to confinement in a fortress for fifteen years. Soltikoff had become the friend, the confidant and the counsellor of M. and Madame Tchoglokoff. Assuredly no person in his senses could ever have submitted to so hard a task as that of listening to two proud, arrogant, and conceited fools, talking nonsense all day long, without having some great object in view. Many, therefore, were the guesses, many the suppositions, as to what this object could be. These reached Peterhoff and the ears of the Empress. Now at this period it often happened that when her Majesty wished to scold any one, she did not scold for what she might well complain of, but seized some pretext for finding fault about something which no one would ever have thought she could object to. This is the remark of a courtier; I have it from the lips of its author, Zachar Czernicheff. At Oranienbaum, every one of our suite had agreed, men as well as women, to have, for this summer, dresses of the same colour; the body gray, the rest blue, with a collar of black velvet, and no trimmings. This uniformity was convenient in more respects than one. It was on this style of dress that she fixed, and more especially on the circumstance that I always wore a riding habit, and rode like a man at Peterhoff. One court-day the Empress said to Madame Tchoglokoff that this fashion of riding prevented my having children, and that my dress was not at all becoming; that when she rode on horseback she changed her dress. Madame Tchoglokoff replied, that as to having children, this had nothing to do with the matter; that children could not come without a cause; and that, although their Imperial Highnesses had been married ever since 1745, the cause nevertheless did not exist. Thereupon her Imperial Majesty scolded Madame Tchoglokoff, and told her she blamed her for this, because she neglected to lecture, on this matter, the parties concerned; and on the whole, she showed much ill-humour, and said that her husband was a mere night-cap, who allowed himself to be worn by a set of dirty-nosed brats (des morveux). All this, in four-and-twenty hours, had reached their confidants. At this term of morveux, the morveux wiped their noses; and, in a very special council held on the matter by them, it was resolved and decreed that, in order to follow out strictly the wishes of her Imperial Majesty, Sergius Soltikoff and Leon Narichkine should incur a pretended disgrace at the hands of M. Tchoglokoff, of which perhaps he himself would not be at all aware; that under pretext of the illness of their relatives, they should retire to their homes for three weeks or a month, in order to allow the rumours which were current to die away. This was carried out to the letter, and the next day they departed, to confine themselves to their own houses for a month. As for me, I immediately changed my style of dress; besides, the other had now become useless. The first idea of this uniformity of attire had been suggested to us by the dress worn on court-days at Peterhoff. The body was white, the rest green, and the whole trimmed all over with silver lace. Soltikoff, who was of a dark complexion, used to say that he looked like a fly in milk, in this dress of white and silver. I continued to frequent the society of the Tchoglokoffs as before, although it was now dreadfully wearisome. The husband and wife were full of regrets for the absence of the chief attractions of their society, in which most assuredly I did not contradict them.

THE PATERNITY OF THE GRAND DUKE PAUL: 1753

In the meanwhile, Madame Tchoglokoff, who never lost sight of her favourite project of watching over the succession, took me aside one day and said: "Listen to me, I must speak to you with all sincerity." I opened my eyes and ears, and not without cause. She began with a long preamble, after her fashion, respecting her attachment to her husband, her own prudent conduct, what was necessary and what was not necessary for ensuring mutual love and facilitating conjugal ties; and then she went on to say, that occasionally there were situations in which a higher interest demanded an exception to the rule. I let her talk on without interruption, not knowing what she was driving at, a good deal astonished, and uncertain whether it was not a snare she was laying for me, or whether she was speaking with sincerity. Just as I was making these reflections in my own mind, she said to me, "You shall presently see whether I love my country, and whether I am sincere; I do not doubt but you have cast an eye of preference upon some one or other; I leave you to choose between Sergius Soltikoff and Leon Narichkine—if I do not mistake, it is the latter." Here I exclaimed, "No, no! not at all." "Well, then," she said, "if it be not Narichkine, it is Soltikoff." To that I made no reply, and she went on saying, "You shall see that it will not be I who will throw difficulties in your way." I played the simpleton to such a degree, that she scolded me for it several times, both in town and in the country, whither we went after Easter. . . .

In the course of the month of May, I again had indications of pregnancy. We went to Liberitza, an estate of the Grand Duke, twelve or fourteen verstes from Moscow. The stone house which was on it had been built a long time ago by Prince Menchikoff, and was now falling to decay, so that we could not live in it. As a substitute, tents were set up in the court, and every morning, at two or three o'clock, my sleep was broken by the sound of the axe, and the noises made in building a wooden wing, which was being hurriedly erected, within two paces, so to speak, of our tents, in order that we might have a place to live in during the remainder of the summer. The rest of our time we spent in hunting, walking, or riding. I no longer went on horseback, but in a cabriolet. About the Feast of St. Peter we returned to Moscow. I was seized with such drowsiness that I slept every day till noon, and then it was only with difficulty that I was awakened in time for dinner. The Feast of St. Peter was kept in the usual way: I was present at mass, at the dinner, the ball, and the supper. Next morning I felt great pains in my loins. Madame Tchoglokoff summoned a midwife, who predicted the miscarriage, which actually occurred the following night. I might have been with child two or three months. For thirteen days I was in great danger, as it was suspected that a portion of the after-birth had remained behind. This circumstance was kept a secret from me. At last, on the thirteenth day, it came away of itself—without pain, or even a struggle. In consequence of this accident I had to keep my room for six weeks, during which the heat was insupportable. The Empress came to see me the day I fell ill, and appeared to be affected by my state. During the six weeks that I kept my room I was nearly tired to death. The only society I had was Madame Tchoglokoff, who came but rarely, and a little Kalmuck girl, whom I liked for her pretty, agreeable ways. I frequently cried from ennui. As for the Grand Duke, he was mostly in his own room, where one of his valets, a Ukrainian, named Karnovitch, a fool as well as a drunkard, did his best to amuse him; furnishing him with toys, with wine, and such other strong liquors as he could procure, without the knowledge of M. Tchoglokoff, who, in fact, was deceived and made a fool of by every one. But in these nocturnal and secret orgies with the servants of the chamber, among whom were several young Kalmucks, the Grand Duke often found himself ill-obeyed and ill-served; for, being drunk, they knew not what they did, and forgot that they were with their master, and that that master was the Grand Duke. Then his Imperial Highness would have recourse to blows with his stick, or the blade of his sword; but in spite of all this, he was ill-obeyed; and more than once he had recourse to me, complaining of his people, and begging me to make them listen to reason. On these occasions I used to go to his rooms, give them a good scolding, and remind them of their duties, when they would instantly resume their proper places. This made the Grand Duke often say to me, and also to Bressan, that he could not conceive how I managed those people; for, as for himself, though he belaboured them soundly, yet he could not make them obedient, while I, with a single word, could get them to do whatever I wished. One day when I went for this purpose into the apartments of his Imperial Highness, I beheld a great rat, which he had had hung—with all the paraphernalia of an execution—in the middle of a cabinet, formed by means of a partition. I asked him what all this meant. He told me that this rat had committed a crime; one which, according to the laws of war, was deserving of capital punishment: it had climbed over the ramparts of a fortress of cardboard which he had on the table in this cabinet, and had eaten two sentinels, made of pith, who were on duty at the bastions. He had had the criminal tried by martial law, his setter having caught him, and he was immediately hung, as I saw, and was to remain there exposed to the public gaze for three days, as an example. I could not help bursting into a loud laugh at the extreme folly of the thing; but this greatly displeased him. Seeing the importance he attached to the matter, I retired, excusing myself on account of my ignorance, as a woman, of military law; but this did not prevent his being very much out of humour with me on account of my laughter. In justification of the rat, however, it may at least be said, that he was hung without having been questioned or heard in his own defence.

THE BIRTH OF THE GRAND DUKE PAUL: 1754

We went to Peterhoff. I walked a great deal, but in spite of this my melancholy followed me. In the month of August we returned to the city, to occupy again the Summer Palace. It was a death blow to me when I learned that, for my accouchement, they were preparing apartments close to, and forming part of those belonging to the Empress. Alexander Schouvaloff took me to see them; I found two rooms, gloomy, and with only one issue, like all those of the Summer Palace; the hangings were of ugly crimson damask, there was scarcely any furniture, and no kind of convenience. I saw that I should be isolated there, without any sort of company, and thoroughly wretched. I said so to Soltikoff and to the Princess Gagarine, who, though they bore no love to each other, had nevertheless a point of union in their friendship for me. They saw the matter as I did, but it was impossible to remedy it. I was to go on the Wednesday to these apartments, which were far removed from those of the Grand Duke. I went to bed on Tuesday evening, and in the night awoke with labour-pains. I called Madame Vladislava, who went to fetch the midwife. She pronounced that I was in labour. The Grand Duke, who was sleeping in his own room, was awakened, as also Count Alexander Schouvaloff. The latter sent word to the Empress, who was not long in coming. It was about two o'clock in the morning. I was very ill. At last, towards noon the next day, the 20th September, I gave birth to a son. As soon as it was dressed, the Empress called in her confessor, who gave the child the name of Paul, after which the Empress immediately bade the midwife take the child up and follow her. I remained on the bed on which I had been confined. Now this bed was placed opposite a door through which I could see the light; behind me were two large windows which did not close properly, and on the right and left of this bed were two doors, one of which opened into my dressing-room, and the other into the room in which Madame Vladislava slept. As soon as the Empress left, the Grand Duke also went away, as likewise did M. and Madame Schouvaloff, and I saw no one again until three o'clock in the afternoon. I had perspired a great deal, and begged Madame Vladislava to change my linen, and put me into my own bed, but she told me that she dared not. She sent several times to call the midwife, who, however, did not come. I asked for something to drink, but still received the same answer. At last, after three hours, the Countess Schouvaloff arrived, very elaborately dressed. When she saw me lying just where she had left me, she was angry, and said it was enough to kill me. This was very consolatory, certainly. I had been in tears from the time of my delivery, pained by the neglect in which I was left, after a severe labour; uncomfortably accommodated, lying between doors and windows, which did not shut close, no one daring to lift me into my bed, which was not two paces off, and to which I had not the strength to crawl. Madame Schouvaloff departed immediately, and went, I think, to fetch the midwife; for the latter came in about half an hour afterwards, and told us that the Empress was so taken up with the child that she would not let her go away for a moment. As for me, no one gave me a thought. This forgetfulness or neglect was not at all flattering. I was dying of thirst. At last they placed me on my bed, and I did not see a living soul for the rest of the day, nor did any one send even to ask after me. The Grand Duke, for his part, did nothing but drink with all he could find, and the Empress was taken up with the child. In the city and throughout the empire the joy at this event was great. The next day I began to feel an excruciating rheumatic pain, from the hip down the thigh and left leg. This pain prevented me from sleeping, and this brought on a violent fever. In spite of all this the attentions I received next day were just of the same character. I saw no one, and no one inquired after me. The Grand Duke, indeed, did come into my room for a moment, and then went away, saying, that he had not time to stop. I did nothing but weep and moan in my bed. Nobody was in my room but Madame Vladislava; in her heart she was sorry for me, but she had not the power to remedy this state of things. Besides, I never liked to be pitied nor to complain. I had too proud a spirit for that, and the very idea of being unhappy was insupportable to me. Hitherto

I had done whatever I could not to appear so. I might have seen Count Alexander Schouvaloff and his wife, but they were such insipid and tiresome people that I was always delighted when they were not present. . . .

At last the Grand Duke, growing weary of his evenings passed without my ladies of honour, came and proposed to spend an evening in my room. At this time he was courting the very ugliest of these ladies, Elizabeth Voronzoff. On the sixth day, my son's baptism took place. He had already come near dying of the thrush. It was only by stealth that I could get any account of him; for to have inquired about him would have passed for a doubt of the Empress' care, and would have been very ill received. Besides, she had taken him into her own room, and whenever he cried she herself would run to him, and, through excess of care, they were literally stifling him. He was kept in a room extremely warm, wrapped up in flannel, and laid in a cradle, lined with black fox furs; over him was a coverlet of quilted satin, lined with wadding, and above this one of rose-coloured velvet, lined with black fox skins. I saw him myself, many times afterwards, lying in this style, the perspiration running from his face and whole body, and hence it was that, when older, the least breath of air that reached him chilled him and made him ill. Besides, he had in attendance on him a great number of aged matrons who, by their ill-judged cares, and their want of common sense, did him infinitely more harm than good, both physically and morally.

THE RETURN OF SOLTIKOFF: 1755

Thus commenced the year 1755. From Christmas-day to Lent there was nothing but fêtes in the city and the court. It was still, in every case, in honour of the birth of my son that they were given. Every one in turn, vied with his neighbour—all eager to give the most splendid dinners, balls, masquerades, illuminations, and fire-works. Under the plea of illness, I did not assist at any of them.

Towards the end of Lent, Serge Soltikoff returned from Sweden. During his absence, the High Chancellor, Count Bestoujeff, sent me all the news he received of him, as well as the despatches of Count Panine, at that time Envoy of Russia to the Swedish Court. They reached me through Madame Vladislava, who received them from her step-son, chief clerk to the High Chancellor, and I sent them back by the same way. I further learned by the same channel, that it was decided that on his return, Soltikoff should be sent to Hamburg as resident minister of Russia, in place of Prince Alexander Galitzine, who was appointed to the army. This new arrangement did not diminish my sadness.

On his arrival, Serge Soltikoff requested me, through Leon Narichkine, to let him know if there was any possibility of his coming to see me. I spoke to Madame Vladislava, who consented to our interview. He was to come to her rooms, and thence to mine. I waited for him until three o'clock in the morning, and was in deadly anxiety as to what could have prevented his coming. I learned next day that he had been enticed by Count Roman Voronzoff into a lodge of Free Masons, and he pretended that he could not get away without giving rise to suspicions. But I questioned and cross-questioned Leon Narichkine to such a degree, that I saw as clear as the day that he had failed in his engagement from carelessness and want of interest, regardless of all I had so long suffered solely from my attachment to him. Leon Narichkine himself, although his friend, did not offer much, if any, excuse for him. To tell the truth, I was greatly annoyed, and wrote him a letter, in which I complained bitterly of his indifference. He answered it, and came to see me. He had little difficulty in appeasing me, for I was only too well disposed to accept his apologies. He recommended me to go into public: I followed his advice, and made my appearance on the 10th of February, the birthday of the Grand Duke, as well as Shrove Tuesday. I had prepared for the occasion a superb dress of blue velvet, embroidered with gold.

MADAME LA RESSOURCE: 1755

It was at Whitsuntide, I think, that we were recalled from Oranienbaum to the city; and it was about the same time that the English Ambassador, the Chevalier Williams, came to Russia. He had in his suite Count Poniatowsky, a Pole, the son of the one who had followed the fortunes of Charles XII of Sweden. After a short stay at the capital, we returned to Oranienbaum, where the Empress ordered us to keep the Festival of St. Peter. She did not come herself, because she did not wish to celebrate the first fête of my son Paul, which fell on the same day. She remained at Peterhoff, and there placed herself at a window, where she remained, it would seem, the whole day; for all who came to Oranienbaum said they had seen her at that window. A very large company assembled. The dance took place in the hall at the entrance of my garden, and we afterwards supped there. The foreign ambassadors and ministers were present. I remember that the English Ambassador, the Chevalier Williams, sat near me at supper, and that we kept up a conversation as agreeable as it was gay. As he was lively and well-informed, it was not difficult to carry on a conversation with him. I afterwards learned that he had been as much pleased as myself at this soirée, and had spoken of me in high terms. This, indeed, was what always happened when I chanced to be with those who suited me in mind and character, and, as at that time, I did not excite so much envy, I was generally well spoken of. I was looked upon as a woman of mind;

and many of those more intimately acquainted with me, honoured me with their confidence, depended on me, asked my advice, and found themselves the better for following it. The Grand Duke had long since named me Madame la Ressource, and however angry or sulky he might be, if he found himself at a loss on any point, he would come running to me, in his usual style, to get my advice, and then be off again as fast as he could. I likewise remember, at this same feast of St. Peter, at Oranienbaum, that seeing Count Poniatowsky dancing, I spoke to the Chevalier Williams about his father, and the mischief he had done to Peter I. The English Ambassador spoke very favourably of the son, and confirmed to me what I was already aware of, namely, that his father and the Czartoriskys, his mother's family, then formed the Russian party in Poland; that the son had been placed under his care, and sent here in order to be brought up in the feelings of his family towards Russia; and that they trusted he would succeed in this country. He might then be about twenty-two or twenty-three years old. I replied that, in general, I looked upon Russia as the stumbling-block of merit for strangers, and considered that those who succeeded in Russia might safely calculate upon success in every other part of Europe. This rule I have always considered as infallible, for nowhere are people more quick in detecting the weak points, absurdities, and defects of a stranger than in Russia. A stranger may be sure that nothing will be overlooked, for, naturally, no Russian really likes a foreigner.

THE GRAND DUKE PETER: 1755

At this period, and for a long time afterwards, the principal plaything of the Grand Duke, while in town, consisted of an immense number of little dolls, representing soldiers, formed of wood, lead, pith, and wax. These he arranged on very narrow tables, which took up an entire room, leaving scarcely space enough to pass between them. Along these tables he had nailed narrow bands of brass, to which strings were attached, and when he pulled these strings the brass bands made a noise which, according to him, resembled the roll of musketry. He observed the court festivals with great regularity, making these troops produce their rolling fire; besides which, he daily relieved guard, that is to say, from every table was picked out the dolls that were assumed to be on guard. He assisted at this parade in full uniform, boots, spurs, gorget, and scarf. Such of his domestics as were submitted to this precious exercise were obliged to appear in similar style.

2
Catherine's Lovers

Catherine participated in a series of liaisons while Grand Duchess, and, as Empress, continued her relationships with many official favorites. The first of the following letters was written to Stanislas Poniatowsky, a Pole with whom Catherine had an affair before becoming Empress, and the second was written to the most famous of her lovers, Gregory Potemkin.

CATHERINE TO PONIATOWSKY [1]

On August 2, 1762, Catherine wrote to Stanislas Poniatowsky, the former lover of her difficult days as Grand Duchess, and described the events that had recently brought her to power. Within two years, Catherine's troops would have insured the election of Stanislas Poniatowsky as the last King of Poland.

. . . It is six months ago since my accession to the throne was first put in hand. Peter III. had lost the little wit he had. He ran his head against everything. He wanted to break up the Guards, and with that intent led them out to war; he meant to substitute for them the Holstein troops which were to have remained in town. He wanted to change his religion, marry Elizabeth Vorontsov and shut me up.

The day of the celebration of the peace with [Prussia], after having publicly insulted me at table, he ordered my arrest the same evening. My uncle, Prince George, got this order retracted, and from thenceforth I lent an ear to the propositions which had been made to me [ever] since the death of the Empress [Elizabeth].

The [original] design was to seize him in his apartments and shut him up as was done with the Princess Anne and her children. He went off [however] to Oranienbaum. We were sure of a great number of the captains of the Guards. The fate of the secret was in the hands of the three brothers Orlov. . . . They are extremely determined people and much beloved by the common soldiers, having served in the Guards. I

[1] From R. N. Bain, *Peter III: Emperor of Russia* (New York: E. P. Dutton and Co., 1902), pp. 191–97.

am under great obligation to these people, all Petersburg is my witness.

The minds of the Guards were made up and at last 30 to 40 officers and 10,000 of the common soldiers were in the secret. There was not a traitor to be found among them during the three weeks [before the revolution], there were four separate parties among them, whose chiefs met together as an executive; the real secret was in the hands of the three brothers. Panin wanted the revolution to be in favour of my son, but they would not consent anyhow.

I was at Peterhof, Peter III. was making merry and dwelling at Oranienbaum. It had been agreed that in case of treason, his return should not be proclaimed. Their zeal for me did what treason might have done. On the [27th July, O. S.] a report spread among the troops that I was arrested. The soldiers began to stir, one of our officers calmed them. Then a soldier went to a captain called Passek, chief of one of the [four] parties, and told him that it was certainly all up with me, he assured him he had news [to that effect]. This soldier, alarmed about me, then went to another officer, who was not in the secret, and told him the same thing. Alarmed to hear that an officer had sent away this soldier without arresting him, he posted off to his major. The major caused Passek to be arrested—and the whole regiment was instantly agog. The report [of this affair] was sent the same night to Oranienbaum. All our conspirators were alarmed. They immediately resolved to send the second brother Orlov to me to bring me into town, and the other two [Orlovs] secured the town, telling everybody I was coming.

The Hetman [Razumovsky], Volkonsky and Panin were in the secret. I was sleeping calmly at Peterhof at 6 o'clock in the morning of the 28th [July, O. S.]. The day had been a very disturbing one for me as I knew all that was going on. [Suddenly] Alexius Orlov enters my room and says quite gently: "It is time to get up; all is ready for your proclamation." I demanded some details. "Passek is arrested," said he. I hesitated no longer. I dressed myself quickly without making my toilet and got into the carriage which he had brought with him. Another officer, dressed up as a valet, was at the carriage door, a third met us some versts from Peterhof.

Five versts from the town I met the elder Orlov with the younger Prince Bariatinsky. Orlov gave up his carriage to me, for my horses were done up, and we got out at the barracks of the Ismailovsky Regiment. [At the gates] were only twelve men, and a drummer, who began sounding an alarm, when the soldiers came running out, kissing me, embracing my hands and feet and clothes, and calling me their deliverer. Then they began swearing allegiance to me. When this had been done, they begged me to get into the carriage, and the priest, cross in hand, walked on in front. We went [first] to the [barracks of the] Semenovsky Regiment, but the regiment came marching out to meet us, crying, Vivat! Then we went to the church of Kazan, where I got out. Then the Preobrazhensky Regiment arrived, crying, Vivat! "We beg your pardon," they said to me, "for being the last. Our officers stopped us, but here are four of them whom we have arrested to shew you our zeal. We want what our brothers want." Then the horse-guards arrived frantic with joy, I never saw anything like it, weeping and crying at the deliverance of their country. . . . I went to the new Winter Palace where the Synod and the Senate were assembled. A manifesto and a form of oath were hastily drawn up. Then I went down and received the troops on foot. There were more than 14,000 men, guards and country regiments. As soon as they saw me they uttered cries of joy which were taken up by an innumerable crowd. I went on to the old Winter Palace to take [my] measures and finish [the business], there we took counsel together, and it was resolved to go to Peterhof, where Peter III. was to have dined with me, at their head. All the great roads had been occupied and rumours came in every moment.

I sent Admiral Talisin to Cronstadt [to secure that fortress]. Then the Chancellor Vorontsov arrived to reproach me for my departure [from Peterhof]; they took him off to church to swear him in. Prince Trubetskoi and Count Shuvalov also arrived from Peterhof in order to collar the regiments and kill me. They were taken off to swear the oaths without the least resistance.

After having sent off our couriers and taken every precaution, towards 10 o'clock in the evening I put on a uniform of the Guards. Having been proclaimed Colonel, with inexpressible acclamations, I took horse and we left only a very few of each regiment behind to protect my son, whom we left in town. I set out at the head of the troops, and we marched all night towards Peterhof. On reaching a little monastery on the way, the Vice-Chancellor arrived with a very flattering letter from Peter III. I had forgotten to say that on leaving town, three soldiers of the Guards, sent from Peterhof to distribute a manifesto among the people, came to me and said: "Here! take what Peter III. has entrusted us with, we give it to you. We are very glad of the opportunity of joining our brethren."

After the first letter came a second, the bearer whereof, General Michal Ismailov, threw himself at my feet and said: "Do you take me for an honest man?" On my replying, "Yes!" "Well," says he, "it is pleasant to have to do with sensible folk. The Emperor offers to resign. I will bring to you [a form of abdication] after a very few alterations. I will save my country from a civil war without any difficulty."

I charged him with this commission, and off he went to accomplish it. Peter III. abdicated, at Oranienbaum, in full liberty, surrounded by 5000 Holsteiners, and came with Elizabeth Vorontsov, Gudovich and Ismailov to Peterhof, where, to protect his person, I gave him five officers and some soldiers. . . . Thereupon I sent the deposed Emperor to a remote and very agreeable place called Ropsha, 25 versts from

Peterhof, under the command of Alexius Orlov, with four officers and a detachment of picked good-natured men, whilst decent and convenient rooms were being prepared for him at Schlusselburg. But God disposed otherwise. Fear had given him a diarrhœa which lasted three days and passed away on the fourth; in this [fourth] day he drank excessively, for he had all he wanted except liberty. Nevertheless, the only things he asked me for were his mistress, his dog, his Negro and his violin; but for fear of scandal [sic] and increasing the agitation of the persons who guarded him, I only sent him the last three things.

The hemorrhoidal colic which seized him affected his brain: two days he was delirious, and the delirium was followed by very great exhaustion, and despite all the assistance of the doctors, he expired whilst demanding a Lutheran priest. I feared that the officers might have poisoned him, so I had him opened, but it is an absolute fact that not the slightest trace of poison was found inside him. The stomach was quite sound, but inflammation of the bowels and a stroke of apoplexy had carried him off. His heart was extraordinarily small and quite decayed. . . .

It would take a whole book to describe the conduct of each of the leaders. The Orlovs brilliantly distinguished themselves by their faculty of ruling the minds of men, by their prudent audacity, by [their attention to] great and petty details, and by their presence of mind. They have a great deal of common-sense and generous courage. They are enthusiastic patriots, very honest folk, passionately attached to my person and united as never brothers were united before. There are five of them in all, but only three were here. . . . The Princess Dashkof, younger sister of Elizabeth Vorontsov, though she would like to attribute to herself all the honour [of the affair], being acquainted with some of the chiefs, was looked upon askance because of her parentage, and being but 19 had no authority at all, and although she pretends that she was the chief intermediary all along, yet the real fact is that everyone had been in [direct] communication with me six months beforehand, before she even knew their names. But she has a meddlesome humour together with a great deal of ostentation, and our principal men hate her exceedingly. It was only a few feather-brains who let her into the secret and told her all they knew, which was very trumpery. Nevertheless, they say that Ivan Ivanovich Shuvalov, the lowest and most cowardly of men has written to Voltaire that a woman 19 years old, has changed the government of this Empire. I beg of you to undeceive this great writer. Five months before she knew anything it was necessary to conceal from the Princess Dashkov [the nature of] the modes of communication between myself and others, and during the last four weeks she was told as little as possible.

The strength of mind of Prince Bariatinsky, who concealed the secret from his dearly beloved brother, the late Emperor's adjutant . . . deserves praise.

In the Horse-Guards, an officer named Chitrov, aged 22, and an under officer, 17 years old, named Potemkin, directed everything with discernment, courage and energy.

That is pretty much the history of this affair and I assure you that everything was done under my direct personal orders. At the last moment I hurried up because the departure [of the Emperor] for the country prevented the execution [of the plot], and everything had been ripe for a fortnight.

The late Emperor, when he heard of the tumult in town, was prevented by the young women of his suite from following the advice of old Field Marshal Münnich, who advised him to throw himself into Cronstadt, or set off for the army with a few followers. When he *did* go in his galley to Cronstadt the fortress was already ours in consequence of the good conduct of Admiral Talizin, who caused General Devier to be disarmed, this Devier being already on the spot on the Emperor's behalf when Talizin arrived. An officer of the port, on his own initiative, threatened to fire point-blank at the galley of this unfortunate Prince.

At last, then God has brought everything to pass according to His pre-disposition. The whole thing is rather a miracle than a fact foreseen and arranged beforehand, for so many felicitous combinations could not have coincided unless God's hand had been over it all.

. . . Be assured, too, that hatred of foreigners was the leading principle of the whole affair, and that Peter III. himself passed for a foreigner.

Adieu, there are some very strange situations in this world.

CATHERINE TO POTEMKIN [2]

Gregory Potemkin, former Guardsman and favorite of the Empress for only two years, nevertheless remained her closest friend and advisor for the rest of his life. Catherine wrote to Potemkin in 1774 expressing her love, and then made notes on his reply apologizing for a quarrel.

MARIA CHOGLOKOVA could see that there was nothing more between us than there had been before our marriage. But as she was often

[2] From Dominique Maroger, ed., *The Memoirs of Catherine the Great*, translated by Moura Budberg (New York: Collier Books, 1961), pp. 280–82. (Copyright © 1955 by Hamish Hamilton Ltd. Reprinted by permission of The Macmillan Company and Hamish Hamilton Ltd.

being scolded by the Empress Elizabeth for doing nothing about the situation, she found nothing better than to offer both parties a choice, according to their wish, among the persons she had in mind. On the one hand, the widow Groot was chosen, who is now married to Artillery Lieutenant-General Miller, and on the other S.S.; the latter because of his obvious inclination and the advice of Maman, driven to this by dire necessity. Two years later S.S. was sent away as Ambassador, having behaved indiscreetly, and Choglokova was unable to keep him at the big Court. A year passed in great grief and then came the present King of P. We took no notice of him to begin with, but other kind people, with their puerile gossip, forced us to take into account that he existed, that his eyes were of unparalleled beauty, and that he turned them (though they were so myopic that they could not see further than his nose) more often in one direction than in another. This one was both loving and loved from 1755 till 1761 including an absence of three years, that is from 1758, and then the repeated entreaties of Prince G.O. whom kind people again brought to our attention, changed my state of mind.

This one would have remained for ever had he not been the first to tire; I learnt this on the day of his departure to the Congress from Tsarskoe Selo and simply decided that I could no longer trust him, a thought that hurt me cruelly and forced me, from desperation, to take a step which I deplore to this day more than I can say, *especially at the moments when other people usually feel happy*. All caresses provoke nothing in me but tears, so that I believe I have never cried since my birth as I have in these eighteen months. I thought at first that I would get accustomed to the situation but things grew worse and worse; on the other side, they sulked sometimes for three months and to tell the truth I was never happier than when they got angry and left me in peace, as the caresses only made me cry.

Then came a certain Hero (*bogatir*); this hero, through his valour and demeanour, was already very close to our heart; on hearing of his arrival people began to talk of his staying here, not knowing that we had already written to him, on the quiet, asking him to do so, with the secret intention, however, of not acting blindly when he did come, but of trying to discover whether he really had the inclination of which Countess Bruce said that many suspected him, the inclination I wanted him to have.

Now, Sir Hero, after this confession, may I hope that I will receive absolution for my sins; as you will be pleased to see, there is no question of fifteen but only of one-third of that figure of which the first occurred unwillingly and the fourth in despair, which cannot be counted as indulgence; as to the other three, God is my witness that it was not through wantonness, for which I have no leanings, and had I been destined as a young woman to get a husband whom I could have loved,

I would have never changed towards him. The trouble is that my heart is loath to remain even one hour without love; it is said that human vices are often concealed under the cloak of kindness and it is possible that such a disposition of the heart is more of a vice than a virtue, but I ought not to write this to you, for you might stop loving me or refuse to go to the Army fearing I should forget you, but I do not think I could do anything so foolish, and if you wish to keep me for ever, show me as much friendship as affection, and continue to love me and to tell me the truth.

[The letter from Potemkin[3] which follows can serve as an appendix to the one above. The annotations on the right are Catherine's.]

Allow me, my dearest, to say these last words to end our 'row.' Do not be surprised that I am so anxious about our love. Apart from the innumerable gifts you have bestowed on me, you have given me your heart.

I allow.
The sooner the better.

Do not be anxious.
When you wash your hands one hand rubs the other.
You are and will be this for ever.

I wish to be preferred to all the former ones, to make you understand that no one has ever loved you as much as I, and as I am the work of your hands, I wish that my repose should also be the work of your hands; that you should find joy in being kind to me, that you should try everything for my consolation and find consolation in me for the great work you have to accomplish, because of your high calling.

I can see it and do believe it. My heart is happy.

My primary joy.
It will come of its own accord.
Let the mind rest in order that the feelings should be free, they are all love, they themselves will find the best path.
The end of our quarrel. Amen.

[3] In Russian. (T.)

3
Catherine and the Enlightenment

History has classified Catherine II as one of the "enlightened despots" of her century, alongside Joseph II of Austria and Frederick II of Prussia. Catherine carefully cultivated the philosophes *such as Voltaire and Diderot, and the artists of the age such as Falconet, and in return, these intellectuals created for her, in Europe, the image of a great cultural patron. Catherine read the great works of the period, and they were reflected in the content, vocabulary, and style of her famous* Instruction. *Many historians have emphasized the shallowness of Catherine's attachment to the ideas of the enlightenment, her concern only for a glorious public image, and her reluctance to actually implement any of the reforms that she professed to admire. The French Revolution of 1789 played a role in Catherine's attitude toward the Enlightenment, and she tended more and more to blame the excesses of that revolution on those thinkers whom she had previously admired and patronized.*

CATHERINE AND VOLTAIRE [1]

Catherine initiated an enduring correspondence with Voltaire shortly after her accession to the Russian throne. She supported the great philosophe *while he glorified her name through Europe. Nothing better exemplifies the relationship of these two preeminent figures of the age than the following letter, in which the Empress grants the philosopher's request for financial aid for his two most famous civil rights clients in France while indicating her willingness to have him advertise her liberality.*

Sir, The brightness of the northern star is a mere aurora borealis. It is nothing more than giving to a neighbour something of our

---

[1] From William Tooke, *Life of Catherine II, Empress of All the Russias* (London, 1802), vol. 1, p. 425.

own superfluity. But to be the advocate of human kind, the defender of oppressed innocence; by this you will be indeed immortalized. The two causes of Calas and Sirven have procured you the veneration due to such miracles. You have combated the united enemies of mankind, superstition, fanaticism, ignorance, chicane, bad judges, and the power lodged in them, all together. To surmount such obstacles, required both talents and virtue. You have shown the world that you possess both. You have carried your point. You desire, sir, some relief for the Sirven family. Can I possibly refuse it? Or, should you praise me for the action, would there be the least foundation for it? I own to you, that I should be much better pleased if my bill of exchange could pass unknown. Nevertheless, if you think my name, unharmonious as it is, may be of any service to those victims of the spirit of persecution, I leave it to your discretion; and you may announce me, provided it be no way prejudicial to the parties.

AN INTERVIEW WITH DIDEROT [2]

The famous philosophe *Diderot, editor of* L'Encyclopedie, *was patronized by Catherine II. He visited the Empress at Saint Petersburg in 1773–74, and recorded the following interview.*

First Question: The population of Russia is estimated sometimes at eighteen million souls and other times at twenty million. Where do these various estimates come from, and what is the actual population? *First Answer:* The variety in the estimations of our population come from the fact that no one knows precisely what it is; but here is something which may serve as a guide. There are nine million men who pay the head tax (women do not pay it). The following provinces and peoples do not pay it any more: Livonia, Estonia, Narva and its territories, the government of Petersburg or Ingria, the Lapons, the Samoyeds, Finland, Little Russia or Ukraine, New Russia, all the Cossacks of whatever names, all the pastoral peoples of Siberia, the Kalmucks, and the foreign colonists established not only in this kingdom but everywhere in the empire (and their number is large). In addition, nobles are excluded from the head tax, as well as foreign families living in the empire for several centuries, and free peasants. Every twenty years we make a new census which we call a revision of the head tax. We include in these revisions all living men including new born infants; each person included in the revision pays seventy *sols* per head. Thus, the living pay for the dead between revisions, but,

[2] "Questions de Diderot et réponses de Catherine II sur la situation économique de l'Empire Russe," in Maurice Tourneux, *Diderot et Catherine II* (Paris: Calmann Lévy, 1899), pp. 532–41; translated by L. Jay Oliva.

on the other hand, the new-borns during the twenty years help their brothers in work and these are not yet paying the head tax.

Second Question: The number of monks has been estimated at seven million three hundred thousand, and the number of nuns at five million three hundred thousand, and we are told that this number is diminishing. Is this true? Is this decline the result of the laws of Peter I, who fixed the age of taking vows at thirty years for men and fifty years for women?

Second Answer: The number of monasteries in Ukraine is sixty-two; in the rest of Russia there are one hundred and sixty-three. Thus, the whole of Russia has only one hundred and one monasteries more than the whole province of Ukraine. The number of convents in this pious province amounts to eighteen, while in the rest of Russia there are sixty-eight. In all, there are three hundred and eleven monasteries and convents in the Russian empire. White Russia is not included in this calculation. The number of monks and other religious has diminished prodigiously over the past ten years; a monk and a nun receive no more support than a soldier, and although the number in each convent is fixed, it profits the convent to have less than its fixed number because then the resources allotted to the vacant places remains to be shared by the occupants. There are very few monasteries in which the number of monks amounts to fifty; the majority do not have more than ten. The laws of Peter the Great doubtless have caused great reforms, but during the twenty years of the reign of his daughter they were neglected. However, since the lands of the monasteries are now regulated by a College, and as it is very difficult to receive permission to take vows, the number of religious is diminishing and controls have been reorganized. Ukraine is a privileged province, where religious fervor abounds. However, the vigilance of Marshal Count Rumiantsev, who was governor of that province, benefitted Ukraine up to the time of the war when he left the province in order to command an army.

Third Question: Entry into Russia was forbidden to the Jews in 1764; then this interdict was lifted. Are there Jews here? If there are, in what condition are they? Are they treated as other foreigners? And about how many Jews are there?

Third Answer: The Jews were routed from Russia by the Empress Elizabeth at the beginning of her reign, about 1742. In 1762 there was a question of allowing them to return, but the proposition was badly made and things remained where they were. In 1764, the Jews were declared merchants and inhabitants of New Russia. They abound in White Russia. There are three or four in Petersburg; for eight or nine years, they lodged in the residence of one of my confessors. They are tolerated despite the law, and people seem to make believe they do not exist. As for the rest, their reintegration into Russia could do great harm to our small merchants, and would produce more anguish than profits by their return.

Fourth Question: Some authors have distributed the inhabitants of Russia into four groups: Church, Nobility, Free Men, and Peasants. Is this distribution exact? What is the population according to these classes?

Fourth Answer: I do not know why it has pleased some authors to distribute the inhabitants of Russia in this way. One could just as reasonably, I think, distribute them thus: Church, Nobility who alone have the right to possess lands, inhabitants of cities and towns who alone have the right to engage in commerce, and peasants who could be divided into two groups: those possessing lands and cultivating them with their own hands, and those who are subjects of the nobility and dependent upon them or who are the immediate subjects of the empire (those peasants on the Crown or on domain lands, veterans, or those who could be called "possessors of [single] households" [odnodvortsy]). . . . There are entire districts where peasants do not sit down at table without having a goose in their pots, and chicken is a very common thing. I have seen those peasants whose granaries were filled with the wheat from six years of harvests, and they did not sell it because the price had fallen. These would be ranged under the first category and the peasants of the nobility under the second. The population by classes would be very nearly according to the following guidelines of peasants and inhabitants of towns under the head tax described above. The clergy could not really be counted except by parishes, of which there was, in 1763, a very inexact count. This count showed for Russia, without Ukraine and the conquered provinces, nineteen thousand. There are also parishes which have several priests, but there is at least one priest in each parish and one or two lectors. The nobility could be the most difficult to count, but assuredly there are more than ten thousand gentlemen in service, and nearly three thousand gentlemen in the regiments of the guards. In the army and in the three corps of cadets, there are about three thousand nobles (there are continually complaints against the cadet corps that they do not accept all those who present themselves). The navy and the artillery have their complement, without counting the civil servants and all their dependents at court. And even greater numbers of nobles still live on the lands and in the provinces, in the capital, but above all at Moscow and at Kazan.

These three classes of nobles, townsmen, and peasants use the most noble words to defend their privileges; the landed lord invokes the rights of property, the merchants those of liberty, and the people those of humanity.

What we must fear more is a return to the spirit of faction, that spirit which alone reigns when the sciences are still new, when justice is partial and which attaches itself in an opinionated way to whatever it seizes upon in the shadows, which abandons nothing because it distinguishes nothing with precision, and which rarely allows itself to develop because opinions only become flexible when they are formed in doubt and nourished with thought.

Every law made for a nation ought to find its origin in the general good; when force and ignorance destroy this principle, these are acts of despotism and error against which reason and equity cry out; these are the days of calamity whose end one awaits impatiently.

Landowners, guaranteed in their fortune, draw only advantages from an increase in the population: For example, they may have destined the income from two hundred arpents of land to buy the work of ten artisans, and this payment buys for each one of these artisans good clothes, agreeable food, and some leisure. But when the number of laborers is increased, the crowd which results allows the landowner to reduce the recompense for work to the barest essentials. Then, with the same quantity of arpents, the landowners support perhaps twice as many workers and procure for themselves new enjoyments, and this increase in work is devoted only to their pleasures.

The bread which nourishes the people, the religion which consoles them, these are the only ideas of the people. They will be always as simple as nature. The prosperity of the state, the coming centuries, the next generation, these are words which have no meaning for them. These people are held in society only by its bonds, and of that immense space which we call the future they do not even perceive tomorrow. The people is deprived by its misery of any wider interest.

Fifth Question: Authors say that foreign merchants find many difficulties in establishing themselves in Russia and many obstacles to the exercise of their commerce. Is this true? What is the source of these obstacles? Is it possible to stop these abuses?

Fifth Answer: If these difficulties exist they can come only from ignorance of the language, of the laws of the country, and of the jealousy and obstacles imposed by other foreigners established here. The laws are not at all opposed to foreigners. They allow them large-scale commerce and reserve only the lesser commerce to our native merchants. But if the foreigner registers himself among the merchants of our country, which he can do whenever the fancy takes him, he can share in this domestic commerce which, usually, is forbidden to foreigners, although there is not a wig-maker or some other Frenchman acting as a tutor or governess who does not practice it at the risk of suffering confiscation. It is perhaps the dangers of this forbidden commerce which makes these people who have tried it and who have lost say that the exercise of commerce is submitted in Russia to numerous obstacles and difficulties. On the other hand, it is usual in Europe to look upon Russia and the commerce which foreigners make here as if we were another Peru, which is designed only to be exploited.

Landed Proprietors

First Question: Is the nobility the only proprietor of lands? Are there nobles and also free peasants?
First Answer: The nobility alone has the right to own lands. Large manufacturers formerly had the right to buy lands, but in 1763 this law was abolished and we have forbidden manufacturers to buy lands because they forced men of the fields to become textile workers and the lands remained fallow. This is a result which provides no profit for the state.

Second Question: What are the privileges of the landed proprietors?
Second Answer: By law there are very few except the maintenance of taverns, but in fact they control on their lands everything that seems proper to them, except the death sentence which is forbidden to them.

Third Question: What are the conditions now prevailing between masters and slaves in the cultivation of the land?
Third Answer: There is a law of Peter the Great which forbids naming the subjects of the nobility as slaves. Formerly, all of the inhabitants of Russia were free. From their origin they were composed of two kinds of people: those who descended from pastoral people and those who were made prisoners of war. At the death of Tsar Ivan Vasilovich, his son, Fyodor Ivanovich, by an ordinance, attached or fixed all peasants to the land that they cultivated and which someone else possessed. There are no laws regulating the relation of masters and their subjects, but every master who has common sense, far from demanding too much, herds his cows in order to milk them easily without wearying them. When something is not regulated by law, natural law takes its place, and often in this way things are less evil, because at least they are arranged according to the natural development of things.

Fourth Question: Does not the servitude of the peasants influence Russian culture? Does not this lack of peasant land ownership produce bad effects?
Fourth Answer: I do not know if there is a country where the peasant loves his land better and his household better than he does in Russia. Our free provinces never produce more grain than those which are not; each nation has its faults, its vices, and its inconveniences.

Fifth Question: What is the price of land, or how much annual revenue is equal to the capital, the property, or the sum required to buy a piece of land?

Fifth Answer: The revenue of a piece of land that one buys ordinarily produces six percent of the capital investment. These lands have been substantially increasing in price for the past twelve to fifteen years. At the same time, the revenues from land have grown prodigiously. A piece of property which produced, for example, sixty years ago, four hundred rubles of revenues, produces at this time eight thousand. The increase in the money supply, in commerce, in the development of textiles, and in the exportation of grain, all have contributed. At the same time, the price of everything is going up.

CATHERINE AND FALCONET [3]

Falconet, famous sculptor and philosophe *of eighteenth century France, worked in Russia under the patronage of Catherine II from 1767 to 1778. Falconet was a close friend of Diderot and of the collaborators in the* Encyclopedie; *Catherine maintained a continuous correspondence with him while he was in Russia. In the first letter, Catherine is critical of an article that has been included in the* Encyclopedie; *in the second, she tries to convince the sculptor to cast his equestrian statue of Peter the Great, the splendid "Bronze Horseman" made famous by Pushkin; in the third, she rejects Falconet's intervention on behalf of a foreign officer.*

February 18, 1767

Yesterday, in the article "On Religious Orders" in *L'Encyclopedie,* I read that your Saint Louis said that if he could spilt himself into two parts he would give half to the Order of Preachers [Dominicans, ed.] and half to the Friars Minor [Franciscans, ed.]. You can see very well that there is not much left for this good king to give to his kingdom. I am mistaken in saying "good king"; I should have said "good man," because a good man can make such plans but a good king does better to give himself completely to his kingdom rather than sharing his halves with mendicant religious orders. Still, if Saint Louis had spoken as *Chimene* in *Le Cid* [a play by Racine, ed.], naming his two halves and marching off with a third, we could believe that this was rhetoric and that in reality he kept something of himself for his royal work. But, on the contrary, Saint Louis spoke quite positively:

[3] Letters of Catherine to Falconet; February 18, 1767; September 18, 1769; March 14, 1773; in Louis Réau, ed., *Correspondance de Falconet avec Catherine II, 1767–1778* (Paris: Edouard Champion, 1921), pp. 4–5, 100–101, 197–98; translated by L. Jay Oliva.

he had two halves and he disposed of them. Of course, he has been rewarded for his generosity; he has been canonized as the best of kings. All virtues have been ascribed to him and he is proposed as a model to all those whom anyone wishes to reshape. It is true that nothing is more praiseworthy than such recognition. Receive my compliments on it: it is good to thus encourage merit with elevating examples. . . .

September 18, 1769

Monsieur Falconet, I have spent the last twenty-four hours searching for the letters that Monsieur Voltaire has written to me, but I do recall that you delivered them to me in the first place. Is it possible that I returned them to you? I can't remember anything about them. You can tell me when you see me tomorrow or the day after; meanwhile, I will keep searching.

You can also tell me then why you do not wish to cast the statue [of Peter the Great on horseback, ed.] yourself. I do not wish to displease you, but there is no good reason that I can see in the letter to M. Betzki [Catherine's advisor, ed.]; I presume you have some better reasons which you have kept to yourself. But if you can conquer the obstacles, it would be a good and useful thing. And what man of genius doesn't follow through to the end? Further, who has convinced you that a professional foundryman would be better than yourself? Please recall how many able foundrymen have failed! You will tell me that this is their business, but I really don't think that you would enjoy the destruction of your work by someone else. I believe that if you are willing to bear the difficulties of casting the statue, it will be a success and that you will be much less displeased than you would be with someone else.

Monsieur, I would never contradict your views, but truly and sincerely I tell you what seems to me to be the truth. We will discuss this matter at length one of these days.

March 14, 1773

I swear to you that I am not only astonished, but also that it is a most peculiar thing to hear the plaintive tone which this M. Lascaris is continually employing. One would think, on hearing him, that he had suffered the greatest wrongs in the world? Well, so that you will know the truth, find out how many years M. Lascaris was a minor officer galloping around with M. Betzki in a campaign regiment; if my memory does not deceive me, he was a lieutenant or at most a captain. Betzki, finding some qualities of intelligence or talent in him, took him under his wing and used him as an adjutant. He served thus about seven or eight years.

He has never been advanced by seniority turns, but always, as he has told you, either by the protection of his commander or by doing his job as he was told. He has always had in his character, as I have remarked a hundred times to his commanders, traits of bad humor and aggressiveness, forever demanding more and never happy. Surely he has been passed by in promotion by others, but assuredly not by anyone who has not won his promotion at the cost of his blood; and surely there are a great many more whom M. Lascaris has passed by who had more seniority than he.

The first words out of his mouth have always been his promotion or his resignation; I have always said that we should let him make up his mind, since we should not restrict his movements nor allow him to lay the law down to us.

I have not mentioned the other gifts he has received, because he will say that they are due to him for services rendered; but I would like to know what nation would have given him more or even as much? M. Lascaris is hated as a toady in the Corps of Cadets; we had to install another commander before they would accept him. I do not know what his commander has promised him, but I do know that I cannot find anything for him to complain about. We never give promotion to a foreigner who is resigning. According to our military law, which is excellent, this honor is reserved to Russians; I consider this a just practice for reasons too long to go into here. We have, then, all his vain pretensions; I do not consider him to have been retarded in rank at all for having risen from captain to lieutenant-colonel in seven years; we have some captains in the army who are facing the enemy every day who have been in their ranks since the last war against Prussia [1762 ed.].

CATHERINE'S INSTRUCTION 4

The Empress, working and writing between 1764 and 1767, prepared a lengthy Nakaz, *or* Instruction, *to guide a commission to be established for the recodification of Russian laws. The contents of the* Instruction *were drawn from the great philosophers of the century, especially Montesquieu and Beccaria. The more than five hundred articles were designed to utilize the wisdom of Western Europe in solving Russian problems, and to inspire a law code that would lead the Russian citizenry to the natural order of society. The document is revealing of Catherine's own education and early hopes, although its expectations were never fulfilled.*

4 From *The Grand Instruction to the Commissioners Appointed to Frame a New Code of Laws for the Russian Empire, Composed by Her Imperial Majesty Catherine II,* edited by M. Tatischeff (London, 1768), chapters 1–5, 11, and conclusion.

O Lord my God, hearken unto me, and instruct me; that I may administer Judgment unto thy People; as thy sacred Laws direct to judge with Righteousness!

**The Instructions to the Commissioners
for Composing a New Code of Laws**

1. The Christian Law teaches us to do mutual Good to one another, as much as possibly we can.

2. Laying this down as a fundamental Rule prescribed by that Religion, which has taken, or ought to take Root in the Hearts of the whole People; we cannot but suppose that every honest Man in the Community is, or will be, desirous of seeing his native Country at the very Summit of Happiness, Glory, Safety, and Tranquillity.

3. And that every Individual Citizen in particular must wish to see himself protected by Laws, which should not distress him in his Circumstances, but, on the Contrary, should defend him from all Attempts of others that are repugnant to this fundamental Rule.

4. In order therefore to proceed to a speedy Execution of what *We* expect from such a general Wish, *We,* fixing the Foundation upon the above first-mentioned Rule, ought to begin with an Inquiry into the natural Situation of this Empire.

5. For those Laws have the greatest Conformity with Nature, whose particular Regulations are best adapted to the Situation and Circumstances of the People for whom they are instituted.

This natural Situation is described in the three following Chapters.

Chapter I

6. Russia is an European State.

7. This is clearly demonstrated by the following Observations: The Alterations which *Peter the Great* undertook in Russia succeeded with the greater Ease, because the Manners, which prevailed at that Time, and had been introduced amongst us by a Mixture of different Nations, and the Conquest of foreign Territories, were quite unsuitable to the Climate. *Peter the First,* by introducing the Manners and Customs of Europe among the European People in his Dominions, found at that Time such Means as even he himself was not sanguine enough to expect.

Chapter II

8. The Possessions of the Russian Empire extend upon the terrestrial Globe to 32 Degrees of Latitude, and to 165 of Longitude.

9. The Sovereign is absolute; for there is no other authority but that which centers in his single Person that can act with a Vigour proportionate to the Extent of such a vast Dominion.

10. The Extent of the Dominion requires an absolute Power to be

vested in that Person who rules over it. It is expedient so to be that the quick Dispatch of Affairs, sent from distant Parts, might make ample Amends for the Delay occasioned by the great Distance of the Places.

11. Every other Form of Government whatsoever would not only have been prejudicial to Russia, but would even have proved its entire Ruin.

12. Another Reason is; That it is better to be subject to the Laws under one Master, than to be subservient to many.

13. What is the true End of Monarchy? Not to deprive People of their natural Liberty; but to correct their Actions, in order to attain the *supreme Good.*

14. The Form of Government, therefore, which best attains this End, and at the same Time sets less Bounds than others to natural Liberty, is that which coincides with the Views and Purposes of rational Creatures, and answers the End, upon which we ought to fix a stedfast Eye in the Regulations of civil Polity.

15. The Intention and the End of Monarchy is the Glory of the Citizens, of the State, and of the Sovereign.

16. But, from this Glory, a Sense of Liberty arises in a People governed by a Monarch; which may produce in these States as much Energy in transacting the most important Affairs, and may contribute as much to the Happiness of the Subjects, as even Liberty itself.

Chapter III

17. *Of the Safety of the Institutions of Monarchy.*

18. The intermediate Powers, subordinate to, and depending upon the supreme Power, form the essential Part of monarchical Government.

19. *I have* said, that the intermediate Powers, subordinate and depending, proceed from the supreme Power; as in the very Nature of the Thing the Sovereign is the Source of all imperial and civil Power.

20. The Laws, which form the Foundation of the State, send out certain Courts of Judicature, through which, as through smaller Streams, the Power of the Government is poured out, and diffused.

21. The Laws allow these Courts of Judicature to remonstrate, that such or such an Injunction is unconstitutional, and prejudicial, obscure, and impossible to be carried into Execution; and direct, beforehand, to which Injunction one ought to pay Obedience, and in what Manner one ought to conform to it. These Laws undoubtedly constitute the firm and immoveable Basis of every State.

Chapter IV

22. There must be a political Body, to whom the Care and strict Execution of these Laws ought to be confided.

23. This Care, and strict Execution of the Laws, can be no where

so properly fixed as in certain Courts of Judicature, which announce to the People the newly-made Laws, and revive those which are forgotten, or obsolete.

24. And it is the Duty of these Courts of Judicature to examine carefully those Laws which they receive from the Sovereign, and to remonstrate, if they find any Thing in them repugnant to the fundamental Constitution of the State, etc., which has been already remarked above in the third Chapter, and twenty-first Article.

25. But if they find nothing in them of that Nature, they enter them in the Code of Laws already established in the State, and publish them to the whole Body of the People.

26. In Russia the Senate is the political Body, to which the Care and due Execution of the Laws is confided.

27. All other Courts of Judicature may, and ought to remonstrate with the same Propriety, to the Senate, and even to the Sovereign himself, as was already mentioned above.

28. Should any One inquire, wherein the Care and due Execution of the Laws consists? I answer That the Care and due Execution of the Laws produces particular Instructions; in consequence of which the before-mentioned Courts of Judicature, instituted to the End that, by their Care, the Will of the Sovereign might be obeyed in a Manner conformably to the fundamental Laws and Constitution of the State, are obliged to act, in the Discharge of their Duty, according to the Rules prescribed.

29. These Instructions will prevent the People from transgressing the Injunctions of the Sovereign with impunity; but, at the same Time, will protect them from the Insults and ungovernable Passions of others.

30. For, on the one Hand, they justify the Penalties prepared for those who transgress the Laws; and, on the other, they confirm the Justice of that Refusal to enter Laws repugnant to the good Order of the State, amongst those which are already approved of, or to act by those Laws in the Administration of Justice, and the general Business of the Whole Body of the People.

Chapter V

31. *Of the Situation of the People in general.*

32. It is the greatest Happiness for a Man to be so circumstanced, that, if his Passions should prompt him to be mischievous, he should still think it more for his Interest not to give Way to them.

33. The Laws ought to be so framed as to secure the Safety of every Citizen as much as possible.

34. The Equality of the Citizens consists in this; that they should all be subject to the same Laws.

35. This Equality requires Institutions so well adapted as to prevent the Rich from oppressing those who are not so wealthy as themselves,

and converting all the Charges and Employments intrusted to them as Magistrates only to their own private Emolument.

36. General or political Liberty does not consist in that licentious Notion, *That a Man may do whatever he pleases.*

37. In a State or Assemblage of People that live together in a Community, where there are Laws, Liberty can only consist *in doing that which every One ought to do,* and *not to be constrained to do that which One ought not to do.*

38. A Man ought to form in his own Mind an exact and clear Idea of what Liberty is. *Liberty is the Right of doing whatsoever the Laws allow:* And if any one Citizen could do what the Laws forbid, there would be no more Liberty; because others would have an equal Power of doing the same.

39. The political Liberty of a Citizen is the Peace of Mind arising from the Consciousness that every Individual enjoys his peculiar Safety; and in order that the People might attain this Liberty, the Laws ought to be so framed that no one Citizen should stand in Fear of another; but that all of them should stand in Fear of the same Laws. . . .

Chapter XI

250. A Society of Citizens, as well as every Thing else, requires a certain fixed Order: There ought to be *some* to *govern,* and *others to obey.*

251. And this is the Origin of every Kind of Subjection; which feels itself more or less alleviated, in Proportion to the Situation of the Subjects.

252. And, consequently, as the Law of Nature commands *Us* to take as much Care as lies in *Our* Power of the Prosperity of all the People; we are obliged to alleviate the Situation of the Subjects as much as sound Reason will permit.

253. And therefore, to shun all Occasions of reducing People to a State of Slavery, except that the *utmost* Necessity should *inevitably* oblige us to do it; in that Case, it ought not to be done for our own Benefit; but for the Interest of the State: Yet even that Case is extremely uncommon.

254. Of whatever Kind Subjection may be, the civil Laws ought to guard, on the one Hand, against the *Abuse* of Slavery, and, on the other, against the *Dangers* which may arise from it.

255. Unhappy is that Government which is compelled to institute *severe* Laws. . . .

260. A great Number of Slaves ought not to be infranchised all at once, nor by a general Law.

261. A Law may be productive of public Benefit, which gives some *private* Property to a Slave.

262. Let us finish all this, by repeating that *fundamental Rule;* that

the government which most resembles that of Nature is that whose
particular Disposition answers best to the Disposition of the People,
for whom it is instituted.

263. However it is still highly necessary to prevent those Causes
which so frequently incited Slaves to rebel against their masters; but
till these Causes are discovered, it is impossible to prevent the like
accidents by Laws; though the Tranquillity, both of the one and of the
other, depends upon it. . . .

Conclusion

523. *Perhaps some Persons may object, after perusing these Instructions, that they will not be intelligible to every one. To this it may
be answered: It is true, they will not be readily understood by every
Person after one slight Perusal only; but every Person may comprehend
these Instructions, if he reads them with Care and Attention, and selects occasionally such Articles as may serve to direct him, as a Rule, in
whatever he undertakes. These Instructions ought to be frequently
perused, to render them more familiar: And every one may be firmly
assured that they will certainly be understood; because,*

524. Assiduity *and* Care *will* conquer *every Difficulty; as, on the*
Contrary, Indolence *and* Carelessness *will* deter *from every laudable*
Attempt.

525. *To render this difficult Affair more easy; these Instructions are
to be read over once, at the Beginning of every Month, in the Commission for composing the New Code of Laws, and in all the subordinate
Committees, which depend upon it; particularly the respective Chapters and Articles intrusted to their Care, till the Conclusion of the Commission.*

526. *But as no perfect Work was ever yet composed by Man; there-
fore, if the Commissioners should discover, as they proceed, that any
Rule for some particular Regulations has been omitted, they have
Leave, in such a Case, to report it to Us, and to ask for a Supplement.*

The Original signed with Her Imperial Majesty's *own Hand, thus,*

Moscow, *July* 30, 1767.   Catherine

CATHERINE AND REVOLUTION [5]

*Catherine responded to the events of the French Revolution,
which began in 1789, by ending her involvement with the liberal
philosophies of France. She wrote the following memorandum in*

[5] "Catherine II: The Revolution Combatted," in Herbert H. Rowen, ed., *From
Absolutism to Revolution: 1648–1848* (New York: The Macmillan Company, 1968),
pp. 221–24. Translated from the French by Herbert H. Rowen. Copyright © 1968
by The Macmillan Company. Reprinted by permission of the publisher.

*1792 advocating a military solution to the French menace. She
herself, however, was actually completely unwilling to send her
own troops for the task; rather she utilized Europe's preoccupa-
tion with France to accomplish the Second Partition of Poland.*

The cause of the king of France is every king's cause.

Europe's interest lies in having France regain the place which is
proper for a great kingdom.

At the present moment a corps of ten thousand men would be strong
enough to cross France from one end to the other.

A half million in money would suffice to establish this force, and
such a modest sum could be obtained at Genoa. France would pay off
this debt over a period of time.

The regions bordering on the Rhine which belong to the bishops of
Speyer and Strasbourg, or to some other princes concerned, would
be best situated for assembling this force. As the proverb says, "If you
have the money, you can have the Switzers too." All the expatriate
nobles would join this corps without fail and perhaps the troops of
the princes of Germany too. With this force France could be rescued
from the bandits; the monarchy and the monarch would be re-estab-
lished; the impostors would be driven out and a few scoundrels punished; the kingdom would be saved from oppression; and a general
amnesty and indulgence would be quickly published for all who submit and return to the obedience of their legitimate master. In the beginning a fortified town would be needed, but even the smallest would
provide a sufficient base. The clergy of France will have returned to
them whatever portion of their property remains unsold; the nobles
will regain the privileges on which their rank depends; and the provinces with representative assemblies [*pays d'États*] will obtain their demands.

It will be necessary to hold firm on the question of order and obedience, but force should be used only against resistance. If the National
Assembly declares these actions to be a crime against the nation, we
should reply by declaring its actions harmful to the kingdom, destructive of the monarchy, and contrary to its laws and principles, to be a
crime against divine and human majesty. The Parlements would make
no difficulty about confirming our declarations. . . .

It is obvious that at the very beginning foreign troops will prove
better in service than native French forces. Nonetheless, many of the
French nobility will assemble, sword in hand, to form a squadron
under the name of the Royal Guard, and will act to rescue the king
and the kingdom from the oppression, the pillage and the ruin of
tyrants and bandits. General officers will take command of this force

as it is formed. This Royal Guard composed of the nobility should not be abolished; if it had existed earlier, it is probable that the royal authority would not have been defeated. Never were there a cause more just nor incentives greater and more capable of arousing zeal and courage. There is no denying that the only result of success will be to restore to its legitimate possessor the authority which is properly his over an almost ruined kingdom. But by means of a wise system of government he will be able to reduce misfortune and make good its losses. Did not the reigns of Henry IV and Louis XIV re-establish the stability of the realm after the greatest of misfortunes? Did not the repute which France regained under the latter reign endure among the public until our own day? . . .

Since our purpose is to re-establish monarchical government in France, the ancient customs which inspire respect for rank in the public must be neither neglected nor treated with contempt. For example, no soldier should be permitted to come before princes or superior officers in the field unless in military uniform. Persons of superior rank should never appear in the theater or in public except when wearing their distinctive insignia, like cordons, etc., and full decorations. The princes should admit to their presence no one in a dress-coat, or dressed otherwise than with the decorations befitting the rank and quality of each in the kingdom, so as to repudiate the idea of perfect equality. They should re-establish the dignity which befits their rank on all occasions. This dignity will in no wise interfere with their being polite, winning and affable in manner with all, for what is involved is not vanity but the place which is proper to each in the monarchy.

It would be desirable for the liberator of France to take precautions that the money and troops will be employed for their proper purpose, that is, to re-establish the monarchy and to maintain the Roman Catholic religion, and for no other aim; in order to achieve this, it will not be useless to agree upon certain points and *even to make an agreement on these with the expatriate princes.* . . .

It is also obvious that there is a principle in this affair which should not be neglected, that is, to be particularly on guard against the frivolous and flighty spirit and the inborn recklessness of the French nation, which have become stronger than ever in this time of misfortune; but these traits may also be a means to bring them under control so long as we do not allow ourselves to be swept along; for of a certainty great affairs are not brought to success by frivolous epigrams, recklessness, and imprudence.

All reports are agreed on one point, that no two of the French who most favor the re-establishment of the monarchy have the same opinion on other matters; it has therefore been held that a proclamation of principles could provide the basis of unity. Those who sign this proclamation of unity will accept the following principles:

1. The maintenance of the Roman Catholic religion in its integrity.
2. Fidelity to the king.
3. His rescue.
4. The re-establishment of the government according to the unanimous wishes of the nation as set forth in the *cahiers* of the provinces, and hence the maintenance of the three Estates in their existence, their property and their security.
5. All contrary oaths shall be declared null and void.
6. A promise to obey the chief of the federation as the basis of the unity of those whose wills are now divided.
7. A promise to contribute to the re-establishment of public peace and tranquility.
8. A promise to maintain military order and discipline.

All points on which it will be difficult to reach agreement should be kept out of this formal proclamation of unity which they will sign, but no one should be accepted for service as an officer under the king and the princes without giving his signature upon his honor.

The most recent reports say that the Princes of the Blood are busy with counterrevolution, but they are said to be downcast, abandoned and pitiful. Such an attitude can only harm their purpose. In order to succeed, they must show a noble and confident air, a serene visage, a firm conviction in the justice of their cause and their enterprise, speaking little of what they really have in mind, but letting it be felt that great-hearted men of intelligence and courage always have at their disposal resources of which the ordinary man is not aware and hence that they always know far more about events than the ordinary person; let them add to this bearing that politeness and benevolence which win men's minds, and they will make great progress; let their bearing encourage, attract and console their fellows. All France is sick with discouragement.

In such a great affair as this of which we have just spoken, what matters is to be possessed utterly by one's purpose, to desire it passionately, and then to communicate one's own convictions to others; hence to act without hesitation as soon as a decision has been taken and thereafter to show the greatest calm in the midst of trouble and never to show agitation or anxiety over events.

This is what the truest, most sincere and purest intentions dictate. These ideas may be imperfect, but they are inspired by the purest desire to seek the triumph of the good and just cause.

4

Catherine's Government

*Catherine's government ultimately rested on her sup-
port of the Russian nobility and the maintenance of peasant
serfdom. Her first decree, announcing her accession, explained
the reasons for her seizure of power. The treatment of the peasantry ultimately caused her involvement in the suppression of a
popular revolt and in the confirmation of the powers and privileges of the Russian gentry. The last document in this section, the
Charter of the Gentry of 1785, embodies the main outlines of
Catherine's government.*

CATHERINE'S ACCESSION MANIFESTO [1]

*The new empress announced her triumphant coup d'état on
June 28, 1762, and described for public consumption the conditions that, she felt, justified her seizure of power.*

By the grace of God, Catharine II, empress and autocratrix of all
the Russias, &c.

All true sons of Russia have clearly seen the great danger to which
the whole Russian empire has actually been exposed. First, the foundations of our orthodox Greek religion have been shaken, and its traditions exposed to total destruction; so that there was absolutely reason
to fear, that the faith which has been established in Russia from the
earliest times, would be entirely changed, and foreign religion introduced. In the second place, the glory which Russia has acquired at
the expense of so much blood, and which was carried to the highest
pitch by her victorious arms, has been trampled under foot by the
peace lately concluded with its most dangerous enemy. And lastly, the
domestic regulations, which are the basis of the country's welfare, have
been entirely overturned.

For these causes, overcome by the imminent peril with which our
faithful subjects were threatened, and seeing how sincere and express
their desires on this matter were: we, putting our trust in the Almighty

[1] From Tooke, *Life of Catherine II*, vol. 1, pp. 518–19.

and his divine justice, have ascended the sovereign imperial throne of all the Russians, and have received a solemn oath of fidelity from all our loving subjects.

CATHERINE'S DECREE ON THE DEPORTATION OF SERFS TO HARD LABOR [2]

While Catherine was renowned in Europe as an "enlightened despot," she hardly earned such a reputation with the Russian peasantry, who were subject to decrees such as the following issued in 1765.

We herewith make it publicly known:

Following Her Imperial Majesty's confirmation, which on January 17, [1765] was presented to the Senate, it was decreed that in case any landowner wants to deliver for better disciplining in hard labor his serfs who, because of very impudent behavior, deserve a just punishment, the Board of Admiralty will take charge of them and use them for heavy work as long as the landlord concerned desires it. During this whole period these people, together with convicts, will be provided with food and clothing from the treasury. When the landlord shall want them back, they [serfs] are to be returned without question, but under one condition: the clothes and shoes of the people, if they are not completely worn out, are to be collected again for the treasury.

CATHERINE'S MANIFESTO AGAINST PUGACHEV [3]

In 1773, a Cossack named Emilian Pugachev raised the banners of revolt among the Ural Cossacks. Peasants, factory workers, subject nationalities, and Old Believers joined to spread the revolt. The movement threatened the Russian system and certainly cemented Catherine in her ties to the Russian gentry as peace keeper. It required a military effort to suppress the revolt, and Pugachev was finally captured and executed in 1775.

By the grace of God, we Catharine II, empress and autocratrix of all the Russias, &c. make known to all our faithful subjects, that we

---

[2] "Catherine II's Decree on the Deportation of Serfs to Hard Labor, January 17, 1765," in Basil Dmytryshyn, ed., *Imperial Russia: A Source Book, 1700–1917* (New York: Holt, Rinehart and Winston, Inc., 1967), p. 118. Translated by Basil Dmytryshyn. Copyright © 1967 by Holt, Rinehart and Winston, Inc. Reprinted by permission of the publisher.

[3] From Tooke, *Life of Catherine II*, vol. 2, pp. 425–27.

have learnt, with the utmost indignation and extreme affliction, that a certain Kozak, a deserter and fugitive from the Don, named Ikhelman Pugatshef, after having traversed Poland, has been collecting, for some time past, in the districts that border on the river Irghis, in the government of Orenburg, a troop of vagabonds like himself; that he continues to commit in those parts all kinds of excesses, by inhumanly depriving the inhabitants of their possessions, and even of their lives; and that in order to draw over to his party, hitherto composed of robbers, such persons as he meets, and specially the unhappy patriots, on whose credulity he imposes, he has had the insolence to arrogate to himself the name of the late emperor Peter III. It would be superfluous here to prove the absurdity of such an imposture, which cannot even put on a shadow of probability in the eyes of sensible persons: for, thanks to the divine goodness, those ages are past, in which the Russian empire was plunged in ignorance and barbarism; when a Griska, an Outreper, with their adherents, and several other traitors to their country, made use of impostures as gross and detestable, to arm brother against brother, and citizen against citizen.

Since those eras, which it is grievous to recollect, all true patriots have enjoyed the fruits of public tranquillity, and shudder with horror at the very remembrance of former troubles. In a word, there is not a man deserving of the Russian name, who does not hold in abomination the odious and insolent lie by which Pugatshef fancies himself able to seduce and to deceive persons of a simple and credulous disposition, by promising to free them from the bonds of submission, and obedience to their sovereign, as if the Creator of the universe had established human societies in such a manner as that they can subsist without an intermediate authority between the sovereign and the people.

Nevertheless, as the insolence of this vile refuse of the human race is attended with consequences pernicious to the provinces adjacent to that district; as the report of the flagrant enormities which he has committed, may affright those persons who are accustomed to imagine the misfortunes of others as ready to fall upon them, and as we watch with indefatigable care over the tranquillity of our faithful subjects, we inform them by the present manifesto, that we have taken, without delay, such measures as are the best adapted to stifle the sedition: and in order to annihilate totally the ambitious designs of Pugatshef, and to exterminate a band of robbers, who have been audacious enough to attack the small military detachments dispersed about those countries, and to massacre the officers who were taken prisoners, we have dispatched thither, with a competent number of troops, general Alexander Bibikof, general in chief of our armies, and major of our regiment of life guards.

Accordingly we have doubt of the happy success of these measures, and we cherish the hope that the public tranquillity will soon be restored, and that the profligates who are spreading devastation over a part of the government of Orenburg, will shortly be dispersed. We are moreover persuaded, that our faithful subjects will justly abhor the imposture of the rebel Pugatshef, as destitute of all probability, and will repel the artifices of the ill-disposed, who seek and find their advantage in the seduction of the weak and credulous, and who cannot assuage their avidity but by ravaging their country, and by shedding of innocent blood.

We trust, with equal confidence, that every true son of the country will unremittedly fulfil his duty, of the contributing to the maintenance of good order and of public tranquillity, by preserving himself from the snares of seduction, and by duly discharging his obedience to his lawful sovereign. All our faithful subjects, therefore, may dispel their alarms and live in perfect security, since we employ our utmost care, and make it our peculiar glory, to preserve their property, and to extend the general felicity.

THE CHARTER OF THE GENTRY [4]

Catherine the Great issued a Charter to the Russian nobility in 1785 that summarized and guaranteed to the gentry the rights, privileges, and position that they had achieved in the eighteenth century. The Charter determined the structure of the upper classes for the remainder of imperial history, and played a key role in establishing the roots of the Russian intelligentsia.

₹ . . As a result of new gains and the expansion of our Empire, when we everywhere enjoy every kind of internal and external peace, we direct our great deed more and more toward an uninterrupted occupation with delivering to our faithful subjects in all vital branches of internal state administration durable and lasting decrees aimed at the increase of happiness and order for future times; toward that aim we find it appropriate to extend our solicitude to our loyal Russian *dvorianstvo* [nobility], in view of the services, zeal, attention, and undeviating faith to All-Russian autocrats—to ourselves as well as to our throne—which it [the nobility] has shown during troublesome times, in war as well as peace. And following God's examples of justice, mercy, and grace, which have beautified the Russian throne and glorified our ancestors, and being moved by our own motherly love

[4] "Catherine II's Charter to the Nobility, April 21, 1785," in Basil Dmytryshyn, ed., *Imperial Russia: A Source Book, 1700–1917* (New York: Holt, Rinehart and Winston, Inc., 1967), pp. 98–102. Translated by Basil Dmytryshyn. Copyright © 1967 by Holt, Rinehart and Winston, Inc. Reprinted by permission of the publisher.

and distinct gratitude to the Russian nobility, our imperial judiciousness and will orders, decrees, announces, and approves undeviatingly for eternity, for the benefit of Russian nobility, in our and imperial service, the following articles:

1. The title of the nobility is hereditary and stems from the quality and virtue of leading men of antiquity who distinguished themselves by their service—which they turned into merit and acquired for their posterity the title of the nobility.

2. It is to the advantage of both the Empire and the Crown, as it is also just, that the respectful title of the nobility be maintained and approved firmly and inviolably; and therefore, as formerly, now and in the future the title of the nobility is irrevocable, hereditary, and belongs to those honorable families who use it; and accordingly:

3. A nobleman transmits his noble title to his wife;

4. A nobleman transmits his noble title to his children hereditarily;

5. Neither a nobleman nor a noblewoman can be deprived of the title of the nobility unless they forfeit it themselves by an act contrary to the standards of noble dignity.

6. The following acts are contrary to the standards of noble dignity and can deprive one of the title: (a) violation of an oath; (b) treason; (c) robbery; (d) thefts of all sorts; (e) deceitful acts; (f) violations which call for either corporal punishment or a deprivation of honor; (g) incitement of others to commit violations—if this be established.

7. But since the title of the nobility cannot be revoked except as a result of violation, and marriage is an honest [institution] set up by divine law, when a noblewoman marries a non-noble man she does not forfeit her title; but she cannot pass on her nobility to her husband or her children.

8. A nobleman cannot be deprived of his title without due process of law.

9. A nobleman cannot be deprived of his honor without due process of law.

10. A nobleman cannot be deprived of his life without due process of law.

11. A nobleman cannot be deprived of his property without due process of law.

12. A nobleman can be judged by his peers only.

13. A nobleman who has committed a crime and is legally liable to be deprived either of his title, honor, or life, cannot be punished without his case being presented before the Senate and then approved by his Imperial Majesty.

14. All criminal acts of a nobleman which for ten years went either unnoticed or had no action taken on them we decree be henceforth forgotten forever. . . .

15. A nobleman cannot be subjected to corporal punishment.

16. Noblemen who serve as junior officers in our armed forces should be punished according to regulations applicable to senior officers.

17. We confirm freedom and liberty to the Russian nobility on an hereditary basis for eternity.

18. We confirm the right of the nobles now in service to continue their service or to ask freedom from service on the basis of the regulations established for that purpose.

19. We confirm the right of the nobles to enter the service of other European countries friendly to us and to travel abroad.

20. Since the title and privileges of the nobility in the past, present, and future are acquired by service and work useful to the Empire and the throne, and since the very existence of Russian nobility depends on the security of the country and the throne, whenever Russian autocracy needs the service of the nobility for the general well being, every nobleman is then obligated, the moment the autocratic government calls him, to perform fully his duty and sacrifice his life, if need be, to government service.

21. A nobleman has the right to sign his name not only as lord of his *pomestie* estate, granted to him by the state, but also as owner of his *votchina* estate, inherited from his ancestors or granted through grace.

22. A nobleman has the power and the authority to give away to whomever he wishes the property which he acquired legally as first owner, to bequeath this property in his will, to confer it as dowry, or to sell or give it away for his livelihood. He may, however, dispose of inherited property only in conformity with the provisions of the law.

23. The inheritable property of a nobleman who may be convicted of a serious crime should pass on to his legal heirs.

24. No one should attempt to seize or damage arbitrarily a nobleman's property without due process of law or the legal judgment of the appropriate court of justice.

25. If a nobleman has a claim against another nobleman he should bring it before the appropriate court of justice.

26. The nobles have the right to purchase villages.

27. The nobles have the right to sell wholesale whatever their villages grow or their handicrafts produce.

28. The nobles may have factories and mills in their villages.

29. The nobles may build small towns on their estates on which they may organize trade and annual fairs. [This activity must not be] contrary to state laws, must be done with the full knowledge of governor generals and *gubernia* administrations, and must be arranged in such a way as not to conflict with fairs of other local cities.

30. The nobles have the right to have, to build, or to buy homes in cities and to have handicrafts there.

31. In case a nobleman prefers to make use of the municipal code of civil rights, he may subordinate himself to it.

32. The nobles are hereby permitted to sell abroad wholesale the products harvested or made on their property, or to have them exported from the designated harbors.

33. The nobles have the right granted to them by the gracious *ukaz* of June 28, 1782 to ownership of not only the fruits of the land belonging to them, but also all resources found beneath the surface and in waters, and all of their products, as is fully stated in that *ukaz*.

34. The nobles have the right of ownership of forests which grow on their property and of their free utilization as is fully explained in the gracious *ukaz* of September 22, 1782.

35. The homes of the nobility in villages are to be free from quartering of soldiers.

36. A nobleman is personally freed from the soul tax. . . .

37. We grant our faithful nobles the permission to assemble in the *gubernias* where they live, to organize in every *namestnichestvo* [district] an Association of Nobles, and to enjoy the rights, privileges, distinctions, and preferences stated below.

38. Nobles may assemble in the *gubernia* by and with the permission of the governor-general or governor every three years during the winter for the purpose of electing noble representatives as well as to hear proposals of the governor-general or the governor.

39. The meeting of nobles in the *namestnichestvo* has permission to elect a *gubernia* marshal of the nobility; this election will occur every three years at which time the names of two marshals of the *uezd* nobility will be submitted to the imperial representative or administrator. The governor-general or the governor will then designate which will be *gubernia* marshal of the nobility for that *gubernia*.

40. By virtue of article 64 and 211 of the statutes, the *uezd* marshal of the nobility is elected by the nobility of the *uezd* through secret ballot every three years. . . .

47. The Association of Nobles has permission to present its needs and interests to the governor-general or the governor.

48. The Association of Nobles has permission to petition, through its deputies, both the Senate and the Imperial Majesty in accordance with the law. . . .

62. The Association of Nobles cannot elect a nobleman whose annual income from his village is below 100 rubles, or who is under twenty years of age, to perform functions of an elective representative of the nobility.

63. A nobleman who either has no village or is under twenty years of age can participate in the Association of Nobles but cannot have an elective voice.

64. A nobleman who never performed any service or who served but did not attain officer rank (even though officer rank was given to him at retirement) may be a member of the Association of Nobles; but he cannot sit in deliberation with the worthy ones or have the right to elect or be elected. . . .

CATHERINE THE GREAT VIEWED BY HER CONTEMPORARIES

Most of the European world could not ignore Catherine the Great, and each observer found a different image beneath the glittering imperial façade. Her friends and attendants, such as Dashkova and Golovine, saw the flashing spirit of her youth and the motherly concern of her advancing years. Some of her critics, such as Prince Shcherbatov, lamented the decline of morals in Russia. Others, such as Alexander Radishchev, viewed Catherine as a hypocrite and a tyrant who repaid candor with imprisonment. The British and the French embassies, more detached and more analytic, saw a clever and complex politician distracted by romances. Foreign observers were fascinated by the immensity of the empire over which this woman ruled, and by the immensity of her task. The heroes of the Enlightenment, such as Diderot, saw in Catherine a glorious philosopher-queen seemingly willing to translate their abstractions into reality. The astonishing point, in such a survey, is that there was a strong measure of truth in all these views.

5

Dashkova: Her Majesty's Inventive Spirit[1]

Princess Dashkova (1743–1810), a member of the famous Vorontsov family, met Catherine the Great in 1758 while the Empress was still Grand Duchess. The two became close friends, and Princess Dashkova participated actively in the coup d'état that brought Catherine to power in 1762. Dashkova's ac-

---

[1] From *The Memoirs of the Princess Dashkov*, translated and edited by Kyril Fitzlyon (London: Calder and Boyars Ltd., 1958), pp. 72–80, 82–86. Reprinted by permission of the publisher.

count of the coup, in her Memoirs, *is one of the few personal observations of the event.*

Happiness came at last when I learnt that Her Majesty had arrived at the barracks of the Izmailovski Regiment and had been unanimously proclaimed Sovereign, that she had proceeded thence to the Kazan Cathedral where there was a great concourse of people all eager to swear allegiance to her, and that the other regiments, both Guards and of the line, had done so too.

It was six o'clock in the morning when I ordered my maid to make ready the dress I wore on State occasions, and later hastened to the Winter Palace where I knew she had to appear. I shall never be able to describe how I reached her. All the troops that happened to be in Petersburg had joined the Guards Regiments and now surrounded the Palace, filling the great square and sealing off all avenues of approach.

I therefore left my carriage and was about to cross the Square on foot when I was recognised by some officers and soldiers. Suddenly I felt myself borne aloft over the heads of all sorts and conditions of men and heard myself called by the most flattering names. Blessings and wishes of prosperity accompanied me till finally I was carried into Her Majesty's ante-chamber with one sleeve lost, dishevelled and in the greatest possible disarray. But in my state of excitement I imagined all this to represent a sort of Triumph. Besides, I neither could, nor had the time to, put it right and therefore presented myself to the Empress just as I was.

We threw ourselves into each other's arms. 'Thank God', 'Thank Heaven' was all either of us was able to utter.

Her Majesty then told me the story of how she had stolen away from Peterhof. My heart beat faster as I listened to her, and I relived in my own emotions all the hopes and fears she must have felt in those critical moments. I too confided in her how anxious I had been during those hours of distress and pain which were decisive for her fate and for the happiness or unhappiness of the Empire. I told her of the annoying mishap which had prevented my going out to meet her. Again we threw ourselves in each other's arms. No happiness could ever have exceeded mine at that moment. It had reached its summit.

Suddenly I noticed that she was still wearing the Order of St Catherine and had not yet put on the blue ribbon of the Cross of St Andrew. (The blue ribbon was not worn by the wife of the Emperor; she was entitled only to the Order of St Catherine which had been founded by Peter I for his own wife. The Emperor Paul was the first to grant the blue ribbon to his wife and the Emperor Alexander followed his example in this respect.) I ran to Mr Panin to borrow his blue ribbon, which I put on the Empress's shoulder. Thereupon she took off her own insignia of the Order of St Catherine and asked me to put them in my pocket.

After a light dinner we proposed to go with the troops to Peterhof. The Empress and I decided to wear the uniform of one of the Guards regiments; she therefore borrowed Captain Talyzin's uniform for the purpose and I that of Lieutenant Pushkin, as these two officers were roughly similar to us in height. These uniforms, by the way, were those the Preobrazhenski Regiment formerly wore from the time of Peter the Great down to the reign of Peter III, who abolished them in favour of Prussian type uniforms. And it is a peculiar thing that no sooner did the Empress arrive in Petersburg than the soldiers threw off their new Prussian uniforms and donned their old ones which they somehow managed to find.

I went quickly home to change so as to be more useful to the Empress in case of need. When I came back to the Palace, Her Majesty, together with those senators that happened to be in town, was holding a kind of council regarding the manifestoes that should be immediately published, etc., etc. Teplov acted as secretary.

It was more than likely that Peter III had by now been informed of the Empress's flight from Peterhof and of the excitement in town. It therefore occurred to me that he could well have been advised by someone in his entourage to act with courage and determination and to come to Petersburg, if necessary in disguise. This thought struck me so forcibly that I did not want to wait till the sitting of the Council was over. I had no right to force my way into that august assembly, but the two junior officers posted at the door either thought the order they had received not to let anyone in did not apply to me or else it never occurred to them that I should not go in. In any case they opened the door for me. I went quickly up to Her Majesty's chair and whispered into her ear what my apprehensions were, adding that if she wanted to take preventive measures she had better take them now without loss of time. Thereupon Her Majesty summoned Mr Teplov to write out an order and relevant instructions in two copies, to be given to two men who were to be posted at the mouth of the two rivers which formed the only possible approaches to the city.

The Empress, who foresaw the embarrassment that my appearance might cause, explained to those venerable old statesmen, who failed to recognise me, who I was and said that my friendship for her, always on the alert to help, had suggested something she had forgotten.

I looked like a boy of fifteen in my uniform, and the appearance of a young and totally unknown Guards officer in the midst of their sanctuary speaking in Her Majesty's ear must have been strange indeed. But no sooner did she mention my name than they all rose from their seats and gravely bowed to me in solemn welcome. I really did behave rather like a small boy and at this mark of respect I blushed and was overcome with confusion.

Soon after the sitting was over and the Empress had given orders to ensure the safety of the city, we mounted our horses and reviewed the troops, who numbered twelve thousand without counting the volunteers who were increasing every moment.

The troops had been on foot for the past twelve hours and therefore as soon as we reached Krasny Kabak, just over six miles away from the city, we made a three-hour halt. We too were badly in need of rest. I had scarcely slept at all for a whole fortnight, and although I could not have fallen asleep at that actual moment, it was the greatest possible bliss to be able to stretch myself out on a bed and rest my tired limbs. There was only one bed in that house, which was nothing but a wretched tavern, and Her Majesty decided that we should both of us lie on it without undressing. The bed was filthy, and I covered it with a large cloak which I obtained from Colonel Karr; but scarcely did we lie down than I noticed a small door by the Empress's pillow, leading I knew not where. This worried me, and I asked her permission to get up and explore the passage. On opening the door I saw that it led into a dark cubby-hole and thence into the yard outside. I had two sentries of the Horse Guards Regiment posted there with strict orders not to move without my permission and not to let anyone near that door. After this, I went back to bed, and as we could not sleep. Her Majesty read out to me the various manifestoes that she intended to publish on our return to town. We told each other our fears, but henceforth they were overshadowed by our hopes.

In the meantime Peter III could come to no decision, and failed even to listen to the advice of Field-Marshal Münnich who happened to be with him at the time. He came to Peterhof, went back to Oranienbaum, and finally yielded to pressure from his friends who urged him to go to Kronstadt and make himself master of the place and of the fleet. But he arrived too late. Admiral Talyzin, who had been despatched by the Empress, was already in command and refused Peter III permission to land. He was therefore forced to return to Oranienbaum, whence he sent General Izmailov with overtures couched in the most submissive terms and with offers of abdication.

Izmailov reached us when we were already on our way to Peterhof. His language was very different to that of my uncle the Grand Chancellor, who came at the moment we were leaving the city and remonstrated with the Empress. Seeing that his arguments got him nowhere, he retired to his own house and refused to swear the oath of allegiance to her. He assured Her Majesty that he would undertake nothing against her by word or deed, but at the same time would not betray the oath he had sworn to Peter III so long as the Emperor was alive. He begged the Empress to appoint an officer who would be attached to his person and see everything that took place in his house, and then withdrew with quiet dignity. I admired my uncle's dignified behaviour all the more since I knew in what low esteem he held the Emperor, and how much the true patriot in him was grieved at the sight of the Sovereign's total incapacity to govern and the dire consequences that were likely to follow.

The Empress sent General Ismailov back to the Emperor beseeching him to persuade His Majesty to give himself up and thus avoid all the incalculable mischief which could not otherwise be prevented; she would then undertake to render his existence as pleasant as possible in any residence he might choose some distance away from Petersburg, and would do her utmost to provide for all his desires.

We were approaching Trinity Convent when the Vice-Chancellor Prince Galitzin arrived with a letter from the Emperor, while the number of followers in our wake was swelled every instant by all those who were leaving him of their own accord.

As Oranienbaum is only about six miles away from Peterhof, Peter III arrived very shortly after us, accompanied by General Izmailov and his A.D.C. General Gudovich. He was conducted, unseen by any but a very few, to a remote apartment where dinner was served. Afterwards he left for Ropsha, which had belonged to him when he was Grand Duke and which he now chose in preference to any other residence. The Emperor was accompanied by Alexis Orlov, who had under him Captain Passek, Prince Theodore Baryatinski and Lieutenant Baskakov of the Preobrazhenski Guards, to whom the Empress had entrusted the custody of his person. I did not see him, though I could have done, but I was assured that he was little affected by his situation, enjoyed a good appetite, drank his favourite wine—burgundy—and wrote two or three letters to his august wife. I shall quote only one of them in which his abdication was well and clearly stated; after naming a few persons (including his favourite negro Narcissus) whom he desired to have with him with the Empress's permission, he mentioned also the provisions he would like to have, which were: burgundy wine, a few pipes and tobacco.

But enough on the subject of a prince, unfortunate because placed on a pedestal high above his natural level. He was not wicked, but his incompetence and lack of education, as well as inclination and natural bent, all combined to make of him a good Prussian corporal and not the Sovereign of a great Empire.

Ever since the previous day I had had no rest, but so subordinate are my physical needs to my spiritual and mental preoccupations that I only felt tired whenever I sat down. I had continually to rush from one end of the Palace to the other as well as to make occasional visits to the sentries downstairs posted at the various entrances. On one occasion after speaking to the Empress's cousin, the Princess of Holstein, I went back to ask Her Majesty whether she would consent to see her for a moment. What was my surprise at finding Gregory Orlov, on the pretext of having hurt his leg, stretched out on a sofa in one of the rooms, opening large bundles of papers which I recognised to be communications from the Supreme Council, such as I had seen in my uncle's care during the reign of the Empress Elisabeth. I asked him what he was doing, and he replied:

'The Empress has ordered me to open them.'

'I doubt it', I said, 'since no action need be taken on them for a few more days till the Empress appoints people who will officially deal with them. But neither you nor I are qualified for that work.'

On this I left him to go and argue with the soldiers, who, thirsty and tired, had broken into a cellar and were drinking gallons of Hungary wine straight out of their hats, thinking it to be a kind of light hydromel. I succeeded better than I hoped. The soldiers emptied on the ground all the wine in their hats, rolled the barrels back into the cellar and sent instead for water from a spring. I was all the more surprised by this proof of their esteem and confidence as they had not obeyed their officers who had spoken to them before me. I gave them whatever money I had left, then turned my pockets inside out to show I had no more to give, and promised that on our arrival in town all the taverns would be open to them and they would be able to drink at the expense of the Crown. My arguments were appreciated and had the desired effect.

I should mention here that this was all my own money. I had never asked the Empress for money, nor received any from her, nor for that matter, had I ever accepted any from the French Ambassador as some writers have claimed. It is true that offers of loans—and immense loans at that—had been made to me, but my answer had always been that with my knowledge or consent no foreign money would ever be employed to bring about the revolution in Russia.

When I came back to the Palace I saw in the room in which Gregory Orlov was lying on a sofa a table laid for three. I pretended not to notice. Presently Her Majesty was told that her dinner was served. She invited me to share it, and to my great annoyance I saw it being served by the side of Orlov's sofa. Apparently my face betrayed my emotions which were those of anger, tempered by sadness, for I sincerely loved the Empress. She asked me what the matter was.

'Nothing', I said, 'except that I have had no sleep for the past fortnight and am terribly tired.'

She then begged me to lend her my support against Orlov, who wanted to leave the service.

'Just think', she added, 'how ungrateful I should appear if I allowed him to retire.'

My reply was the opposite of what she wanted it to be. I told her that now she was Sovereign she was in the position to reward him in a manner which would make his fame resound far and wide, without compelling him to stay in the service. It was then I realised with a pang that Orlov was her lover, and that never would she be able to keep it a secret.

After our meal and Peter III's departure, we left Peterhof. We broke our journey at Prince Kurakin's country house, which had only one bed and again we had to share it. Our next stopping place was Katerin-hof where there was a vast concourse of people, and the populace was coming over to our side in droves, ready to defend us in case of a pitched battle between our troops and the Holstenians who were gen-erally hated.

Our entry into the city beggared all description. Countless people thronged the streets shouting and screaming, invoking blessings upon us and giving vent to their joy in a thousand ways, while the old and the sick were held up at open windows by their children to enable them to see with their own eyes the triumph that shone on everyone's face. The music of the regimental bands, the peal of church bells, the holy altars aflame with lights and shining through the open doors of churches from the darkness within, revealing groups of priests in sacred vestments with their crosses held high aloft as if to consecrate the universal joy—such was the general picture which presented itself to my eyes, but which I can but very imperfectly describe, as, over-whelmed by my own emotions and almost oblivious of reality, I rode by the side of the Empress, reflecting on the blessings of a bloodless revolution, and contemplating in this gift of Heaven both a beneficent Sovereign and an adored friend whom my own efforts had helped to rescue from a perilous situation, even, perhaps, from a horrible fate, and to place on the throne of my beloved country.

I was so overwhelmed by a host of different sentiments and by the desire to see my father, my uncle and my daughter, that we no sooner arrived at the Summer Palace than, without leaving the Empress time to enter it, I asked her for permission to take the carriage that had followed us on the way in order to visit them. Her Majesty immediately granted me the permission I asked for and kindly besought me to re-turn as quickly as possible.

On leaving my sister, I went home to kiss my little Nastasie. These three visits had taken a long time, and by then it was very late. I there-fore had no time to change and tidy myself, and I was in a hurry to go to the Palace. My maid told me that she had felt a weight in the pocket of my dressing-gown and found it to be the Order of St Catherine in diamonds. It was the Empress's. I took it. As I entered the room next to that of the Empress, I saw Gregory Orlov and Kakovinsky coming out of it, and when I went up to the Empress I could no longer doubt that Orlov was my enemy. For no one else could have introduced Kakovinsky to the Empress. Besides, Her Majesty immediately reproached me for having spoken to that officer in French in front of soldiers, thus arousing the suspicion that I wanted him to dismiss them.

I answered curtly and my face wore the expression of the most perfect disdain. 'It is too early, Ma'am', I said. 'You have not been on the throne for more than a few hours and your troops, who have shown every sign of trusting me implicitly, could hardly have worried about what I might say in whatever language it might be.' And I handed her back the Order of St Catherine so as to cut short this conversation.

'Come, now', she said, 'you will admit, though, that you ought not to have dismissed the soldiers.'

'True enough, Ma'am', I said, 'in spite of Mr Vadkovski's entreaties I should not have interfered with that fool Kakovinsky, and should have left you with no guard to relieve those who were looking after your safety and the safety of your Palace.'

'Now, now', she said, 'let's leave it at that. So much for your quick temper, and this'—making a move to pin on my shoulder the Order which I had returned to her—'is for your services.'

Far from kneeling to receive the decoration, I said to her: 'Forgive me, Your Majesty, for what I am going to say to you. You are approaching the moment when, for all you may wish to the contrary, truth will be banished from your ears; I implore you not to confer this Order on me, because if it is meant as an ornament you know that I set no store by such things; if it is for my services, then, however mediocre they may appear to some people, in my own eyes they cannot be repaid because I am not to be bought, nor ever shall be, at any price.'

Her Majesty embraced me, with the words: 'At least let friendship enjoy its rights.'

I kissed her hand—and there I was in an officer's uniform, with a ribbon (but no star) across the shoulder, only one spur and for all the world like a little boy of fourteen.

Her Majesty then told me that she had already despatched a Guards lieutenant to my husband, with a note to make him turn back on his tracks and join us as quickly as possible. This news gave me so much pleasure that I immediately forgot all the very justifiable anger I felt towards her.

I stayed for about another hour with the Empress. She told me she would have an apartment ready for me in this same Palace the very next day; I requested that she should leave me at my own house till the arrival of my husband, and that we should then move in together.

The Hetman Count Razumovski and Mr Panin left the Empress's apartments at the same time as I. I repeated to them what I had seen at Peterhof and the conversation she had had with me during dinner, and told them I was sure Orlov was Her Majesty's lover, to which Mr

Panin replied: 'It's lack of sleep for a fortnight at a stretch and your eighteen years of age that have excited your imagination.'

'Very well', I said to him, 'I agree, but as soon as you satisfy yourself that I was right you must allow me to tell you that you are nothing but a couple of fools. You and your cool heads!'

The bargain was struck and I hastened back home and to bed. A wing of chicken which I found—the remains of my child's dinner—was all I ate, and being in a hurry to enjoy the benefit conferred by Morpheus I slipped into bed very quickly. But so much excitement coursed through my veins that whenever I dozed off my legs and arms began to twitch, my whole body shook so violently that it almost leapt in the air, and I awoke with a start.

Here I must mention an incident which I forgot to mention before and which occurred on our way back to town. When we took our seats in the carriage—the Empress, myself, Count Razumovski and Prince Volkonski—in order to rest a while, Her Majesty asked me what she could do for me so as to repay me in some sort.

'Give happiness to my country', I said, 'continue to have for me the sentiments which are responsible for my own present happiness, and I shall be content.'

'But this is merely my duty', she replied, 'and I want to lighten the weight which I feel upon my conscience.'

'I never thought', I retorted, 'that the service of friendship could be a burden to you.'

'Well, anyway', said Her Majesty, 'tax me with anything you like, but I shall have no peace of mind unless you let me know this instant what I could do to give you pleasure.' She embraced me as she spoke.

'Well then', I said to her, 'restore to life an uncle of mine who does not happen to be dead.'

'This is an enigma', she said.

'Prince Volkonski will explain it to you', I replied, for though I was not soliciting this favour for myself it cost me a lot to ask for it.

Prince Volkonski told Her Majesty that General Leontiev, my husband's uncle, while serving with distinction in the army sent against the Prussians, had been deprived, through his wife's intrigues, of a seventh of his land and a quarter of his furniture and cash—which she should have received at his death (as is the right of widows in Russia). Peter III became all the more readily party to this injustice, as he felt a resentment against all generals who had served well against Frederick.

The Empress admitted the justice of the case, and promised me that this would be one of the first Orders-in-Council she would sign.

'Well, Ma'am', I said, 'I shall be excellently rewarded by Your Majesty, as he is my mother-in-law's only brother whom she holds most dear.'

I was very pleased thus to give the Prince's mother proof of my attachment to the family and overjoyed at successfully evading the receipt of a bounty, as this went against my principles.

The following day Mr Panin was granted the title of Count and a pension of five thousand roubles, and Prince Volkonski and Count Razumovski received the same pension. The rest of the conspirators of the first class were to receive six hundred peasants and a pension of two thousand roubles, or else twenty-four thousand roubles in lieu of land. To my great surprise I found myself in that class. I did not want to take advantage of the choice that was given of accepting land or twenty-four thousand roubles, as my mind was quite made up not to accept either. Many of those who had taken part in the Revolution blamed my disinterestedness, but my friends advised me differently. And so, in order not to swell the general outcry or to annoy the Empress, I asked to be given a list of my husband's debts, and as they amounted to about twenty-four thousand roubles, I ordered this sum to be used for buying back the bonds or papers held by the Prince's creditors. This was done by Her Majesty's Private Office on receipt of my order.

The following day Mass was said in the Great Chapel, and we saw Gregory Orlov wearing the Order of St Alexander. As soon as Divine Service was over I came up to my uncle and Count Razumovski, who did not expect it, and said to them with a meaningful air:

'With all due respect, you are a couple of fools.'

On the fourth day after the accession to the throne, Mr Betskoy requested a moment's audience of Her Majesty, which was granted— I was the only one to be present, together with the Empress. What was our surprise when he fell on his knees and begged her to tell him by whom she thought she had been raised to the throne.

Her Majesty's answer was: 'I owe my accession to God and to my good and faithful subjects.'

'Then', he replied, 'I can no longer wear this ribbon', and he made to take off the Order of St Alexander with which he was decorated. The Empress would not let him and asked him what the matter was.

'I am', he said, 'the unhappiest of men, since you do not know that the guards on that occasion had been posted, and the money distributed among them, by me.'

We thought—not without reason—that he was completely mad. The Empress got rid of him very cleverly by telling him she knew how much she owed him, and that therefore he would be the only person to whom she would entrust the responsibility of looking after the jewellers who were to make the great new crown in diamonds to be used on the day of her coronation. He got up in a rapture of very obvious delight, and left us immediately, apparently in a hurry to communicate this great news to his friends. We had a good laugh about it and I admired Her Majesty's inventive spirit which had rid her of a tiring madman.

6
Countess Golovine: Maternal Solicitude[1]

Countess Golovine was born in 1766 and raised at the court of Catherine the Great. Her memoirs reflect the views of the court nobility whose lives revolved completely about the Empress. The first part of the following selection deals with Countess Golovine's early memories of court life, and the second treats of the death of the Empress.

A grand and entirely new spectacle was opening out before my eyes in the shape of a majestic and imposing Court and a great sovereign, who was plainly drawing me into closer and closer intimacy with her who was to inspire me with an unalterable attachment. The more I had the honour of seeing Princess Louise, the more absolutely devoted to her I became. In spite of her extreme youth, my interest in her did not escape her notice, as I was happy to observe. At the beginning of May the Court left for Tsarskoie Sielo, and the day after her imperial Majesty instructed my husband to send for me to spend the summer there.

I was delighted to receive this command, and started at once so as to arrive before the Empress's evening. As soon as I was dressed I went up to the castle, to be presented to her. She appeared at six o'clock, addressed me very kindly, and said to me: 'I am very glad to see you in our party. From to-day you are "Madame la grosse Maréchale," [2] which will make you seem more imposing.'

I am now going to give some idea of the persons to whom the Empress accorded permission to reside at Tsarskoie Sielo, and who were admitted to her private circle. But before tracing these various portraits, I should like to describe the sovereign who, for thirty-four years made Russia a happy land.

Posterity judges, and will judge, Catherine with all human preju-

[1] *Memoirs of Countess Golovine,* translated by G. M. Fox-Davies (London: David Nutt, 1910), pp. 35–40, 122–28.
[2] This name was given to me because my husband is a little stout. (Author's note.)

79

dice. The new philosophy, by which she was unfortunately influenced, and which was the mainspring of her failings, covered as with a thick veil her great and fine qualities. But it seems only just to dwell for a moment on the period of her splendid dawn, before condemning her and wiping out the memory of her glory and her unspeakable goodness.

The Empress was brought up at the Court of her father, the Prince of Anhalt, by an ignorant governess of low family, who was hardly capable of teaching her to read, her parents troubling neither about her principles nor her education. She was brought to Russia at the age of seventeen, a beautiful girl with much natural grace and charm, witty, clever, and sensitive, and anxious to please and to learn. She was married to the Duke of Holstein, then Grand Duke, and destined to succeed the Empress Elizabeth, his aunt. He was ugly, weak, undersized, fussy, a drunkard, and a debauchee. Elizabeth's Court was nothing but the scene of a debauch, of which she set the example. A clever man, Count Munnich, was the first to perceive Catherine's ability. He persuaded her to study, and she welcomed the idea enthusiastically. The first book he gave her to read was Bayle's Dictionary—a poisonous, dangerous, and seductive work, especially for one who had no conception of the divine truth which confounds a lie.

Catherine read this work three times in the space of a few months. It enflamed her imagination and afterwards brought her into correspondence with all the Sophists. Such was the mind and temper of the princess who became the wife of an emperor whose sole ambition was to be a corporal in the service of Frederic II. Russia groaned under the yoke of feebleness, and Catherine groaned with Russia, for her grand and noble ideas seemed to rise superior to the obstacles in the way of her elevation. Nature was revolted by the depravities of Peter III and the contempt in which he held his subjects. A general revolution was on the point of breaking out, and a regency was demanded. The Empress having already a son ten years of age—afterwards Paul I —it was decided to send Peter III away to Holstein. Prince Orlov and his brother, Count Alexis, who at that time enjoyed the Empress's favours, were commissioned to get him away. Several ships were got ready at Cronstadt, and Peter was to embark with the battalions that he had sent for from Holstein, sleeping at Ropcha, near Oranienbaum, the evening before his departure.

I will not go into the details of the tragic event that ensued, about which only too much has been said, while the main principle directing it has been much misunderstood; but I owe it to the cause of truth to mention here an authentic account which I received from Count Panine, the Minister. His testimony is the more unassailable since it is well known that he was not particularly attached to the Empress. Having been the tutor of Paul I, he had hoped to hold the reins of government himself, under the regency of a woman, and saw his expectations disappointed. The strength with which Catherine grasped the imperial power disappointed his ambitious projects, and he bore her a grudge all his life.

One evening that we were at his house, surrounded by his relatives and friends, he told us a number of interesting anecdotes, and insensibly came to the assassination of Peter III. 'I was in the Empress's cabinet,' he said, 'when Prince Orlov came to announce to her that all was over. She was standing in the middle of the room; the word *over* struck her. "He is gone," she replied at first; then learning the sad truth, she fell into a dead faint. Afterwards she had frightful convulsions, which for a time caused fears for her life. When she recovered, she shed the bitterest tears. "My glory is departed," she repeated; "posterity will never forgive me for this unintended crime!"' The favour in which they were held had stifled in the Orlovs every feeling but that of an unbounded ambition. They had thought that, by killing the Emperor, Prince Orlov might step into his place and induce the Empress to crown him.

It is difficult to do justice to the unshaken firmness with which she ruled and cared for her Empire. She was ambitious, but she covered Russia with glory, while her maternal solicitude extended to the humblest individual, and the private interest of each one of her subjects was near to her heart. None could be more imposing than the Empress at times of state. None could be greater, kinder, or more indulgent than she in her private circle. She hardly made her appearance before fear yielded to a tender respect. People seemed to say: 'I see her, I am happy; she is my protector and my mother.'

When she settled down to her game in an evening she would look all round the room to see that everyone had what they required. She carried her attentions so far as to order a blind to be lowered, if the sun were inconveniencing anyone. The players consisted of the General aide-de-camp in attendance, Count Stroganov, and of M. Tchertkov, an old chamberlain, of whom she was very fond. My uncle, M. de Chouvalov, the Lord Chamberlain, took part in the game sometimes, and at any rate was present, as also M. Plato Zoubov. The evening was over at nine o'clock or half-past.

I recollect that Tchertkov, who was a bad player, once lost his temper with the Empress for having made him miss a trick. Her Majesty was hurt at the manner in which he flung his cards down on the table, and she put an end to the game, but said nothing. It was then about time to withdraw, so she rose and took leave of us. Tchertkov was dumbfounded. The next day was a Sunday, and ordinarily, on that day, there was a large table set for all the Ministers. The Grand Duke Paul and the Grand Duchess Marie also used to come over from Pavlovsk, the castle they resided in, which was only four versts from Tsarskoie Sielo, but when they did not come there was a small select table in the colonnade, to which I had the honour of being admitted. After mass and the reception, when the Empress had withdrawn, the Court Marshal, Prince Bariatinski, read out the names of the persons who were to have the honour of dining with her. Tchertkov, who had the *entrée* to all the small gatherings, sat in a corner, utterly wretched on account of the scene of the previous evening, and not daring to lift his eyes to the man who was to pronounce his doom. But to his surprise he heard his name called out. He ran, he did not walk. When we entered the colonnade we saw her Imperial Majesty seated at the far end. She rose, came up to Tchertkov, took his arm, and walked all round the colonnade with him. When they returned to their starting-point, she said to him in Russian: 'Are you not ashamed to have thought I should sulk with you? Have you forgotten that between friends quarrels are forgotten?' I never saw a man in such a state as this poor old fellow. He burst into tears, and repeated over and over again: 'O Mother, how can I speak to thee; how can I reply to such goodness? I would like to die for thee all the time!'

The use of *thee* and *thou* is very energetic in Russian, and detracts in nothing from the respectfulness of language.

A round table used to stand near the Empress's during the evenings at Tsarskoie Sielo, and Princess Louise, already betrothed to the Grand Duke, sat between the Princess, her sister, and me. Mlle. de Chouvalov, afterwards Princess v. Dietrichstein, and the nieces of Countess Protassov completed the princesses' circle.

The Empress had pencils, pens, and paper brought to us, and we used to draw or play at secretary. Her Majesty used sometimes to ask to see the products of our imagination, and would be greatly amused. Countess Chouvalov played some game with Mlle. Protassov and the lords in waiting, and sometimes also with Countess Braniçka, who came occasionally to Tsarskoie Sielo.

Some presentiments are stronger than our reason. Even if we say to ourselves that we must take no notice of them, we are none the less disturbed by them, and we cannot dismiss them from our thoughts. They pursue us like a shadow, alarm us, and are constantly before our eyes.

A very few days later, at ten o'clock in the morning, while my mother was taking breakfast, a Court lackey, in attendance on my uncle, came in and asked my mother's permission to wake him. 'The Empress had an apoplectic fit about an hour ago,' he said. I uttered a frightful cry and hurried to tell my husband, who was downstairs in his own rooms. I had the utmost difficulty in getting down the stairs, for I was trembling all over, and could hardly put one foot before the other.

When I entered my husband's room, I had to force myself to utter the fatal words: *The Empress is dying.*

My husband was dumbfounded. Then he asked for his things so that he could go as quickly as possible to the castle. I could neither cry nor speak, still less think. M. Tarsoukov, the nephew of the Empress's head waiting-woman, came in, and said to me in Russian:

'All is at an end, she and our happiness.'

Then Count and Countess Tolstoy arrived, and the latter remained with me while her husband went to the castle with my husband. We spent, until three o'clock in the morning, the most wretched hours of my life. Every two hours my husband sent me a little note, and at one time our hopes revived a little, but only momentarily. The Empress lay for thirty-six hours in an apoplectic fit, her body alive, but her mind dead, and on 6 November she ceased to breathe.

I will insert here the detailed account of her last days and of the events which took place in the palace the first few hours after her end. They were reported to me by the same person whom I have already quoted.

The Empress's disappointment over the non-success of her projects with regard to the King of Sweden had reacted upon her in a manner that was very apparent to all those immediately round her. She changed her whole mode of life, seldom appearing, except on Sundays, for mass and dinner, and very rarely admitted her circle into the Diamond-room or to the Hermitage at all. She spent almost every evening in her bedroom, to which no one was ever admitted, except the few persons whom she honoured by her special intimacy. The Grand Duke Alexander and his wife, who usually spent all their evenings with the Empress, only saw her once or twice during the week, with the exception of Sundays. They often received commands to remain at home and often, too, she persuaded them to go to the town theatre to see the new Italian opera.

On Sunday, 2 November, the Empress appeared in public for the last time, almost as if to bid farewell to her subjects. Everybody was struck, after the event, by the impression she produced that day. Although the public assemble every Sunday in the Knights Guards' Hall and the Court in the attendants' room at the side, the Empress rarely came out through the Guard-room. Usually, she went straight from the attendants' room, through the dining-room, into the chapel; or else sent the Grand Duke, her son, or her grandson, when his father was not present, and heard mass from the entresol, an inner room, a window of which looked down into the chapel.

On 2 November the Empress went to mass through the Guard-room. She was in mourning for the Queen of Portugal, and looked better than she had done for a long time. After mass she held a lengthy reception; Mme. Lebrun had just completed a full-length portrait of the Grand Duchess Elizabeth, which she presented to the Empress that day, and her Majesty had it placed in the Throne-room, and stopped a long time in front of it, examining it and criticising it with the persons invited to dine with her. There was a large table, as was usual on Sundays, and the Grand Dukes Alexander and Constantine and their wives dined with her.

This was not only the last dinner she had with them, but it was the last time she saw them, and they received commands not to go in to her in the evening. On Monday the 3rd and on Tuesday the 4th the Grand Duke Alexander and the Grand Duchess Elizabeth were at the opera. On Wednesday the 5th, at eleven o'clock in the morning, when the Grand Duke Alexander had gone out for a walk with one of the Princes Czartoryski, Count Saltykov sent word to the Grand Duchess to ask where he was, and begged her to tell him whether she was aware at what time he would be in. But she did not know. Shortly afterwards the Grand Duke came in, very much upset at the message from Count Saltykov, who had sent after him into every corner of St. Petersburg. He had already been told that the Empress was ill, and that Count Nicholas Zoubov had been sent to Gatchina.

He was thunderstruck, and the Grand Duchess no less than he, at the news, and they spent the day in a state of unspeakable anxiety. At five o'clock in the evening the Grand Duke Alexander, who had with difficulty restrained himself so long, obtained permission from Count Saltykov to enter the Empress's apartments. This consolation had at first been refused him, for no good reason, though for motives readily apprehended by anyone who was acquainted with Count Saltykov. When the Empress was alive it had been rumoured that she intended to debar her son from the succession and to appoint the Grand Duke Alexander her heir. Never, I am sure, did such a thought even occur to the Empress but its having been mentioned was sufficient to make Count Saltykov prohibit the Grand Duke Alexander from entering his grandmother's apartments before his father's arrival. As the Grand Duke Paul could not, however, be much longer in arriving, the Grand Duke Alexander and the Grand Duchess Elizabeth came to the Empress's apartments between five and six in the evening, the only persons they then encountered in the outer rooms being a few servants with sorrowful faces.

The persons waiting in the Empress's dressing-room were a picture of concentrated despair. At last they were admitted, and saw the Empress lying unconscious on the ground, on a mattress with a screen round it. She was in her bedroom, which was only very dimly lighted, and at her feet were Mlle. Protassov, the first lady-in-waiting, and Mlle. Alexeiev, one of the principal waiting-women, the sound of whose sobs mingled with the Empress's frightful death rattle, and alone broke the profound silence.

The Grand Duke Alexander and his wife did not remain long, for they were very much overcome, but passed on through the Empress's rooms. The Grand Duke's kind heart prompted him to go to Prince Zoubov, whose rooms adjoined those of the Empress, and as the same corridor led to the apartments of the Grand Duke Constantine, the Grand Duchess Elizabeth went to see her sister-in-law. They were not able to remain together long, for they had to prepare to receive the Grand Duke, their father, who arrived at about seven o'clock, and, without calling at his own palace, took up his abode with the Grand Duchess in the Empress's apartments. He only saw his sons; his daughters-in-law were commanded to remain at home.

The Empress's apartments filled up at once with servants devoted to the Grand Duke Paul, for the most part persons of obscure origin, to whom neither their talents nor their birth gave any right to aspire to the places and favours that in imagination they already saw being showered upon them. The crowd in the ante-rooms grew from moment to moment. The *Gatchinese* (as the persons I have just alluded to were called) ran about and knocked up against the courtiers, who asked each other in amazement who these Ostrogoths could be, who alone had the right of entry to the inner rooms, whereas formerly they had never been seen even in the ante-rooms.

The Grand Duke Paul had installed himself in a small room beyond his mother's bedroom, so that all those to whom he gave orders had to pass the Empress, who was still breathing, as if she no longer lived. This profanation of sovereign Majesty, this irreligion—for it would have been the same in the case of the humblest human being—shocked everyone, and showed up the character of the Grand Duke Paul, who authorised it, in a very unfavourable light. Thus the night passed: there was a moment's hope once, for the remedies seemed to be taking effect, but this hope was soon extinguished. The Grand Duchess Elizabeth spent the night fully dressed, waiting, expecting every moment to be sent for. Countess Chouvalov went backwards and forwards, bringing news of the Empress's condition. The Grand Duke Alexander had not returned home since his father's arrival, but towards three o'clock in the morning they both came in to see the Grand Duchess Elizabeth. A new uniform had already been ordered, that of the battalions of the Grand Duke Paul, which became the models after which the whole army was reorganised. Very trivial incidents sometimes bring about greater results than others that are more important in themselves. The sight of these uniforms—forbidden outside the limits of Pavlovsk and Gatchina, and which the Grand Duchess had never seen her husband put on, except privately, because the Empress did not like her grandsons to take the Prussian army, with its undue attention to petty details, as a model—the sight, I say, of these uniforms, that the Grand Duchess had made fun of a thousand times, destroyed in a moment the illusion that she was trying to cling to. Her feelings were harrowed, and she burst into tears, the first that she had been able to shed, for she seemed to have passed suddenly from a pleasant, safe and convenient abode into a prison.

The Grand Dukes made a very short stay. Towards morning the order to put on Russian dress was received, which meant that the Empress's end was approaching. However, the whole day passed in suspense; she had a long and agonised passing, without a moment's return of consciousness, but on the 6th, at eleven o'clock in the evening, the Grand Duchess Elizabeth and her sister-in-law, who was in her own apartments, were sent for. The Empress Catherine was no more. The Grand Duchesses passed through the crowd, hardly seeing what was round them, and the Grand Duke Alexander came to meet them, to tell them to kneel down when they kissed the hand of the new Emperor. They found him, with the Empress Marie, at the entrance to the bedroom. After having greeted him, they had to go through this bedroom, pass by the remains of the Empress without stopping, and enter the adjoining room, where they found the young Grand Duchesses in tears. Meanwhile the Empress Marie was superintending the dressing of the deceased Empress and the arrangement of the room with great activity and ability.

The defunct Empress was laid on a bed and dressed in *négligé,* after which the Imperial family assembled, to be present at the funeral service, which was recited in the room itself: then, after having kissed her hand, they repaired to the chapel, where the oath was taken to the Emperor in person. These mournful ceremonies were only over at two o'clock in the morning.

7

Radishchev: The Groans of Thy Subject People[1]

A. N. Radishchev (1749–1802), a publisher and writer who came strongly under the influence of enlightened ideas, published his work, A Journey from Saint Petersburg to Moscow in 1790. In more tranquil times he might have escaped retribution for his exposure of the evils of Russian society, especially autocracy and serfdom. But the Revolution was raging in France and the Empress Catherine was withdrawing her former interest in the critical works of the Enlightenment. Radishchev was imprisoned for his work. The following selection examines the question of Russia's monarch.

While I was sleeping, the humors stirred up by my thoughts streamed to my head and, stimulating the tender substance of my brain, aroused a variety of images. In my dream appeared innumerable pictures, but they disappeared like light vapors in the air. At last, as often happens, a certain fiber of my brain, firmly touched by the fluids arising from the internal vessels of my body, throbbed more than the others, and this is what I dreamed.

I imagined that I was a tsar, shah, khan, king, bey, nabob, sultan, or some such exalted being, sitting on a throne in power and majesty.

My throne was of pure gold and, cleverly set with varicolored precious stones, it shone resplendent. Nothing could compare with the luster of my raiment. My head was crowned with a laurel wreath. Around me lay the regalia of my power. Here lay a sword on a column wrought of silver, on which were represented battles at sea and on land, the capture of cities, and other triumphs of this sort; everywhere my name could be seen on high, borne by the Genius of glory, who was hovering over all these exploits. Here one could see my scepter resting upon sheaves heavy with abundant ears of grain, wrought of pure gold and perfectly imitating nature. A pair of scales hung from

[1] From A. N. Radishchev, *A Journey From Saint Petersburg to Moscow*, translated by Leo Weiner, edited by Roderick Page Thaler (Cambridge, Mass.: Harvard University Press, 1958), pp. 66–76. Copyright © 1958 by the President and Fellows of Harvard College. Reprinted by permission of the publisher.

a rigid beam. In one of the scales lay a book with the inscription "The Law of Mercy"; in the other likewise there was a book with the inscription "The Law of Conscience." The orb was carved from a single stone and was supported by a circlet of cherubim sculptured in white marble. My crown was raised above everything else and rested on the shoulders of a mighty giant, and its rim was supported by Truth. A serpent of enormous size, forged of gleaming steel, wound all about the foot of my throne and, holding the tip of its tail in its jaws, represented eternity.

Not these lifeless emblems alone proclaimed my power and majesty. About my throne stood the estates of the realm, timidly submissive and anxious to catch my glance. At some distance from my throne crowded a countless multitude of people, whose various attires, facial features, bearing, appearance, and stature indicated their diversity of race. Their trembling silence assured me that they were all subject to my will. On the sides, upon a somewhat higher level, stood a great number of charming, splendidly garbed women. Their glances expressed their delight upon seeing me, and their very wishes strove to anticipate mine ere they arose.

The deepest silence reigned in this assembly; it seemed that all were anxiously expecting an important event upon which depended the peace and happiness of the whole commonwealth. Self-centered and bored to the bottom of my soul by the cloying monotony of existence, I paid my debt to nature and, opening my mouth from ear to ear, I yawned with all my might. They all responded to my mood. Suddenly confusion spread its somber veil over the face of joy, the smile flitted away from the lips of tenderness and the sparkle of merriment from the cheeks of pleasure. Twisted and furtive glances betrayed the sudden approach of terror and imminent misfortune. Sighs were heard, the stinging forerunners of grief; and groans, restrained by fear. Despair and mortal terror, more agonizing than death itself, rushed in with giant strides to take possession of all hearts. I was moved to the depths of my soul by this sad spectacle; my facial muscles involuntarily contracted toward my ears and, stretching my lips, produced in my features a twitch that resembled a smile, after which I sneezed loudly. Just so the midday sun breaks through the thick, dark, foggy atmosphere. Its vital heat disperses the condensed moisture, which, divided into its component particles, is in part lightened and swiftly borne into the immeasurable space of ether, while the rest, retaining in itself only the weight of its earthly particles, swiftly falls down. The darkness, which had prevailed everywhere before the radiant globe broke through, suddenly disappears and, hastily throwing off its impenetrable shroud, flies away on rushing wings, leaving no trace of its presence. Even thus my smile dispelled the looks of sadness which had settled on the faces of the assembled company; joy quickly filled the hearts of all, and not an oblique sign of displeasure was left. All began to cry: "Long live our mighty Sovereign! May he live forever!" Like the gentle midday breeze which stirs the foliage and produces an amorous whisper in the oak grove was the joyful murmur that passed through the gathering.

One said in a low voice: "He has subdued our enemies abroad and at home, he has expanded the frontiers of the fatherland, he has subjected thousands of men, of many races, to his power." Another exclaimed: "He has enriched the realm, he has expanded internal and foreign commerce, he is a patron of the arts and sciences, he encourages agriculture and industry." Women tenderly said: "He has saved thousands of useful citizens from destruction by preventing their death even at the breast." One announced with dignity: "He has increased the income of the government, he has reduced the people's taxes, he has provided the people with a secure livelihood." Youths, ecstatically raising their hands to heaven, cried: "He is merciful and just, his law is equal for all, and he considers himself its first servant. He is a wise legislator, a righteous judge, a zealous executive, he is greater than all other kings, he gives liberty to all men."

Speeches like these, striking my eardrum, resounded loudly in my soul. To my mind the praises seemed true, since they were accompanied by outward expressions of sincerity. Receiving them as such, my soul rose above the usual circle of vision, expanded in its essence, and, embracing all, touched the threshold of divine wisdom. But nothing could be compared with my self-satisfaction as I uttered my commands. I ordered my commander-in-chief to proceed with an innumerable host to the conquest of a country separated from me by a whole celestial zone. "Sovereign," he replied, "the glory of thy name alone will conquer the people who inhabit that land. Terror will go before thine arms, and I will return bearing the tribute of mighty kings." To my lord admiral I spake: "Let my ships spread sail over all the seas, so that strange peoples may see them; let my flag become known in the north, east, south, and west." "It shall be done, Your Majesty." And he flew to execute my command like a wind sent to swell the sails of a ship. "Proclaim to the farthest limits of my realm," I said to the keeper of the laws, "that this is the day of my birth; let it be forever famous in the chronicles as the day of universal amnesty. Let the prisons be thrown open, set the prisoners free to return to their homes as people who have strayed from the true path." "Thy mercy, O Sovereign, is the mark of an infinitely generous being. I hasten to publish the glad tidings to the fathers grieving for their children, to the wives grieving for their husbands." To my chief architect I said, "Let magnificent buildings be erected as homes for the Muses, let them be adorned with various imitations of nature; and may they be as inviolate as the celestial beings for whom they were built." "O wise ruler," he replied, "even as the elements have obeyed thy commands and, joining forces, have in swamps and solitudes founded vast cities which surpass in magnificence the most famous cities of antiquity, so this labor will be light to the zealous executors of thy commandments. Thou hast spoken, and the raw building materials are already hearkening to thy voice." "Let the hand of generosity be opened now," I said, "and let the surplus of superabundance flow out to the needy, let the treasure which we do not need return to its source." "O most gracious ruler, given us by the Almighty, father of thy children, enricher of the poor, thy will be done!" At each of my commands all the people there shouted for joy, and applause not only accompanied my speech but even anticipated my thoughts. Of all this company, one woman alone, who stood leaning hard against a column, sighed grievously, while scorn and anger flashed across her countenance. Her features were stern and her garments simple. Her head was covered with a hat, while all the others stood with their heads bare. "Who is she?" I asked one who was standing near me. "She is a pilgrim, a stranger to us; she says she is an oculist, named Clear-of-Eye. But she is a very dangerous witch who carries venom and poison, and gloats over grief and affliction; she is always frowning, and she scorns and reviles everyone; in her abuse she spares not even thy sacred head." "Wherefore, then, is this evildoer tolerated in my realm? But we shall deal with her tomorrow. This is a day of grace and rejoicing. Come, my comrades in bearing the heavy burden of government, receive the rewards your labors and accomplishments deserve." Then I arose from my throne and conferred various honors upon those present; nor were the absent ones forgotten, but those who had received my commands with joyful countenance were granted ampler signs of grace.

Then I continued my speech: "Let us go, props of my power, buttresses of my rule, let us go and be merry after our labor. For he who has labored deserves to partake of the fruit of his labors. The Monarch should partake of joy, since he dispenses joy so bountifully to all. Show us the way to the feast you have prepared," I said to the master of the revels. "We shall follow you." "Wait," the pilgrim called to me from her place, "wait, and come to me. I am a physician sent to thee and thy like to open thine eyes. Oh, what blindness!" she exclaimed. An invisible power urged me to approach her, although all those who surrounded me held me back and some even used force.

"On both thine eyes there are cataracts," said the pilgrim, "and yet thou hast passed unhesitant judgment upon everything." Then she touched both my eyes and took off from them a thick film, like horny skin. "Thou seest," she said to me, "that thou hast been blind, stone-blind. I am Truth. The Almighty, moved to pity by the groans of thy subject people, has sent me down from the heavenly regions to drive away the darkness which impenetrably obscured thy vision. I have done so. Now everything will appear before thine eyes in its true form. Thou shalt see into the heart of things. No longer will the serpent that hides in the deep recesses of the soul escape thee. Thou shalt know thy faithful subjects who, far from thee, love not thee, but their country; who are always ready for thy defeat, if it will avenge the enslavement of man. But they will not stir up untimely sedition to no purpose. Call them to thee, to be thy friends. Drive away this haughty mob that stand before thee and hide the infamy of their souls under gilded garments. They are thy real enemies, who dim thine eyes and bar my entry to thy palace. Once only do I appear to kings during their whole reign, that they may know me in my true form; but I never abandon the dwellings of mortals. My stay is not in royal palaces. The guard that surrounds and watches them with a hundred eyes by day and by night bars my entry thither. If and when I succeed in breaking through this dense crowd, all those who surround thee raise the scourge of persecution and seek to cast me out of thy dwelling; therefore beware lest I leave thee again. For then words of flattery, emitting poisonous vapors, will again bring back thy cataracts, and a film impenetrable to light will cover thine eyes. Then will thy blindness be very great and thy vision barely suffice for one step. Everything will seem joyful to thee. Thine ears will not be troubled by groans; every hour thy hearing will be soothed by sweet songs. The sacrificial incense of flattery will hover about thy vulnerable soul. Thy touch will always feel smooth softness. Never will beneficent roughness irritate thy sense of feeling. Tremble now in the face of this imminent peril. A storm cloud will rise above thy head, and avenging thunderbolts will be ready to strike thee down. But I promise thee, I will remain within the borders of thy realm. Whenever thou desirest to see me, whenever thy soul, besieged by the wiles of flattery, thirsts for the sight of me, call me from afar; wherever my harsh voice is heard, there wilt thou find me. Never be afraid of my voice. If from the midst of the people there arise a man who criticizes thy acts, know that he is thy true friend. With no hope of reward, with no servile trembling, with a sturdy voice he will proclaim me to thee. Beware and do not dare to put him to death as a rebel. Call him to thee, be hospitable to him as to a pilgrim. For everyone who criticizes the Sovereign in the fullness of his autocratic power is a pilgrim in the land where all tremble before him. Treat him well, I say, honor him, so that he may return and tell thee ever more truth. But such stout hearts are rare; hardly one in a whole century appears in the world's arena. But in order that the impassioned delight in the exercise of power may not put thy vigilance to sleep, I give thee this ring, which will warn thee against thine injustice, if thou wilt fight against it. For know that thou hast it in thy power to be the greatest murderer in the commonweal, the greatest robber, the greatest traitor, the greatest violator of the public peace, a most savage enemy who turns his malice against the lives of the weak. Thine is the blame if a mother lament for her son, or a wife for her husband, killed on the field of battle, for the danger of being subjected to a conqueror's yoke hardly justifies the murder called war. Thine the blame if the field be deserted, if the peasant's little ones starve at their mother's breast, withering from lack of food. But look now at thyself and those around thee, observe how thy commands are executed, and if thy soul quake not with terror at the sight, I will leave thee and forget thy palace forever."

As she spoke, the pilgrim's countenance seemed radiantly happy. The sight of her filled my soul with joy. No longer did it feel the surge of vanity and the swell of pride. I felt at peace; the tumult of vainglory and the storm of ambition no longer disturbed my soul. My glittering garments seemed to be stained with blood and drenched with tears. On my fingers I saw fragments of human brains; my feet were standing in slime. The people around me looked still more odious. They seemed all blackened and seared within by the dark flame of greed. At me and at one another they threw fierce looks full of rapacity, envy, sly cunning, and hate. My commander-in-chief, whom I had sent forth to conquer, was wallowing in luxury and pleasure. The army was without discipline; my soldiers were valued less than cattle. No pains were taken to care for their health or their provisioning; their lives counted for nothing; they were deprived of their fixed and proper pay, which was misspent on unnecessary military frippery. A majority of the new recruits died as a result of neglect by their superiors or because of their unnecessary and untimely severity. The money intended for the maintenance of the troops was in the hands of the master of the revels. Medals for military distinction were awarded, not for bravery, but for base servility. I saw before me a renowned military commander, whom I had honored with outstanding marks of my favor. Now I saw clearly that his whole distinction lay in pandering to the lust of his superior. He had had no occasion to show bravery, for he had not even seen the enemy from a distance. From such warriors I had expected new laurels. I turned away from a thousand calamities that unfolded before my eyes.

My ships, which I had ordered to sail the farthest seas, I saw coasting near the mouth of the harbor. The admiral who had flown on the wings of the wind to carry out my orders was stretching his limbs on a soft bed, intoxicated with voluptuous desire, in the embraces of a hired inciter of his lust. On a chart, executed at his command, of a completely imaginary voyage, there were already visible in all parts of the world new islands abounding in fruits appropriate to their various climates. Vast lands and innumerable peoples were created by the pens of these new voyagers. By the gleam of nocturnal lights they had already written a glowing description, in a flowery and splendid style, of this voyage and the discoveries made on it. Golden covers had already been prepared to adorn this very important work. O Cook! Why did you pass your life in travail and privations? Why did you end it so miserably? If you had boarded these ships, you would have begun your voyage in delightful ease, and in delightful ease you would have ended it, and you would have made just as many discoveries while sitting in one place, and (in my kingdom) you would have been just as famous, for you would have been honored by your Sovereign.

The achievement of which, in my blindness, my soul was most proud, namely, the abolition of the death penalty and the granting of amnesty to prisoners, had hardly any visible effect on the vast complex of governmental activities. My commands had either been completely violated by being misapplied, or had not had the desired effect because of distorted interpretation and dilatory execution. Mercy had come to be bought and sold, and the auctioneer's hammer knocked down compassion and generosity to the highest bidder. Instead of being thought merciful by my subjects because of the amnesty I had ordered, I passed among them for a cheat, hypocrite, and wicked play-actor. "Keep thy mercy," thousands of voices shouted, "do not proclaim it to us in high-sounding words, if thou dost not intend to carry it out. Do not add insult to injury, do not make our burden heavier by making us feel it more keenly. We were peacefully asleep; thou hast disturbed our sleep when we did not want to wake up, since we had nothing to wake up for." In the construction of cities I saw only the waste of the government's money, frequently drenched with the blood and tears of my subjects. In the erection of magnificent buildings the waste was often accompanied by a misunderstanding of true art. I saw that their internal and external arrangements lacked even the slightest particle of taste. They seemed to belong to the age of the Goths and Vandals. In the home prepared for the Muses I did not see the inspiring streams of Castalia and Hippocrene; limping art crept, earthbound, scarcely daring to raise its glances above the levels sanctioned by tradition. Bending over the drawings of the building, the architects were not thinking about how to make it beautiful but about how to make money out of it. I was nauseated with my ostentatious vanity and turned my eyes away. But my soul was hurt most of all by the results of my liberality. In my blindness I had thought that public funds not needed for governmental purposes could not be spent in any better way than on succour for the indigent, clothing for the naked, food for the hungry, rescue for those suffering under adverse circumstances, or to reward excellence and merit that do not find their joy in wealth. But how sad it was to see that my generosity poured more wealth upon the rich, the flatterer, the false friend, the murderer, sometimes indeed the secret murderer, the traitor and violator of the public trust, the clever sycophant who knew my desires and pandered to my weaknesses, the woman who gloried in her shamelessness. Barely, almost imperceptibly, the thin wellsprings of my generosity trickled down to modest worth and bashful merit. Tears poured from my eyes and hid from me the miserable objects of my foolish generosity. Now I saw clearly that the honors I had given out always fell into the hands of the unworthy. In the quest for honors, which mortals dream of, inexperienced worth, struck with the first gleam of these supposed blessings, began the race evenly with flattery and meanness of soul. But starting awkwardly, it was always exhausted after the first few steps and was fated to content itself with its own approval, in the conviction that worldly honors are dust and ashes. Seeing that the world was out of joint as a result of my weakness and the trickery of my ministers; that my affection was wasted upon a woman who sought in my love satisfaction only for her vanity and who sought to please me only with her outward appearance, while her heart felt only loathing for me, I shouted in the madness of my anger. "Unworthy criminals, evildoers! Tell me, wherefore have you abused your Sovereign's trust? Stand now before your judge. Tremble, ye who have grown hardened in evil. How can you justify your deeds? What can you say in excuse? Here he is; I will call him from his hut of humility. Come," I called to an old man whom I saw at the border of my vast realm, half-hidden in a moss-covered hut, "come and lighten my burden; come and restore peace to my anxious heart and troubled mind." As I said this, I saw afresh the responsibility of my high office, recognized the vastness of my duty, and understood whence proceeded my right and my power. I trembled inwardly and was terrified by the responsibility of my stewardship. My blood surged wildly, and I awoke. Even before I was fully conscious, I clutched my finger, but it bore no ring of thorns. If only it would always stay on the little finger of a King!

Ruler of the world, if, when you read my dream, you smile scornfully or knit your brow, know that the pilgrim whom I saw has flown far away from you and disdains your palace.

8

Buckinghamshire: The Remains of a Fine Woman[1]

The Earl of Buckinghamshire was the English Ambassador to Russia from 1762 to 1765. The first selection, written in 1762, describes the new Empress; the second, written in 1765, discusses the Empress from the perspective of four years of rule.

Her Imperial Majesty is neither short nor tall; she has a majestic air, and possesses that happy mixture of dignity and ease which at once enforces respect and sets men at their ease. Formed with a mind and a body capable of acquiring every accomplishment, and enforced retirement gave her more leisure to cultivate them than is usually allotted to princes, and qualified her, as she charmed the eye in gay society, to delight the understanding in more serious moments. This period of constraint, which lasted several years, and the agitation of mind and continual fatigues which she has undergone since her accession, have deprived her charms of their freshness. Besides, she has never been beautiful. Her features were far from being so delicately and exactly formed as to compose what might pretend to regular beauty, but a fine complexion, an animated and intelligent eye, a mouth agreeably turned, and a profusion of glossy chestnut hair produce that sort of countenance which, a very few years ago, a man must have been either prejudiced or insensible to have beheld with indifference. She has been, and still is, what often pleases and always attaches more than beauty. She is extremely well made, the neck and hands remarkably beautiful, and the limbs so elegantly turned as equally to become the dress of either sex. Her eyes are blue, their vivacity tempered by a languor in which there is much sensibility and no insipidity. She has the air of paying no attention to what she wears, yet she is always too well drest for a woman who is entirely indifferent to her appearance. A man's dress is what suits her best; she wears it always when she rides on horseback. It is scarce credible what she does in that way, managing horses,

[1] From *The Despatches and Correspondence of John, Second Earl of Buckinghamshire, Ambassador to the Court of Catherine II*, 2 vols., edited by A. D. Collyer (London, 1901), vol. 1, pp. 100–104, 273–76.

even fiery horses, with all the skill and courage of a groom. She excels, too, in the serious as well as livelier dances. She expresses herself with elegance in French, and I am assured that she speaks Russian with as much precision as German, which is her native language, and that she has a critical knowledge of both languages. She speaks and reasons with fluency and precision, and some letters which must have been of her own composing have been admired and applauded by the scholars of the nation in whose language they were wrote.

Reading made her amusement in the retirement in which she lived in the days of the late Empress. The history and the interests of the European Powers are familiar to her. When she spoke to me of English history, I perceived that what had struck her the most was the reign of Elizabeth. Time will show where such an emulation may lead her. Finding herself superior in information and argument to most of those about her, she thinks she is equally so to everybody, and, understanding clearly what she has learnt, she sometimes thinks herself mistress of what she has not. When she was on board the Admiral's ship at Cronstadt, her imperial standard flying, and flattered with the inexperienced grandeur of commanding more than twenty large ships, she disputed with me which end of a man-of-war went first—a circumstance which indeed she was not obliged to know—but the actual situation made the doubt ridiculous.

Much stress is laid upon her resolution, particularly in the instance of dethroning her husband. Desperate situations make cowards valiant. She was compelled either to ruin him or to submit herself to that confinement which she knew had long been in deliberation. Those who know her well say she is rather enterprising than brave, and that her appearance of courage arises sometimes from a conviction of the pusillanimity of her enemies, at others from her not seeing her danger. She certainly is bolder than the generality of her sex, but I have seen her twice very much afraid without reason: once when she was getting out of boat into a ship; the other time, upon hearing a little noise in the ante-chamber at Court. But when the occasion requires it she dares all, and in many critical and dangerous situations her courage has never failed her. Yet she has all the delicacy of her sex. To see her is to know that she could love, and that her love would make the happiness of a lover worthy of her.

Two capital errors, which are equally evident and inexcusable, *are* the meanness with which she submits to the ill-bred inattention of Orlow, and the little affection she shows to the Grand Duke.

The amusements of her retirement, into which she enters with a youthful spirit, are trifling beyond expression, and much the same which children in other countries leave off at twelve years old.

Those who are most in her society assure me that her application to business is incredible. The welfare and prosperity of her subjects, the glory of her empire, are always present to her; and to all appearance her care will raise the reputation and power of Russia to a point which, at present, they have never reached, if she does not indulge too much in farfetched and unpractical theories, which interested or ignorant people are too ready to suggest to her. Her foible is too systematic, and that may be the rock on which she may, perhaps, split. She embraces too many objects at once; she likes to begin, regulate, and correct projects all in a moment. Indefatigable in everything that she undertakes, she obliges her ministers to work incessantly. They argue, make plans, and sketch out a thousand schemes, and decide upon nothing. Among those who hold the first rank in her confidence, some will be found who have experience, but few if any who possess superior talents. There is, however, one of her Majesty's secretaries who has knowledge, wit, and even application, when women and the pleasures of the table—which always demand his first cares—give him any leisure for business.

Unwilling to touch so tender a string, I have deferred till the last speaking of the Revolution and the most melancholy catastrophe which succeeded.

The Empress has frequently talked to me of her husband, and, without exaggerating his indiscretions, pointed out those which principally occasioned his ruin. Once, in her absence, I saw his picture in her cabinet; it was without a frame and stood upon the floor, as if brought in for her to look at. The Vice-Chancellor told me it was a strong likeness. I examined it with attention, and could not help running over in my mind the hard fate of the heir of Russia, Sweden, and Holstein, who, with many defects in his understanding, had none in his heart.

The Vice-Chancellor seemed surprised at my silent attention, and asked me what employed my thoughts. Was it so difficult to guess?

When this is considered as a portrait drawn by one who knew her and who wished with candour to steer the middle course between calumny and adulation, who will not mourn the steps she took to raise herself to Empire, and the fatal measures which the worst of her followers judged necessary to secure her in that throne she fills so well?

Many, and some of the deepest hue, are the blemishes which shade a character otherwise so amiable. Her enemies, and particularly the French and Austrians, have taken every method to place them in the strongest light, and, not contented with those which were known to be true, and others but too probably, they have sought to blacken her still more with fictions which have almost been generally received, even by those from whom her political disposition might claim a fairer hearing. She is accused of dethroning her husband; of usurping that empire of which, even from her own declaration, she could only pretend to be

Regent; of causing her husband to be put to death; of changing the whole system of her Empire in order to make one of her former lovers king of Poland; and, lastly, of contriving the murder of the late Prince Ivan. That her present favourite is the fourth person she has distinguished is as certain as that she was persuaded to receive the first by the Empress Elizabeth, who thought her nephew incapable of begetting children; and possibly anyone who is acquainted with the abandoned scenes which passed at that Court will wonder that a young, lively woman, who had long seen debauchery sanctified by usage and the highest example, should want any persuasion at all. When I allow that the seizing the Crown herself does not admit of justification, nor even of palliation, that adopting the most favourable and improbable supposition that her husband was put to death, not only without her order, but contrary to her intention, her not clearing up the fact and punishing the guilty at any risk is unpardonable. Shall I incur a suspicion of partiality when I assert that the folly and imprudence of the ill-fated Emperor, his avowed intention of confining her, his further plan of setting aside the Great Duke, his ill-conceived expedition against the Danes, his mean, subservient adulation of the King of Prussia, which in the end must have been destructive to his country, and lastly, the insults she was hourly exposed to from his abandoned mistress—too powerful an incentive of that feminine resentment which so often decides the fate of empires—may, in a great measure, apologise for her conduct so far as removing him from the throne?

To assert that some time ago I should have thought it an easy task to draw a full and just character of the Empress, and that now, having frequent opportunities of seeing her in the hours of dissipation when the veil of restraint and ceremony was thrown off, the undertaking puzzles and embarrasses me, has something the air of a paradox, which, however, is easily solved by mentioning that then I knew only the great outlines and was unacquainted with the little weaknesses and inconsistencies which almost efface some and shade many of those eminent qualities which adorn her. It is impossible to consider the general tenour of her conduct, since she placed herself upon the throne, without tracing evident marks of a laudable ambition to distinguish herself; to make her subjects happy at home and respectable abroad; to encourage arts, sciences and commerce; to form by a liberal education the young nobility of both sexes; to extend in a great degree the same advantages to inferior ranks; to improve the public revenue without oppressing individuals; to check the tyranny with which the clergy distressed their vassals; and to introduce that ease of society, that urbanity and general good breeding which prevail in other European nations; in a word, to transmit her name with glory to posterity, and by the use she makes of empire to palliate the means by which she has acquired it.

In the course of two years, though hourly alarmed by the attempts of her enemies, she has exerted her good offices for the general pacification of Europe; she has given a King to Poland, established a sovereign in Courland, and greatly contributed to the overturning of the so long prevailing French system in Sweden. These are facts of which it is as necessary to labour the proof as it would be vain to contest the reality, and surely it is greatly to be lamented that vanity, self-sufficiency, avarice, and a taste for trifling pleasures should cloud so bright a future?

The expenses of the Court are in some instances retrenched to a degree of meanness, and many persons of the first rank seize officiously the first pretence to retire from Petersburg, as, receiving no longer the same presents from the Sovereign, they cannot afford to pay the daily-increasing price of every article of consumption.

Political intrigue and fruitful imaginations have variously accounted for her most imprudent journey to Riga; in fact, it was determined by the desire of a little mind to make a naval parade, to enjoy the pageantry and adulations with which the provinces received her, and to see a sovereign of her own creating at her feet. Deaf to the friendly advice which combated her inclination, she was obstinate to prove her steadiness.

Her face and figure are greatly altered for the worse since her accession. It is easy to discover the remains of a fine woman, but she is now no longer an object of desire. The many who wish to arraign the conduct and vilify the character of this Princess tax her with the same disposition to debauchery as sullied the reign of her predecessor. This makes it necessary to say something on the subject, and succinctly state such information as upon the strictest inquiry I have obtained, which when candidly considered may palliate though not justify her conduct. She had been married some years to the Grand Duke without being with child, and, as this was supposed to arise from the inability of her husband, distant hints were thrown out by the Empress, which were not taken. At last she sent her confidante, Madame Shouvalow, to inform the Grand Duchess that if she did not soon contrive to produce an heir to the Empire she must expect to be divorced. After some hesitation she yielded. One Soltikow (now abroad) was the man pitched upon, and he is said to be the father of the present Grand Duke. The first scruples being got over, the rest followed but too naturally. Soltikow having left the country, the solitude in which she generally lived made every possible amusement necessary, and General Chernichow and, soon after, Poniatowski enjoyed her favour. Orlow was one of the young people who entered early into the conspiracy to place her upon the throne. She saw him frequently; the beauty of his person, and his particular affection for her, of which she has since declared she had long been sensible, induced her to yield. Her being with child at the time of the Revolution was a circumstance which, as her husband never approached her, made it necessary to hasten that event. She was brought to bed of a son at Moscow some months after. The child is under the care of Schurin at Petersburg, where her Imperial Majesty has sometimes visited him.

9

Shcherbatov: Arbitrary Worldly Principles[1]

Prince Shcherbatov (1733–90), was born of an ancient Russian noble family with a long tradition of state service. He was a confirmed opponent of absolute monarchy and an advocate of the role of the old noble families. He saw army service, was a participant in the Legislative Commission of 1767, and served in a variety of bureaucratic posts; in the latter part of his life, he devoted himself to writing a series of unpublished essays which were highly negative evaluations of Catherine's reign. The following view of Catherine's reign, in which he saw the decline of his own class, was written sometime before 1787, but not uncovered until the 1850s, and only published in 1896.

A woman not born of the blood of our sovereigns, who deposed her husband by an armed insurrection, she received, in return for so virtuous a deed, the crown and sceptre of Russia, together with the title of 'Devout Sovereign', in the words of the prayer recited in church on behalf of our monarchs.

It cannot be said that she is unqualified to rule so great an Empire, if indeed a woman can support this yoke, and if human qualities alone are sufficient for this supreme office. She is endowed with considerable beauty, clever, affable, magnanimous and compassionate on principle. She loves glory, and is assiduous in her pursuit of it. She is prudent, enterprising, and quite well-read. However, her moral outlook is based on the modern philosophers, that is to say, it is not fixed on the firm rock of God's Law; and hence, being based on arbitrary worldly principles, it is liable to change with them.

In addition, her faults are as follows: she is licentious, and trusts herself entirely to her favourites; she is full of ostentation in all things, infinitely selfish, and incapable of forcing herself to attend to any mat-

[1] From Prince M. M. Shcherbatov, *On the Corruption of Morals in Russia*, edited and translated with an introduction and notes by A. Lentin (London: Cambridge University Press, 1969), pp. 235–57, odd pages only. Reprinted by permission of the publisher.

ters which may bore her. She takes everything on herself and takes no care to see it carried out, and finally she is so capricious, that she rarely keeps the same system of government even for a month.

For all that, once on the throne, she refrained from taking cruel vengeance on those who had previously vexed her. She had with her her favourite, Grigory Grigor'evich Orlov, who had helped her to accede to the throne. He was a man who had grown up in alehouses and houses of ill-repute. He had no education, and had hitherto led the life of a young reprobate, though he was kind and good-hearted.

This was the man who reached the highest step which it is possible for a subject to attain. Amid boxing-matches, wrestling, card-games, hunting and other noisy pastimes, he had picked up and adopted certain rules useful to the state. His brothers did likewise.

These rules were: to take vengeance on no one, to banish flatterers, to leave each person and government-organ in the uninterrupted execution of their duties, not to flatter the monarch, to seek out worthy men and not make promotions except on grounds of merit, and finally, to avoid luxury. These rules were kept by Grigory Grigor'evich Orlov (later Count and finally Prince) to the day he died.

Finding that gambling can bring others to ruin, he gave it up. Although Counts Nikita and Pyotr Ivanovich Panin were his sworn enemies, he never did them the least harm; on the contrary, on many occasions, he did them favours, and defended them from the monarch's wrath.

He not only forgave Shvanvich, the man who treacherously attacked his brother, Alexei Grigor'evich, but even did him favours. The many flatterers who tried to exploit his pride, were never successful; on the contrary, it was easier to gain his affection by outspokenness than by flattery. He never interfered with the administration of any government-organ which did not belong to him; and if he did make a request on someone's behalf, he was never angry if his request was turned down. He never flattered his sovereign, for whom he had a genuine zeal, and would tell her the whole truth with a certain outspokenness, and always moved her heart to mercy, as I myself witnessed on many occasions. He liked to seek out worthy men as far as he was able, but he disliked making promotions except on the grounds of merit—this, not only in the case of those whom he benefitted for their worth alone, but even in the case of his boon-companions; and the first sign of his favour was to force a man to serve the nation with zeal and to employ him in the most dangerous situations, as he did in the case of Vsevolod Alexeevich Vsevolozhsky, whom he took with him to Moscow during the Great Plague, and whom he set to work there.

Although he had been dissolute and luxurious in his youth, there was later no trace of luxury to be seen in his house; his house contained nothing exceptional by way of furnishings; his table could not compare with those of the epicures; there was nothing extraordinary about his carriages, though he was fond of horses and racing; and, finally, at no time in his life did he ever wear gold or silver on his clothes.

But all his good qualities were overshadowed by his licentiousness. He scorned his duty to his sovereign and the monarch's Court, and turned the Royal Court into a den of debauchery. There was hardly a single maid-in-waiting at Court who was not subjected to his importunings—and how many of them were weak enough to yield to them! —and this was tolerated by the monarch. Finally, he ravished his thirteen-year-old cousin, Ekaterina Nikolaevna Zinov'ev, and although he later married her, he did not thereby conceal his vice, for he had already publicly revealed his action, and by the marriage itself he broke every law of church and state.

However, during his period of favour, affairs were quite well conducted, and the monarch, imitating her favourite's simplicity, was indulgent to her subjects. There were not many distributions of largesse; duties were carried out, and the monarch's pleasure served instead of rewards. Men were not insulted by being passed over when it came to awarding ranks, and the monarch's pride was often quelled by the truthfulness of her favourite.

However, since virtue is not as prone to imitation as vice, the praiseworthy sides of his conduct were little followed. Seeing the licentiousness of Orlov and his brothers, women prided themselves in striving to become their mistresses, and decency and modesty, already impaired in the time of Peter III, were completely extinguished by long habit during the Orlovs' period of favour, the more so since this was also a means of acquiring the monarch's favour.

His removal, rather than fall, from the position of favourite, gave others the chance to take his place at the side of the licentious Empress, and it may be said that each favourite, however brief his period of favour, has put Russia in debt to the tune of millions of roubles by some vice or other (apart from Vasil'chikov, who did neither good nor evil). Zorich introduced the custom of immoderate gambling; Potyomkin—love of power, ostentation, pandering to all his desires, gluttony and hence luxury at table, flattery, avarice, rapaciousness, and it may be said, all the other vices known in the world, with which he himself is full and with which he fills his supporters, and so on throughout the Empire. Zavadovsky brought base Malorussians to office; Korsakov increased brazen licentiousness among women; Lanskoy made cruelty a mark of honour; Ermolov did not succeed in doing anything, but Mamonov is introducing arbitrariness in the distribution of ranks and favouritism for his own kinsmen.

The Empress herself, selfish woman that she is, wishes, it seems, to increase the power of vice, not only by her own example but by her actual encouragement of it. Fond of glory and ostentation, she loves flattery and servility.

Among her entourage is Betsky, a man of small intellect, but sufficiently cunning to deceive her. Knowing her love of glory, he established many institutions, such as the Foundlings' Homes, the Convent for Young Ladies, the reorganized Land Cadet Corps and the Academy of Arts, and the Loan and Orphans' Bank. In this he behaved like the architect of Alexandria who built the Pharos; on which building he fashioned in alabaster the name of Ptolemy, the king who provided the money for the building; but beneath the alabaster he carved his own name in marble, so that when with the passage of time the alabaster fell away, his name alone should be visible.

So Betsky too, though he made it seem that everything he did was for the glory of the Empress, yet not only does his name appear as chief founder of all his schemes, which have been printed in various languages, but he did not even leave the monarch the power of choosing the directors of these institutions, but he himself was supreme director in every one of them, that is, until his credit collapsed.

And in order to hide this, all methods were used by him in order to flatter her: her praises were sung everywhere, in speeches, in writings and even in ballets performed at the theatre. Once, at a performance at the Cadet Corps of the ballet 'The Battle of Chesme', I myself heard her say to me: 'Il me loue tant, qu'enfin il me gâtera.'

She would have been fortunate if a change of heart had accompanied these words, but no, when she said this, her soul was drunk with pomp and flattery.

Ivan Perfil'evich Elagin took no less pains in order to flatter her in public and in private. He being Director of the Court Theatre, various works were written in her honour; her deeds were celebrated in ballet-dances; sometimes 'Fame' announced the arrival of the Russian fleet in the Morea, sometimes the battle of Chesme was celebrated; sometimes 'The Soldiery' danced with Russia.

Prince Alexander Alexandrovich Vyazemsky, a man of small intellect, but extremely cunning, also used a most artful means of flattery, being Procurator-General and holding in his hands the state revenues. He pretended to be stupid, he pointed out to her the excellent administration of the state perfected under her rule, and said that he himself was stupid, and that everything that he did was on her instructions and under her inspiration. Sometimes he not only compared her wisdom with that of God but said that it was greater; by this means he gained the upper hand over her.

Bezborodko, her secretary, now already a Count, a member of the College of Foreign Affairs, High Chamberlain and Postmaster-General, makes it an invariable rule as far as the administration is concerned, never to contradict her, but to praise and carry out all her orders. For this he has received an immoderate number of awards.

Flattery having reached such a peak at Court among men employed in affairs of state, people have begun to flatter in other ways. If anyone builds a house with money partly given by her or that he has stolen, he invites her to the housewarming, where he writes the following words in illuminations: 'A Gift to You from Your Subjects'; or else he inscribes on the house: 'By the Generosity of Catherine the Great', forgetting to add: 'But to the Ruination of Russia.' Or else, festivals are given in her honour, gardens are built, with impromptu spectacles and decorations, everywhere showing flattery and servility.

To add to the corruption of women's morals and of all decency, she has set other women the example of the possession of a long and frequent succession of lovers, each equally honoured and enriched, thus advertising the cause of their ascendancy. Seeing a shrine erected to this vice in the heart of the Empress, women scarcely think it a vice in themselves to copy her; rather, I suppose, each thinks it a virtue in herself that she has not yet had so many lovers!

Although she is in her declining years, although grey hair now covers her head and time has marked her brow with the indelible signs of age, yet her licentiousness still does not diminish. She now realizes that her lovers cannot find in her the attractions of youth, and that neither rewards, nor power, nor gain can replace for them the effect which youthfulness can produce on a lover.

Trying to conceal the ravages of time, she has abandoned her former simplicity in dress, and though in her youth she disliked cloth-of-gold, and criticized the Empress Elisabeth Petrovna for leaving a wardrobe large enough to clothe a whole army, she herself has started to show a passion of her own for inventing suitable dresses and rich adornments for them, and has thus given rise to the same luxury, not only in women but also in men.

I remember, when I entered the Court in 1768 there was only one coat in the whole Court that was embroidered in gold—a red cloth coat, belonging to Vasily Il'ich Bibikov. In April 1769, the Empress was angry with Count Ivan Grigor'evich Chernyshov for arriving at Czarskoe Selo on her birthday in an embroidered coat; but in 1777 when I retired from Court, everyone wore clothes of cloth-of-gold with embroidery even on ordinary days, and were now almost ashamed to have embroidery only on the edge of their garments.

It cannot be said that the Empress is particular about food; on the contrary, it may be said that she is too moderate. But her former lover, who has remained her all-powerful friend, Prince Grigory Alexandrovich Potyomkin, is not merely particular about food, but a positive glutton. The negligence of the High Marshal of the Court, Prince

Nikolai Mikhailovich Golitsyn, in neglecting to prepare some favourite dish of his, subjected him to Potyomkin's vile abuse, and forced him to retire. From this let everyone judge whether it is not a fact that Prince Golitsyn's successors, Grigory Nikitich Orlov and Prince Fyodor Serge-evich Boryatinsky, are not now making every effort to satisfy this all-powerful glutton. And certainly the royal table has become much more magnificent and is far better today.

And also, in order to please this friend of the monarch, people every-where have begun to try to increase magnificence at table (though it was sufficient even before his time), and this disease of luxury and the desire to glut oneself on the finest fare has spread from the highest to the lowest.

Generally speaking, women are more prone to despotism than men; and as far as she is concerned, it can justly be averred that she is in this particular a woman among women. Nothing can irritate her more than that when making some report to her, men quote the Laws in opposition to her will. Immediately the retort flies from her lips: 'Can I then not do this irrespective of the laws?'

But she has found no one with the courage to answer that she can indeed, but only as a despot, and to the detriment of her glory and the nation's confidence. Many law-suits attest to her arbitrariness: (1) the restoration to Mar'ya Pavlovna Naryshkin by Talyzin of certain estates, which had been confirmed as his property by the title-deeds and by ac-tual possession; (2) the case of the children of Prince Boris Vasil'evich Golitsyn concerning the wrongful confiscation of the estates of their grandfather, Streshnev; although this injustice was recognized by the Senate, and a report was submitted requesting permission for them to be restored to the rightful heirs, and although the postscript on the report 'So be it' seemed to indicate that their claim was being justly satisfied; yet later the explanation came from the Empress's study that the words 'So be it' meant 'Let them remain confiscated'.

Akim Ivanovich Apukhtim reported to her through the College of War about the retirement of a certain Major-General; he received the order that the man was to be retired without promotion. When he began to point out that the Laws specifically laid it down that Major-Generals were to be promoted upon retirement, he received the answer that 'She was above the Laws, and did not choose to grant him this reward'.

Such examples, seen in the monarch herself, certainly encourage the grandees to similar arbitrariness and injustice, and Russia, groaning from such outrages, shows daily signs of how infectious the monarch's example is.

Such an attitude of mind, and particularly in a person devoted to her favourites, naturally brings with it bias and injustice. I could sup-ply many examples of both of these; but it is sufficient if I tell how, because of her dislike of Sakharov, on the grounds of his immorality (though he had long been her valet-de-chambre and had enjoyed her confidence, though he was no better then) his case was placed in the archives without consideration. As if immorality was to be punished in a property-suit, a case in which even a dissolute man may be in the right, and where the point at issue is not morals and character, but purely and simply—who owns what.

Then there was the case of Wachtmeister, concerning the wrongful confiscation of his grandfather's estates in Livonia. Though his case was upheld by all the departments of the Senate, the verdict he received was that, since the estates had been already given to General Browne, they should remain his property. Count Roman Larionovich Vorontsov, an avowed bribe-taker all his life, was appointed Viceroy of Vladimir, where he did not cease to practice his usual corruptions. These did not escape the notice of the monarch, but she merely rebuked him with an ambiguous hint, by sending him a large purse. Only when he was already dead and the people's ruin had gone to extremes, was the order given for an inquiry into his conduct and that of the governor; and although the people's ruin had lasted seven years, the inquiry was only authorized to cover two years.

Do not such examples, which are of frequent occurrence, encourage the citizens to indulge in similar conduct for their own advantage? I have read in a certain book the following clear symbol: that it is vain to try and draw a true circle when the centre is uncertain and wavering; the line of the circle will never meet exactly; there are also the words of the Holy Writ, which also clearly signify the duty of those in authority: 'Teacher, Reform Thyself!'

Is it possible to imagine that a monarch who makes such large distributions of largesse, a monarch who is the main recipient of the treasures of the entire state, could be avaricious? Yet so it is; for what else can I call the introduction of that habit, so much censured by all political writers, the habit of selling offices for money? There are many examples of this: the dissolute and avaricious leaseholder, Lukin, having donated 8,000 roubles to the Court out of his ill-gotten gains, and presenting them in the cause of a school for the common people, received the rank of Captain. Then there was Prokofy Demidov, who was almost brought to the scaffold for his lampoons. Though he had been under investigation for the crime of attacking a secretary of the College of Justice in his own house, and though he was responsible for incessant outrages and practical jokes, offensive to any well-constituted government, yet, for donating money to the Foundlings' Home (and thereby insulting his own children), he received the rank of Major-General; and for donating 5,000 roubles in the cause of public education, gratitude was expressed to him publicly in the newspapers. As if the monarch could not establish useful institutions without taking money from corrupt men, and as if dissolute morals could be atoned for with money!

This example has become even more infectious than the others. All offices can be bought, official positions have begun to be given not to those most worthy, but to those who pay most for them, and even these men, once they have paid, have started to recoup their loss by exacting bribes from the people.

Merchants, enriched by peculation of state property, have received high rank; for example, Loginov, a leaseholder, who not only robbed through his leases, but was actually convicted for embezzlement of commissariat funds, received civil rank. Faleev, who as purveyor to the monarch always charged three times too much, has not only received civil rank and a title of nobility for himself, but has also had all his minions promoted to the ranks of staff officer.

Trade has fallen into disrepute, and unworthy men have been made nobles, thieves and rascals have been rewarded, dissoluteness encouraged, and all this before the eyes of the monarch and with her connivance. Is it possible, then, in view of this, to expect justice and impartiality from the ordinary magistrates?

The whole reign of this monarch has been marked by events relating to her love of glory. The many institutions founded by her apparently exist for the good of the nation. In fact they are simply symbols of her love of glory, for if she really had the nation's interest at heart, she would, after founding them, have also paid attention to their progress. But she has been content simply with their establishment and with the assurance that she will be eternally revered by posterity as their founder; she has cared nothing for their progress, and though she sees their abuses she has not put a stop to them.

This is attested by the establishment of the Foundlings' Home, the Convent for the Education of Young Ladies of the Nobility, the reorganization of the Cadet Corps, and so on. In the first of these, a large number of infants have died, and even today, after over twenty years, few or hardly any artisans have emerged. In the second, the young ladies have emerged with neither learning nor morals, apart from what nature has provided them with, and their education has consisted in acting comedies rather than in the improvement of their hearts, morals and reason. From the third, the pupils have emerged with little knowledge and with an absolute aversion to all discipline.

The wars that have been started attend to this still more. Poniatowski was raised to the Polish throne out of favouritism; it was wished to provide him with an autocratic form of government, contrary to the Polish liberties. The protection of the Dissidents was undertaken; and instead of striving to invite these victims of religious persecution to join their co-religionists in Russia, and thereby to weaken Poland and strengthen Russia, occasion was given for a war with Turkey, fortunate in its events, but costing Russia more than any previous war. The Fleet was sent to Greece and under God's protection won a victory; but the only motive behind this expedition was love of glory. Poland has been partitioned, thereby strengthening the houses of Austria and Brandenburg, and losing Russia her powerful influence over Poland. The Crimea has been acquired, or rather, stolen, a country which, because of its difference of climate, has proved a graveyard for Russians.

Measures have been drawn up which men are not ashamed to call laws, and the new provincial governorships have been filled indiscriminately, to the ruin of all that went before, to the detriment of society, to the increase of sharp practice and the ruin of the people; and no watch is kept over these governors to see whether they carry out their instructions exactly.

Laws have been concocted, called Rights of the Nobility and Municipal Rights, which contain a deprivation rather than a granting of rights, and lay a universal burden on the nation.

Such an unbridled love of glory is also encouraging the growth of an enormous number of large buildings everywhere. Farmers have been attracted away from their land by the prospect of greater employment and gain; yet the state revenues scarcely suffice for such buildings, which even when built, will be a burden to maintain. Private men, too, are copying this passion, founded on love of glory, that their names, inscribed on a building, should survive for many centuries, and have plunged madly into the erection of such buildings and their decoration.

One man, out of affluence, will spend many thousands of roubles in building houses, gardens and summer-houses for his comfort and pleasure; a second does the same out of ostentation, and a third, following this pernicious example, does the same in order not to fall behind the others, and spends beyond his means. All three, though they may find themselves comfort and pleasure, are gradually brought to ruin by this luxuriousness. They become a burden to themselves and the state, and often make up their losses by bribe-taking and other deplorable means.

My conscience assures me that all my descriptions, however black they may be, are unbiased; truth alone and the corruption into which all my fellow-subjects have fallen and from which my country groans, have compelled me to commit them to paper. And so, from a fair description of the morals of the Empress, it is quite possible to see the disposition of her heart and soul.

True friendship has never resided in her heart, and she is ready to betray her best friend and servant in order to please her lover. She has no maternal instincts for her son, and her rule with everyone is to cajole a man beyond measure and respect him as long as he is needed, and then in her own phrase 'to throw away a squeezed-out lemon'.

Examples of this are as follows: Anna Alexeevna Matyushkin, who was always loyal to her even during her period of oppression, was finally banished. Count Alexei Petrovich Bestuzhev, who had helped her when she was Grand Duchess in all her designs, and had suffered misfortune on her behalf, was deprived of all her trust at the end of his life, and after his death she reviled him. Count Nikita Ivanovich Panin, who had helped her to accede to the throne, saw all his offices taken away from him in his old age, and perhaps it was this that brought about his death. Nikolai Ivanovich Checherin, who served her with all possible zeal and enjoyed her favour, was in the end so victimized by her that he ended his life prematurely.

Prince Alexander Mikhailovich Golitsyn, the Field Marshal, the silent executor of all her orders, died without any regret on her part; for though the news of his death was known in the morning, yet that day she went merrily to a concert, and, having indulged her merriment, asked her lover, Lanskoy, on the way out, how Prince Alexander Mikhailovich was; and on receiving the news of his death, she then pretended to burst into tears; this certainly shows, incidentally, what a false heart she has. Countess Praskov'ya Alexandrovna Bruce, who was long her favourite and friend, was finally banished from Court, and died of grief. Let each judge from this whether pure sentiments of friendship can abide in the subjects after such examples.

Having painted this sad picture, I do not think I need to state whether she has faith in God's Law, for if she had, then God's Law itself might improve her heart and set her steps on the path of truth. But no: carried away by her indiscriminate reading of modern writers, she thinks nothing of the Christian religion, though she pretends to be quite devout.

However much she conceals her thoughts, these are frequently revealed in her conversation, and her deeds prove it even more. Many books by Voltaire, undermining religion, have been translated by her order, such as *Candide, The Princess of Babylon,* and others; and Marmontel's *Belisaire,* which makes no distinction between pagan and Christian virtue, was not merely translated by a society at her order, but she herself took part in translating it.

And her tolerance of, or rather, permission for unlawful marriages, such as those of Princes Orlov and Golitsyn with their cousins, and of General Bauer with his step-daughter, proves this most of all. And so it may be said that even this indestructible bastion of conscience and virtue has been destroyed in her reign.

10

The French Embassy: Paternity of Grand Duke Paul[1]

The paternity of Catherine's son, the Grand Duke, later Tsar Paul, is a much debated mystery of Russian history. Catherine's memoirs seem to indicate Serge Saltykov as the father of her son, and thus confirm the end of the Romanov dynasty. Catherine's testimony is the main evidence. The following document, prepared by the French Embassy in Russia, recounts the contemporary opinion on these matters, and gives some notion of the intrigue that suffused the Russian court.

The ceremony of marriage between the Grand Duke Peter and the Grand Duchess Catherine was about to take place [1745, ed.] when the Grand Duke came down with small-pox. This illness ravaged him so frightfully that he emerged from his sick room completely unrecognizable. His face had become hideous. . . . The Grand Duchess did not see him before their wedding; finally, on the wedding day, despite some care to warn the young girl of the Grand Duke's ugliness, her first glance of his face froze her on the spot. She turned away moaning, and the Princess of Zerbst [her mother, ed.] threw herself into the arms of the Grand Duke and held him in her embrace for a long while to give her daughter time to recover from the shock. . . . Finally they celebrated the marriage, but the Grand Duke was incapable of having children due to an obstacle which circumcision remedies among eastern peoples. The Grand Duke, however, thought his case was without remedy. The Grand Duchess, who had no interest in him and was not yet impressed with the need for children, accepted his malady with some relief. . . .

The Grand Duchess Catherine then met Serge Saltykov [1754, ed.] and became pregnant by him. Saltykov was frightened by his predicament and sought means to protect himself. He was well aware of the Grand Duke's condition, and confided to the Princess Narishkin, his sister-in-law, that it could be remedied. The Empress, talking one day

[1] Notes from Saint Petersburg, September 8, 1758, *Archives of Foreign Affairs of France, Russian Correspondence,* vol. 57; Edited and translated by L. J. Oliva.

to the Princess Narishkin who was herself pregnant, indicated that the good lady ought to communicate some of her fertility to the Grand Duchess. Narishkin then told the Empress that such might be possible, and informed the Empress of Saltykov's proposal. The Empress gave her permission to try.

Serge Saltykov then proceeded to attempt to convince the Grand Duke to do all that was necessary to give himself heirs. He conveyed to him also a completely new idea of pleasure. The same day he arranged a supper with persons whom the Grand Duke enjoyed and admired, and, in a moment of gaiety, everyone united to press the Grand Duke to consent. At the same time, Boerhave entered with a surgeon, and, in a moment, the operation was performed and succeeded very well. Saltykov received, on this occasion, a very beautiful diamond from the Empress. . . . Everyone at court insinuated that this operation was only a ruse to hide an accident which had happened to the Grand Duchess. The Empress, hearing the rumors, was becoming suspicious. However, the Grand Duke, now able to sleep with the Grand Duchess, resented these insinuations. He was persuaded by Saltykov to reassure the Empress on the matter. So, the morning after the marriage was consummated, the Grand Duke . . . provided proofs to the Empress. Thus the Grand Duchess and Saltykov were free to continue their arrangements for several years. . . .

11
Richardson: Love of Fame[1]

William Richardson was a Scot who accompanied the British Ambassador to Russia as a secretary in the years 1768 to 1772. Upon his return, he published his Anecdotes of the Russian Empire *from which the following description of Catherine the Great is taken.*

1. FAIRER THAN HER DAUGHTERS

August 19, 1768: The Empress of Russia is taller than the middle size, very comely, gracefully formed, but inclined to grow corpulent; and of a fair complexion, which, like every other female in this country, she endeavours to improve by the addition of rouge. She has a fine mouth and teeth; and blue eyes, expressive of scrutiny, something not so good as observation, and not so bad as suspicion. Her features are in general regular and pleasing. Indeed, with regard to her appearance altogether, it would be doing her an injustice to say it was masculine, yet it would not be doing her justice to say, it was entirely feminine. As Milton intended to say of Eve, that she was fairer than any of her daughters, so this great Sovereign is certainly fairer than any of her subjects, whom I have seen. . . . Her demeanour to all around her seemed very smiling and courteous.

2. AN IMPERIAL DAY

Nov. 7, 1768: Her Majesty . . . rises at five in the morning, and is engaged in business till near ten. She then breakfasts and goes to prayers: dines at two: withdraws to her own apartments soon after dinner: drinks tea at five: sees company, plays at cards, or attends public places, the play, opera, or masquerade, till supper: and goes to sleep at ten. By eleven every thing about the palace is as still as midnight. Whist is her favourite game at cards. She usually plays for five imperials

[1] "Extracts from Anecdotes of the Russian Empire," in Peter Putnam, ed., *Seven Britons in Imperial Russia 1698–1812* (Princeton: Princeton University Press, 1952), pp. 145–48. Copyright 1952 by Princeton University Press. Reprinted by permission of the publisher. Footnotes have been omitted.

(ten guineas) the rubber; and as she plays with great clearness and attention, she is often successful: she sometimes plays, too, at picquet and cribbage. . . . In the morning between prayers and dinner, she frequently takes an airing, according as the weather admits, in a coach or a sledge. On these occasions, she has sometimes no guards, and very few attendants; and does not chuse to be known or saluted as Empress. It is in this manner that she visits any great works that may be going on in the city, or in the neighbourhood. She is fond of having small parties of eight or ten persons with her at dinner. . . . When she retires to her palaces in the country, especially to Zarskocelo [Tsarskoe Selo] she lays aside all state, and lives with her ladies on the footing of as easy intimacy as possible. Any one of them who rises on her entering or going out of a room, is fined a ruble, and all forfeits of this sort are given to the poor. You will easily perceive, that by her regular and judicious distribution of time, she is able to transact a great deal of business; and that the affability of her manners renders her much beloved.

3. PHILANTHROPIST OR PEACOCK?

I will not yet say anything very positive concerning her character and principles of action. For, she may be very social, and very affable and "smile and smile and"—you know the rest.

I may, however, very safely affirm, that a great number of her actions, so great indeed as to constitute a distinguishing feature in her character, proceed either from the desire of doing good, or the love of fame. If from the last, it must also be acknowledged, that the praise she is so desirous of obtaining, is, in many instances, the praise of humanity. Sometimes, indeed, there is a sort of whim or affectation of singularity, in the manner of conferring her favours, that looks as if the desire of being spoken of, fully as much as the desire of doing good, is the fountain from which they flow.

January 1769: I assure you, my dear Sir, I do not find it an easy matter to obtain information. . . . No intelligence of a political nature, but such as the court chuses to communicate; no views of men and manners, and no anecdotes of incidents in domestic life, can be collected from the news-papers. How unlike England! that land enlightened by the radiance of Chroniclers, Advertisers, and Gazetteers. The half of Russia may be destroyed, and the other half know nothing about the matter. . . .

I have to contend, too, with another difficulty. I perceive that the same objects are seen in very different lights by different persons. . . . I was lately present at a distribution of prizes to the students educated in the Academy of Arts and Sciences. . . . There were . . . present many ladies and gentlemen of the Court. Count Betskoy began the ceremony by addressing a speech to the Grand Duke, in which he recommended the seminary to his protection. To this His Imperial Highness replied: "As the welfare of Russia shall ever be the object nearest my heart; and as the proper education of youth is of so much consequence in every well-ordered state, it claims, and shall ever obtain, my most constant attention." . . .

I was told that the Empress was present among the ladies. . . .

Tell me now, would not a stranger, on witnessing such a scene, on seeing one of the most powerful Sovereigns on earth and the presumptive heir of this mighty empire so attentive to the welfare and improvement of their people, would he not feel rapture, approve, and applaud? Yet, when I expressed those sentiments, there were persons who shake their heads. . . . This Academy has subsisted for many years, but what have they done? It may be mentioned, with ostentatious pomp, in a news-paper, or by Voltaire, and nothing else is intended.

4. EMANCIPATOR OR AUTOCRAT?

November 1768: I was lately present at a meeting of the deputies summoned by the Empress from all the nations of her empire, and who have been assembled to assist Her Majesty in forming a system of legislation. There is something magnificent in this idea: and if she really intends what she professes, to give equitable laws to all her subjects and dependents, from the Baltic to the wall of China, and from Lapland to the Caspian, she deserves admiration. . . .

The meeting consists of about six hundred members. They meet in the palace, where they have one large hall for the whole assembly; and several adjoining rooms for committees. They consist of representatives of the nobility, the peasantry, and the inhabitants of towns or cities. . . . The chief officers in this assembly are a Marischal, who presides; and a Procureur General for the Crown. . . .

In transacting business, the following method is observed. The Procureur lays before the deputies some principle or subject of law proposed by the Empress, and concerning which they are to give an opinion. They then adjourn; and the committee to whom that subject particularly belongs, prepare it for the next general meeting. Then all the members are permitted to deliver their opinions in a written speech, and to determine the point before them, by the plurality of votes. But whatever their determinations may be, it remains with the Empress to ratify them or not, as she pleases. Two of the subjects lately discussed in this assembly were, "Whether any but the nobility had a right to buy lands?" and, "Whether any but the nobility had a right to buy slaves?"

I have heard that freedom of extemporaneous speaking was allowed in some of the first meetings of this assembly; but that that being likely to occasion too much disorder, it was discontinued. At present, it is expected that no person, unless his views be very well known, shall deliver a speech without previously consulting the Marischal; and if he disapproves of it, the orator, though he had the powers of a Cicero, must keep his speech in his pocket. Indeed, this assembly has no pretensions whatever to freedom of debate, and scarcely any tendency towards establishing political liberty. The members, in general, are chosen by the will of the sovereign: by her the subjects of debate are proposed: she keeps in her own hands the right of ratifying every determination: and the assembly, convoked by her sole authority, may be dismissed at her pleasure.

12
Diderot: Portrait of the Empress[1]

Diderot, one of the best known of the philosophes *and the editor of the renowned* Encyclopedie, *maintained a long correspondence with Catherine II, and visited her in 1773–74. Below are, first a letter from Diderot to Catherine, from Paris, October 17, 1774; and second a series of comments on Catherine II made by Diderot and recorded by his friend Suard.*

DIDEROT TO CATHERINE

Dear Madame: From the bosom of my family I have the honor to write to Your Majesty. Father, mother, brothers, sisters, children, grandchildren, friends, and acquaintances throw themselves at your feet and thank you for all the kindnesses which you have extended to me at your court. As they have shared my happiness, it is just that they should also share my memories. I must tell Your Majesty, because I feel it in the depths of my heart, that I merit the praise that I am going to give myself; this is the advantage which sovereigns gain when they confer their interests on a good man: they spread joy in the hearts of a great number of others. The talents and the virtues of Your Majesty have become the conversational topics of our evenings. Everyone wishes to know everything. No circumstance appears too minor for the speaker or for his hearers. I am forced to tell the same story ten times over.

"Is she then noble of feature?"
"One could not be more noble."
"Do you say that she is full of grace and affability?"
"All those who have approached her will tell you the same as myself."
"And you did not tremble on entering the room with her?"
"Excuse me, but that could not last long; since she is not cognizant

[1] "Diderot to Catherine II, October 17, 1774," and "Propos de Diderot sur l'imperatrice de Russie," in Maurice Tourneux, *Diderot et Catherine II* (Paris: Calmann Lévy, 1899), pp. 495–98, 579–82. Translated by L. J. Oliva.

of her own rank or grandeur, she makes others forget it at the same time."

"Is she strong?"

"She herself tells me that there were moments of peril in her life in which she rediscovered her soul."

"Does she love the truth?"

"So much so that I would send to the executioner those who would not dare to tell it to her."

"Is she knowledgeable?"

"More knowledgeable in her empire, as vast as it is, than you are about your own domestic affairs."

"Is she well read?"

"She speaks our language at least as well as we do, and our great authors are her friends."

"And who has instructed her?"

"I asked her this question and here is her response: two great instructors have conducted her along her road, and both have lived with her during twenty years—unhappiness and solitude."

"Does she permit people to contradict her?"

"As much as they wish."

"Have you contradicted her?"

"Assuredly."

"But doesn't this insult her?"

"She would answer that there can be no insults between equals."

"That is charming. She must turn the head of all those who have the good fortune to meet her?"

"So she does."

"And does she grow angry?"

"Very much so, but this is a secret that she has confided to me; I have never perceived anything except profound judgment and singular penetration in her manner."

"She understood your thoughts immediately?"

"So promptly that in the first words of a discussion she had already foreseen the end of the discussion, however difficult it may have been."

"Is she good?"

"Too good, and this is perhaps her only fault."

"This is not very common in a despot?"

"Not very common, and I remember that I pleased her by swearing to her that I have found myself with the soul of a slave in a country that people call free, and the soul of a free man in a country which people call enslaved."

"Does she believe in God?"

"Yes."

"And does she pardon you for not believing in God?"

"Why not?"

"You arrived in Russia at a very stormy moment. There was an unhappy war and a revolt on the frontier."

"I swear to you that I never noticed that her tranquility was disturbed by these events. She was firmly resolved to make peace with her enemy, and she saw in the rebel only a sot who was awaiting his proper justice."

"Events have proven that she was right."
And then my friends ask questions on the climate and customs, on government, on laws, and the ministers, the priests, sciences, arts, your academy, the education and your schools.
"Does she love glory?"
"It is her passion."
"In that case she ought to be satisfied."

Signed: Diderot.

DIDEROT COMMENTS TO SUARD

M. Diderot returned from Holland, drunk with admiration for the Empress of Russia and expressing his drunkenness in a most amiable and most interesting manner. I have had a long conversation with him and he has spoken to me only of the Empress; he has recorded a multitude of her characteristics. I will try to recall the most curious of them, but they will lose the grace and skill on paper which the words of Diderot himself would convey.

"I left," he said, "for Petersburg with the certainty that I would be well received by the Empress; I was going to her with the recommendation of her good words, and there is no recommendation which is better. When I was presented to her I did not know a word that I said, because I was agitated and greatly troubled, but I felt that she enjoyed our visit because I could see she was very touched and troubled herself. After an hour of conversation she said to me: M. Diderot, you see this door by which you have entered; that door will be opened to you every day between three and five in the afternoon."

Since Diderot has never in his life known what time it was, Grimm insists that he would often arrive after four o'clock in the afternoon, and when the hour came to bring in the people who worked with the Empress, the Empress often had difficulty in getting him to leave.

And since he is very forceful in conversation, he would strike the knees of the Empress incessantly and with so much force that she was obliged to put a table between them. He often took her hands in his and kissed them tenderly, which did not displease the Empress. Princes ought to like these familiarities which come from a lack of manners and not from a lack of respect. If one asks Diderot how he found the Empress he will respond: "She has the soul of Brutus and the body of Cleopatra."

"I was completely astonished," he said to her one day, "to forget in speaking with Your Majesty that I was speaking with a very great sovereign." "Why do you not forget it?", she answered, "I never remember it myself."

"There is nothing so dangerous," said Diderot to her, "as a just, firm and enlightened despot; if he is replaced by another who has the same qualities, it is even a greater evil still, and all hope is lost for a nation if it has a third." "Do you know," answered the Empress, "that you are speaking to a despot?" "Yes, madame, to a just, firm and enlightened despot." Diderot could not prevent himself one day from showing astonishment at how knowledgeable the Empress was on so many subjects. "I have had," she answered him, "two excellent masters, unhappiness and solitude, and I have had them for twenty years." "I would use hell for only one class of men," said Diderot to her. "Which ones?", asked the Empress. "Those who lie to Princes." In this case, the Princess replied in a lively manner, "you are going to tell me the truth. What do they think of me in Paris?"

The question was embarrassing. He hesitated a moment and then said, "Madame, there are people who believe you innocent of the death of Peter III, but they think that it was very well done to depose an imbecile tyrant. Others do not believe you innocent . . ."

And he stopped there. "And those?", demanded the Empress.

"Those," answered Diderot, "think the same as the others."

I think, using the principles of Diderot, that he ought at least to escape from purgatory for that answer.

The Empress said to him: "I see in you sometimes the mind of a man of a hundred years of age, and sometimes that of a child of twelve years."

One day as they argued with a great deal of energy, she said to him, "You have a hot head and I also, we interrupt each other, we do not hear each other and we utter insults." "With this difference," answered Diderot, "that when I interrupt your Majesty I perform a great impertinence." "No," she replied, "between equals how can there be impertinences?"

"I will give," she said one day, "peace to the Turks as it pleases me, but as to Pugachev, he is a sot, and will be hung before three months pass." [2]

I do not know how much of Diderot there is in all these stories, but certainly everything is not, and even so, I prefer novels better than history. For the rest, he defends himself very seriously against having uttered the words which some have ascribed to him, "that the Russians have become rotten fruit before they have ripened," and he is right to defend himself; it would not suit him to say such a thing and I do not even believe he is disposed to think it.

[2] It took the Empress considerably more than three months to capture Pugachev, and, rather than being hung, he was beheaded, drawn, and quartered. [Editor.]

CATHERINE THE GREAT IN HISTORY

Catherine the Great has never attracted as much historical attention as Peter the Great, in the sense that historians have not credited Catherine II with the cataclysmic consequences for Russia and the world that are found in histories of her dynamic predecessor. There is irony in this, since Catherine has always been a more popular figure in history, and her name and reputation are common, while Peter the Great remains more obscure in the public mind. There is further irony in the fact that, though her image is well known across the world, her image is a caricature; Catherine's personality has not yet been penetrated by either popular history or professional biographers.

The following scholars and historians present a variety of perspectives on Catherine the Great, and, as is to be expected, they mirror more of their own times than those of the elusive Empress. The historian Karamzin, plagued by the vision of European revolts, traced the moral decline of Russia in her age, although he viewed the Empress herself in a rather favorable light. Herzen, the revolutionary, found her life magnificent evidence of the corruption of the system, while Klyuchevsky, the penetrating scholar, viewed her as representing the triumphant gentry. Pokrovsky, a Marxist, traced the economic themes that directed her reign, and the Soviets found in her examples of the deep-seated ills that pointed toward revolution. Professors Gershoy and Billington, with the perspective of modern scholarship, tie the Russian past and the European atmosphere into a convincing picture of Catherine's role in the intellectual life of her age.

The reader must, however, construct his own image and understanding of this complex woman. Perhaps, that is the pleasure involved in the examination of Catherine's life. The evidence abounds, but the judgments are not yet formulated. There is always immense pleasure and intellectual satisfaction in resolving a problem for oneself.

13
Karamzin: The Second Architect of the New Russia[1]

Nicholas M. Karamzin (1766–1826), Russian novelist and historian, was unhappy with the revolutionary ferment that rocked his own generation. He sent his Memoir *to Tsar Alexander I in 1811 in an attempt to clarify Russian history for the ruler and to curb his determination for reform.*

Another conspiracy, and the unfortunate Peter III lay in the grave, together with his pitiful vices. . . . Catherine II was the true inheritor of Petrine greatness, and the second architect of the new Russia. The main achievement of this unforgettable queen was to soften autocracy without emasculating it. She flattered the so-called *philosophes* of the eighteenth century, and admired the character of the ancient republicans, but she wished to command like a terrestrial goddess —and she did. Peter, having violated national customs, had to have recourse to cruel methods. Catherine could do without them, to the satisfaction of her gentle heart: for she required of Russians nothing contrary to their conscience or civil tradition, and endeavored only to exalt either the fatherland, given her by heaven, or her own fame— and this she tried to achieve by victories, laws, and enlightenment. Her proud, noble soul refused to be debased by timid suspicion, and so vanished the dread of the Secret Chancery. With it left us also the spirit of slavery, at any rate among the upper classes. We accustomed ourselves to pass judgment, to praise in the actions of the sovereign what was praiseworthy, and to criticize what was not. Catherine listened to our opinions, and there were times when she struggled within herself, but she always overcame the desire for revenge—a virtue of great excellence in a monarch! Catherine was confident of her greatness, and firm, unshakable in her declared purposes. Constituting the sole spirit of all the political movements in Russia, and holding firmly in her hands the reins of power, she eschewed executions and tortures,

[1] From *Karamzin's Memoir on Ancient and Modern Russia,* translation and analysis by Richard Pipes (Cambridge, Mass.: Harvard University Press, 1959), pp. 130–34. Copyright 1959 by the President and Fellows of Harvard College. Reprinted by permission of the publisher.

and imbued the hearts of ministers, generals, and all state officials with a most lively fear of arousing her displeasure, and with a burning zeal to win her favor. For all these reasons Catherine could scorn idle gossip; and when sincerity spoke words of truth, the queen thought—"I have authority to demand silence of this generation of Russians, but what will posterity say? And shall thoughts, confined by fear to the heart, be less offensive to me than the spoken word?" This manner of thought, demonstrated by the actions of a reign which lasted for thirty-four years, distinguished her reign from all those which had preceded it in modern Russian history. That is to say, Catherine cleansed autocracy of the stains of tyranny. This calmed men's hearts, and led to the development of secular pleasures, knowledge, and reason.

Having raised throughout her realm the moral value of man, Catherine re-examined all the inner parts of our body politic, and left none unimproved. She emended the statutes of the Senate, the gubernii, the courts, as well as those of the economy, army, and commerce. Special praise is due to the foreign policy of her reign. Under Catherine Russia occupied with honor and glory one of the foremost places in the state system of Europe. In war we vanquished our foes. Peter had astounded Europe with his victories—Catherine made Europe accustomed to them. Russians began to think that nothing in the world could overcome them—a delusion which brought glory to this great queen! Although a woman, she knew how to choose commanders as well as ministers and administrators. Rumiantsev and Suvorov were equals of the most illustrious generals in the world. Prince Viazemskii earned for himself the reputation of a worthy minister with his prudent political economy and the preservation of order and integrity. Shall we reproach Catherine for her excessive love of military glory? Her triumphs assured the external security of the realm. Let foreigners condemn the partition of Poland—we took what was ours. The queen followed the policy of noninterference in wars which were of no concern to Russia and of no use to herself, yet she succeeded in maintaining in the empire the martial spirit which victories had bred.

In his endeavor to please the gentry, the weak Peter III had granted them the freedom to choose whether or not to enter state service. The sagacious Catherine did not abrogate this law, but she was able to neutralize its politically harmful consequences. The queen wanted to supplant the love of Holy Rus', weakened by the reforms of Peter the Great, with civic ambition. To achieve this end she combined new attractions and benefits with service ranks, and devised symbols of distinction, the value of which she endeavored to maintain by bestowing them only on people of merit. The Cross of St. George could not produce valor, but it did bolster it. Many served in order to keep their seat and the right to speak at Assemblies of the Nobility; many, notwithstanding the spread of luxury, greatly preferred titles and ribbons to material gains. All these factors strengthened the necessary dependence of the gentry on the throne.

But we must admit that the most brilliant reign of Catherine was not without its dark side. Morals continued to deteriorate ever more in the palaces as well as in the cottages—in the former from the example set by the dissolute court, in the latter from the spread of taverns, which brought income to the treasury. Do the examples set by Anne and Elizabeth absolve Catherine? Do the riches of the state belong to a man whose only distinction is a handsome face? A hidden weakness is only a weakness; an overt one is a vice, because it seduces others. The violation of canons of morality diminishes the very dignity of the sovereign's office, for no matter how depraved they may be themselves, people cannot inwardly respect those who are depraved. And is it necessary to demonstrate that the people's sincerest respect for the monarch's virtue helps strengthen his authority? We must regretfully concede that while zealously praising Catherine for the excellencies of her soul, we unwillingly recall her foibles, and blush for mankind. We must also note that justice did not flourish at that time. When a lord knew that he was in the wrong in a law suit against a squire, he used to have the case transferred to the Cabinet, where it went to sleep, never to reawaken. The very political institutions devised by Catherine reveal more sparkle than substance; the choice fell not upon the best in content, but the prettiest in form. This holds true of the institution of the gubernii, which, though elegant in theory, were badly suited to the conditions of Russia. Solon was in the habit of saying: "My laws may not be perfect, but they are the best for the Athenians." Catherine sought in laws theoretical perfection, but she failed to consider how to make them function most smoothly and most usefully. She gave us courts without having trained judges; she gave us principles but without the means with which to put them into practice. Many of the harmful consequences of the Petrine system also emerged more clearly in the reign of this queen. Foreigners secured control over our education; the court forgot how to speak Russian; the gentry sunk into debt from the excessive emulation of European luxury; dishonest deals, inspired by a craving for fancy were more common; the sons of Russian boyars dispersed abroad to squander their money and time on the acquisition of a French or English appearance. We possessed academies, institutions of higher learning, popular schools, wise ministers, a delightful society, heroes, a superb army, an illustrious fleet, and a great queen—but we lacked decent upbringing, firm principles, and social morality. The favorite of a great lord, even though of low birth, was not ashamed to live in splendor; the lord himself was not ashamed of corruption. People traded in truth and ranks. Catherine—a great statesman at principal state assemblies—proved a woman in the minutiae of royal activity. She slumbered on a bed of roses, she was deceived or else deceived herself. She either did not see, or did not wish to see many abuses, perhaps considering them unavoidable, and she felt satisfied with the over-all successful, glorious progress of her reign. Yet when all is said and done, should we compare all the known epochs of Russian history, virtually all would agree that Catherine's epoch was the happiest for Russian citizens; virtually all would prefer to have lived then than at any other time.

The events which occurred after her death silenced those who had severely judged this great queen. For it is true that in her last years, years which were indeed the weakest in principle as well as in execution, we were particularly prone to censure her. Having grown accustomed to the good, we failed to appreciate its full value, and perceived all the stronger its contrary; the good seemed to us to follow naturally, as if inevitably from the order of things rather than from the personal wisdom of Catherine, whereas the bad we blamed on her.

14

Herzen: A Ship Floating on the Ocean[1]

Alexander Herzen (1812–70) was a Russian of aristo-cratic background and European education who exercised a strong influence on the rise of the radical movement in Russia. Through his newspaper, The Bell, *he commented on Russian affairs from his long exile in western Europe. Herzen edited and published the* Memoirs *of Catherine the Great to discredit the monarchy. The following is his introduction to those* Memoirs.

During the Crimean war, the archives were transferred to Moscow. In the month of March, 1855, the present Emperor had the manuscript brought to him to read. Since that period one or two copies have again circulated at Moscow and St. Petersburg. It is from one of these that we now publish the Memoirs. As to their authenticity, there is not the least room for doubt. Besides, it is only necessary to read two or three pages of the text to be quite satisfied on the point.

We have abstained from all corrections of the style, in every case in which it was not evident that the copy presented some fault of transcription.

Passing to the Memoirs themselves, what do we find?

The early years of Catherine II—of that woman-emperor, who occupied for more than a quarter of a century all contemporary minds, from Voltaire and Frederic II to the Khan of the Crimea and the Chiefs of the Kirghis—her young days described by herself! . . . What is there for the Editor to add to this?

In reading these pages, we behold her entering on the scene, we see her forming herself to that which she afterwards became. A frolicsome girl of fourteen, her head dressed "à la Möise," fair, playful, the betrothed of a little idiot, the Grand Duke, she has already caught the disease of the Winter Palace—the thirst of dominion. One day, while "perched" with the Grand Duke upon a window-sill, and joking with him, she saw Count Lestocq enter: "Pack up your things," he said, "you

[1] Alexander Herzen (ed.), *Memoirs of Catherine the Great* (New York: D. Appleton and Co., 1859), pp. v–xv.

are off for Germany." The young idiot seemed but little affected by the threatened separation. "It was pretty nearly a matter of indifference to me also," says the little German girl; "but the crown of Russia was not so," adds the Grand Duchess.

Here we have, in the bud, the Catherine of 1762!

To dream of the crown, however, was quite natural in the atmosphere of that court; natural not only for the betrothed of the Heir Presumptive, but for every one. The groom Biren, the singer Rasoumowsky, the Prince Dolgorouky, the plebeian Menchikoff, the oligarch Volynski—every one was anxious for a shred of the imperial mantle. The crown of Russia, after Peter I, was a res nullius.

Peter I, a terrorist and reformer, before all things, had no respect for legitimacy. His absolutism sought to reach even beyond the tomb. He gave himself the right of appointing his successor, and instead of appointing him, he contented himself with ordering the assassination of his own son.

After the death of Peter, the nobles assembled for deliberation. Menchikoff put a stop to all discussion, and proclaimed as Empress his old mistress, the widow of a brave Swedish dragoon, slain upon the field of battle, the widow of Peter also, to whom Menchikoff had resigned her "through devotion" to his master.

The reign of Catherine I was short. After her, the crown passed from head to head as chance directed: from the once Livonian tavern-keeper, to a street-boy (Peter II); from this street-boy, who died of small-pox, to the Duchess of Courland (Anne); from the Duchess of Courland to a Princess of Mecklenburg (wife of a Prince of Brunswick), who reigned in the name of an infant in the cradle (Ivan); from this boy, born too late to reign, the crown passed to the head of a woman born too soon—Elizabeth. She it is who represents legitimacy.

Tradition broken, the people and the state completely separated by the reforms of Peter I, coups d'état and palace revolutions were the order of the day: nothing was fixed. The inhabitants of St. Petersburg, when retiring at night, knew not under whose government they should awake in the morning; they consequently took but little interest in changes, which, after all, did not essentially concern any but a few German intriguers, become Russian ministers, a few great nobles grown gray in perjury and crime, and the regiment of Preobrajensky, which disposed of the crown like the Pretorians of old. For all others, every thing remained unchanged. And when I say others, I speak only of the nobles and officials; for as to the great silent people—that people prostrate, sad, stupefied, dumb—it was never thought of. The people was beyond the pale of the law, and passively accepted the terrible trial which God had sent it, caring little for the spectres which mounted with tottering steps the ascent to the throne, gliding like shadows, and disappearing in Siberia, or in the dungeons. The people was sure to be pillaged in any case. Its social condition therefore was beyond the reach of accident.

What a strange period! The imperial throne, as we have elsewhere said, was like the bed of Cleopatra. A crowd of oligarchs, of strangers, of panders, of minions, led forth nightly an unknown, a child, a German; placed the puppet on the throne, worshipped it, and, in its name, gave the knout to all who presumed to question the arrangement. Scarcely had the chosen one time to become intoxicated with the delights of an exorbitant and absurd power, and to condemn his enemies to slavery or torture, when the succeeding wave raised up another pretender, and the chosen of yesterday, with all his followers, was ingulphed in the abyss. The ministers and generals of one day, were the next on their way to Siberia, loaded with chains.

This bufera infernale carried away people with such rapidity, that there was not time to get accustomed to their faces. Marshal Munich, who had overturned Biren, rejoined him on a raft, stopped upon the Volga, himself a prisoner, with chains on his feet. It is in the struggle of these two Germans, who disputed the empire of Russia as if it had been a jug of beer, that we may retrace the true type of the coups d'état of the good old times.

The Empress Anne died, leaving the crown, as we have just said, to a child only a few months old, under the regency of her lover Biren. The Duke of Courland was all-powerful. Despising everything Russian, he wished to civilize us with the last. In the hope of strengthening himself, he destroyed, with a cold-blooded cruelty, hundreds of men, and drove into exile more than twenty thousand. Marshal Munich got tired of this; he was a German as well as Biren, and besides a good soldier. One day, the Princess of Brunswick, the mother of the little Emperor, complained to him of the arrogance of Biren. "Have you spoken on this subject to any one else?" asked the Marshal. "I have not." "Very well, then; keep silent, and leave every thing to me." This was on the 7th of September, 1740.

On the 8th, Munich dined with Biren. After dinner he left his family with the Regent, and retired for a moment. Going quietly to the residence of the Princess of Brunswick, he told her to be prepared for the night, and then returned. Supper came on. Munich gave anecdotes of his campaigns, and of the battles he had gained. "Have you made any nocturnal expeditions?" asked the Count de Loewenhaupt. "I have made expeditions at all hours," replies the Marshal, with some annoyance. The Regent, who was indisposed, and was lying on a sofa, sat up at these words, and became thoughtful.

They parted friends.

Having reached home, Munich ordered his aide-de-camp, Manstein, to be ready by two o'clock. At that hour they entered a carriage, and drove straight to the Winter Palace. There he had the Princess awakened. "What is the matter?" said the good German, Anthony Ulrich, of Braunschweig-Wolfenbüttel, to his wife. "I am not well," replied the Princess.—And Anthony Ulrich turned over and slept like a top.

While he slept, the Princess dressed herself, and the old warrior conferred with the most turbulent of the soldiers in the Preobrajensky regiment. He represented to them the humiliating position of the Princess, spoke of her future gratitude, and as he spoke, bade them load their muskets.

Then leaving the Princess under the guard of some forty grenadiers, he proceeded with eighty others to arrest the chief of the State, the terrible Duke of Courland.

They traversed without impediment the streets of St. Petersburg; reached the palace of the Regent; entered it; and Munich sent Manstein to arrest the Duke in his bed-chamber, living or dead. The officers on duty, the sentinels, and the servants looked on. "Had there been a single officer or soldier faithful," says Manstein, in his memoirs, "we were lost." But there was not one. Biren, perceiving the soldiers, endeavoured to escape by creeping under the bed. Manstein had him forced out: Biren defended himself. He received some blows from the butt-ends of their muskets, and was then conveyed to the guard-house.

The coup d'état was accomplished. But something stranger still was soon to follow.

Biren was detested; that might explain his fall. The new Regent, on the contrary—a good and gentle creature, who gave umbrage to no one, while she gave much love to the Ambassador Linar—was even liked a little from hatred to Biren. A year passed. All was tranquil. But the court of France was dissatisfied with an Austro-Russian alliance which the Regent had just concluded with Maria Theresa. How was this alliance to be prevented? Nothing easier. It was only to make a coup d'état, and expel the Regent. In this case, we have not even a marshal reverenced by the soldiers, not even a statesman. An intriguing ambassador, La Chétardie, are sufficient to carry to the throne, Elizabeth, daughter of Peter I.

Elizabeth, absorbed in pleasures and petty intrigues, little thought of overturning the government. She was led to believe that the Regent intended to shut her up in a convent. She, Elizabeth, who spent her time in the barracks of the guards, and in licentious excesses . . . better make herself Empress! So also thought La Chétardie; and he did more than think; he gave French gold to hire a handful of soldiers.

On the 25th of November, 1741, the Grand Duchess, dressed in a magnificent robe, and with a brilliant cuirass on her breast, presented herself at the guard-house of the Preobrajensky regiment. She exposed to the soldiers her unhappy condition. They, reeking with wine, cried out, "Command, mother, command, and we will slaughter them all!" The charitable Grand Duchess recoils with horror, and only orders the

arrest of the Regent, her husband, and their son—the baby-Emperor.
Once again is the old scene repeated.

Anthony Ulrich, of Braunschweig, is awakened from the most profound slumber; but this time he cannot relapse into it again, for two
soldiers wrap him up in a sheet and carry him to a dungeon, which he
will leave only to go and die in exile.

Again is the coup d'état accomplished.

The new reign seems to go on wheels. And once more nothing is
wanting to this strange crown . . but an heir. The Empress who
will have nothing to do with the little Ivan, seeks one in the episcopal
palace of the Prince-Bishop of Lubeck. It is the nephew of the Bishop
whom she selects, a grandson of Peter I, an orphan without father or
mother, and the intended husband of the little Sophia Augusta
Frederica, Princess of Anhalt-Zerbst-Bernburg, who resigned all these
sonorous and illustrious titles to be called simply . . Catherine II.

And now, after all that has been said, let the reader picture to himself what must have been the nature of the medium into which destiny
had cast this young girl, gifted, as she was, not only with great talent,
but also with a character pliant, though full of pride and passion.

Her position at St. Petersburg was horrible. On one side was her
mother, a peevish, scolding, greedy, niggardly, pedantic German, box-
ing her ears, and taking away her new dresses to appropriate them to
her own use; on the other, the Empress Elizabeth, a coarse and grum-
bling virago, never quite sober, jealous, envious, causing every step of
the young Princess to be watched, every word reported, taking offence
at everything, and all this after having given her a husband the most
ridiculous Benedict of the age.

A prisoner in the palace, she could do nothing without permission.
If she wept for the death of her father, the Empress sent her word that
she had grieved enough—"That her father was not a king, that she
should mourn him longer than a week." If she evinced a friendship
for any of her maids of honour, she might be sure the lady would be
dismissed. If she became attached to a faithful servant, still more certain was it that that servant would be turned away.

Her relations with the Grand Duke were monstrous, degrading. He
made her the confidante of his amorous intrigues. Drunk from the age
of ten, he came one night, in liquor, to entertain his wife with a description of the graces and charms of the daughter of Biren; and as
Catherine pretended to be asleep, he gave her a punch with his fist to
awaken her. This booby kept a kennel of dogs, which infested the air,
at the side of his wife's bed-chamber, and hung rats in his own, to
punish them according to the rules of martial law.

Nor is this all. After having wounded and outraged nearly every
feeling of this young creature's nature, they began to deprave her sys-
tematically. The Empress regards as a breach of order her having no

children. Madame Tchoglokoff speaks to her on the subject, insinu-ating that, for the good of the state, she ought to sacrifice her scruples, and concludes by proposing to her a choice between Soltikoff and Narichkine. The young lady affects simplicity and takes both—nay, Poniatowsky into the bargain; and thus was commenced a career of licentiousness in which she never halted during the space of forty years.

What renders the present publication of serious consequence to the imperial house of Russia is, that it proves not only that this house does not belong to the family of Romanoff, but that it does not even belong to that of Holstein Gottorp. The avowal of Catherine on this point is very explicit—the father of the Emperor Paul is Sergius Soltikoff.

The Imperial Dictatorship of Russia endeavours in vain to represent itself as traditional and secular.

One word more before I close.

In perusing these Memoirs, the reader is astonished to find one thing constantly lost sight of, even to the extent of not appearing anywhere —it is Russia and the People. And here is the characteristic trait of the epoch.

The Winter Palace, with its military and administrative machinery, was a world of its own. Like a ship floating on the surface of the ocean, it had no real connection with the inhabitants of the deep, beyond that of eating them. It was the State for the State. Organized on the German model, it imposed itself on the nation as a conqueror. In that monstrous barrack, in that enormous chancery, there reigned the cold rigidity of a camp. One set gave or transmitted orders, the rest obeyed in silence. There was but a single spot, within that dreary pile, in which human passions reappeared, agitated and stormy, and that spot was the domestic hearth; not that of the nation—but of the state. Behind that triple line of sentinels, in those heavily ornamented sa-loons, there fermented a feverish life, with its intrigues and its conflicts, its dramas, and its tragedies. It was there that the destinies of Russia were woven, in the gloom of the alcove, in the midst of orgies, beyond the reach of informers and of the police.

What interest, then, could the young German Princess take in that magnum ignotum, that people unexpressed, poor, semi-barbarous, which concealed itself in its villages, behind the snow, behind bad roads, and only appeared in the streets of St. Petersburg like a foreign outcast, with its persecuted beard and prohibited dress—tolerated only through contempt.

It was only long afterwards that Catherine heard the Russian people seriously spoken of, when the Cossack Pougatcheff, at the head of an army of insurgent peasants, menaced Moscow.

When Pougatcheff was vanquished, the Winter Palace again forgot the people. And there is no telling when it would have been once more remembered, had it not itself put its masters in mind of its existence, by rising in mass in 1812, rejecting, on the one hand, the release from serfdom offered to it at the point of foreign bayonets, and, on the other, marching to death to save a country which gave it nothing but slavery, degradation, misery—and the oblivion of the Winter Palace.

This was the second memento of the Russian people. Let us hope that at the third it will be remembered a little longer.

15

Kliuchevsky: Catherine's Man of Letters[1]

V. O. Kliuchevsky (1841–1911) was one of Russia's most distinguished historians. His Course in Russian History, *taught while he was a professor at the University of Moscow, was later published and had enormous influence. Kliuchevsky's character sketch of Catherine emphasizes the contradictions, in the reign, between her achievement of territorial unity and the subjection of the peasants to serfdom, and between her drive to progress and her willingness to place the responsibility for such progress in gentry hands.*

Catherine ascended the throne at a moment not merely rare, but unique, in our history. The moment had for its direct origin the reforms of Peter I, owing to the manner in which, during the seventeenth century, he decided the essentially economic question of reorganisation of the people's labour, and the therewith inseparably connected State economy. The question of reorganisation of the people's labour lay in raising that labour's capacity to the level of the economic needs of the State, but Peter so decided the question as to evoke a wholly different question, and to leave it undecided. The second question related to the State's rights. Continuously throughout his reforming activity rights remained his weak point—in this regard he only completed the edifice of State which ancient Moscow had founded upon class *tiaglo*. Of the significance of this latter term we shall be reminded by recalling what I have said earlier as to the significance of Peter's work in general: we shall then remember the term *tiaglo*, in this connection, to have connoted a system whereby given obligations of State were apportioned to the several State classes, in order that the State might meet its need both for agents of administration and for resources of finance.

. . . I have alluded to the moment as one not merely rare, but unique, in our history, for the reason that it was then that, for the first

[1] From V. O. Kliuchevsky, *A History of Russia* (London: J. M. Dent & Sons Ltd., 1931), pp. 110, 112–13, 115–19. Reprinted by permission of the publisher.

time, Russia's State life left its accustomed rut, and that, for the first
time, Russia's order of State shifted from its agelong basis. The basis
of the old order had been compulsory, semi-bonded labour of all classes
for the State's benefit. Now one class in particular, on gaining release
from State obligations, took to living for its own benefit alone, and to
acting on behalf of certain corporate, or personal, interests which formerly had constituted part of the country's interests at large. Whence
it is not difficult to imagine the problems arising, and calling for decision, as the community continued upon its historical way. The old
State order might have been harsh, but at least it had been equitable.
Hence one of the community's problems now was to remove that harshness, and yet to retain that equity. That is to say, release of one class in
particular from obligations of State called for release of the other
classes as well, save that the other classes' relief needed to be carried
out on lines differing from those on which the *dvorianstvo* had won to
freedom. As a matter of fact, the *dvorianstvo* not only went on to legislative extension of its freedom until the Law of 18 February, 1762, set
upon it the crown, but previously prepared the way with revolution,
with less than legal action (for assuredly the class would never have
gained such swift and easy emancipation without the *révolutions de
palais* in which it had actively participated), whilst similarly, though
another class too, the bonded *krestiané,* thought to acquire freedom
through a revolutionary method (undoubtedly that was the idea underlying the peasant risings of Catherine's early days, the peasant risings which culminated in the Pugachev affair), that class's emancipation
called, in the interests of the public good, and of public orderliness, to
be accomplished through purely legal, rather than through violent,
means, to the end that, all round, the existing system of chance and
freewill should be succeeded by a system purely legal and just. Herein
lay the problem of State equity involved in the second question to
which Peter's reforms gave rise. The question's proper solution lay in
legal, equitable definition of the relations existing between the *dvorianstvo* and the bonded *krestianstvo.*

Nevertheless, what, as a matter of fact, was the trend communicated
to Russian life by Catherine's legislation? The task confronting her was
to rid the State's structure of the layer of oppression with which it
stood coated, and yet to preserve the structure's equitable bases. Well,
her Accessional Manifesto did, without doubt, adumbrate vaguely such
a policy—it did promise that Russia's State order should come to be
based upon legality: but, for the very reason that she had ascended
the throne through revolutionary means, through a sheer seizure of
authority, her interests stood permanently bound up with those of the
class in particular already mentioned. The effect of her thus having to
show partiality to the politically active, and the politically experienced,

social section in question was to pervert that social section, and to make it lose its political traditions.

Through possession of unpaid labour the *dvorianstvo* never became the motive lever of the nation's industry. And through the position guaranteed to the class by the Government there stood destroyed any need for the class to gain, through useful agrarian authority, the submission and the respect of the local populations. All this opened up to the class an abundant leisure which, in turn, caused independence of thought to decline in the class, even as the absence of equal legality for all caused social relations to become warped in favour of the strongest social section alone, and the one-sided tendency in question to disintegrate social interests by setting some in opposition to others, and rendering amicable class activity in common impossible. Next, that activity's absence gave rise to *dvorianin* frivolity, and to a weakening of *dvorianin* morals: and, with the class become thus, the *dvorianstvo* took to attempting to fill the intellectual void with alien, ready-made ideas; whilst at the same time the class's ability to live upon others' toil destroyed in the class the habit of mental exercise. Such is history's logic in all such cases: and in the fact there stands explained the formula to which I resorted for characterisation of Catherine's reign when beginning the study of her times, when I remarked that the two essential features of those times were an irregular, one-sided development of certain native factors, and an uncalled-for propagation of certain alien ideas to which those native factors stood opposed. The net result of such a trend in Catherine's policy was to evolve two special contradictions, as that policy's eventual consequences. The one contradiction was that at the very moment when Catherine's Empire gained external political unity, and when the south-western branch of the Russian nation attained release from a foreign yoke, the bulk of the root stock of that nation underwent subjection to internal servitude. And the second contradiction lay in the fact that Catherine's policy entrusted further guidance of the Russian community along the road of development to the very class which stood least willing for, and least capable of, the task: that is to say, her policy entrusted it to the cultured *dvorianstvo*.

The more clearly to understand that *dvorianstvo's* then available stock of political means and moral forces, we had better recall once more the chief stages of the *dvorianstvo's* evolution during the eighteenth century. During that century the class's moral and political progress proceeded closely in relation to the class's record as regards service of State. Under Peter there was demanded for such service a military-artisan course of training which, in many cases, never was put to any practical use. And under Peter's successors service of State called, rather, for a course in polite manners, since that, if not absolutely necessary for service, was at least an aid towards service advancement. The inward connection between the study of navigation to which Peter's Guardsman was set and the study of the elegancies which Elizabeth's *petit-maître* traversed is seen in the two studies' equal futility. In Catherine's time neither the one study nor the other was called for, since then service too ceased to be called for. Yet still the class retained, if not a realisation of the necessity of education, at least a measure of educational accustomedness, or a measure of recollection of education as an indispensable acquisition. And, possessed of this recollection, the class proceeded to assume the position which jointly the Law of 1762, Catherine's *gubernia* institutions, and serf proprietorship had created for it. Yet even participation in local administration failed to stir the *dvorianstvo* to acquire serious administrative training: whilst, with that, the ownership of serfs stripped the class of all incentive to accumulate stocks of politico-economic and agricultural knowledge. And, seeing that, also, this position conferred upon many of the class a leisure time needing somehow to be filled, the *dvorianstvo's* sense of pride, nourished by compulsory service; its habituation to service during the years of youthfulness only, and to retirement as soon as the years of maturity approached; and its ideas and habits, come of a short-lived service career, all helped to change the class's interests and tastes, and so to complicate *dvorianin* education that to the demand for *galanterie de salon* Catherine's times added a demand for literary polish, and therefore an addiction to the pursuit of reading. That reading was not, at first, accompanied with any idea of making practical use of what was read; but later the pursuit became more serious, and directed itself at least towards refreshing intellects jaded with ennui, and towards stimulating thought become drowsy with desire, through new and daring ideas.

So the sequence of things was that Peter's artillerist-navigator became Elizabeth's *petit-maître*, and Elizabeth's *petit-maître* gave birth to Catherine's man of letters, and Catherine's man of letters became, towards the close of the century, the philosopher-Freemason-Voltairian. The latter type especially represented the social section which came to be entrusted with the Russian people's further guidance along the road of progress. Let us, therefore, note the principal features of the type. Before the philosopher-Freemason-Voltairian attained his social position, a position based upon injustice, and rounded off with lack of serious occupation, he passed from the hands, probably, of a village deacon into those of the French *gouverneur*, and then, having finished his education in the theatres of Italy and the restaurants of France, applied his acquired knowledge in St. Petersburgan drawing-rooms, and at last, with some book of Voltaire's in hand, ended his days in his Muscovite, or his manorial, study. Truly he presented a strange phenomenon, seeing that his every manner, his every habit, his every taste, his every sympathy, his every faculty, even to his speech, was a thing alien, imported. At home, devoid of any living, organic ties with his surroundings, he saw himself left with absolutely nothing to do in the world. And though, as he was a stranger amongst his own, he strove to become his own amongst strangers, European society always looked upon him as an immigrant, as a Tartar in disguise, even as his people in Russia looked upon him as a Frenchman born upon Russian territory. So much of the tragical was there in this position of a nondescript, of an historical superfluity, that possibly we might have sympathised with the occupant of the position if the position had in any way mortified the occupant himself; but the Catherinian freethinker knew not, as yet, low spirits: it was only in the time of Alexander I that he began to experience depression, and in the time of Nicolas I that he flagged, and in that of Alexander II that, worn out with excitement over the Emancipation, he finally succumbed. No, in Catherine's day he only just—idled. But he idled, at that, quite briskly and cheerfully, for still he was celebrating his release from departmental or military service, for all that his hatred of the special *dvorianin* uniform then conferred upon him could have been equalled only by the hatred of a youngster just set free of duty in a cadet corps. Nor had any of the more serious cares of life yet arisen to confront him. Nor had he yet come really to examine his circumstances. Rather, he was still living intoxicated with his and liberty's honeymoon. True, the very ideas which he held so strongly, and the very books which he read with such enthusiasm, might have been expected to make him feel at odds with his surroundings, and a contradiction in himself; but no—the Catherinian freethinker still was in no way inclined to find fault, in no way disposed to recognise the contradiction involved, since all his head was full to the brim of ideas and literary works which seemed to brighten his brain, and to titillate pleasantly his nerves. Indeed, never at any other period has fine diction so easily moved the cultured Russian to tears. Yet those tears and ecstasies represented only a pathological impulse, only a nervous spasm. Never did they find reflection in an exercise of will; never did they translate ideas into action; never did they make of words facts. Calmly the Catherinian freethinker would give his women serfs readings from a work on human rights, and then repair to his stable premises, and there pass judgment upon his peccant *krestiané*. For him theories and phrases served as sentiments. They exercised no effect upon the social order. All that they did was, without bettering morals and social relations, to mitigate perception. In this divorce between thought and act we see the fundamental characteristic of the educated Russian of Catherine's day. Yet let us not run away with the notion that that Russian's generation proved fruitless completely, or that his form of mental process represented as much an historical futility as did conferment upon him of a uniform at the very moment of his service's cessation. True, he, as a psychological curiosity, still awaits the hand of an artist; but yet he has a place in our history, for he served to show forth a special intellectual influence, and to act as a transitional point between one set of ideas and aspirations and another. Of course, the Catherinian freethinker's generation made no use of its ideas; but at least it conserved those ideas, and therewith educated the next generation, a generation which came to take a more serious view of its problems.

These, then, were the character and the results of the reign of Catherine II.

16
Pokrovsky: The Serfowners' State[1]

Michael N. Pokrovsky (1868–1932) was a Marxist historian before the Russian revolutions of 1917 and the foremost Soviet historian of the 1920s. He emphasized economic determinism, and his orthodox Marxist approach caused much resistance to his work from the rising nationalism of the new Stalinist era. The following analysis of Catherine's reign, stressing the economic control of the serfowners, is from his Brief History of Russia.

Elizabeth left the throne to her nephew, Peter of Holstein, who became after her death the Emperor Peter III. But he only retained the throne for a few months. He was an insignificant man, a drunkard, with the manners of a drill-sergeant. His wife Catherine, by birth a penniless German princess, was a very cunning and ambitious intriguer. She had been selected by Elizabeth who hoped she would turn out to be meek and obedient. She pretended to be demure and devoted; and at the same time she sold Russian military secrets to the enemy (during the Seven Years' War). She deceived her husband as well as the Empress, and gave him a son and heir for whose birth he bore no responsibility. The boy's father was followed by a succession of other "favourites." At the time of Elizabeth's death the post was occupied by Orlov, a clever and daring officer of the Guards, who had many contacts and enormous influence in the Guards. In the meantime, Peter III, in his quality of Duke of Holstein, had quarrelled with Denmark, and decided to take advantage of his position as Emperor of Russia to revenge himself on his Danish neighbour. But the Russian guards had no wish to shed their blood for the interests of Holstein. The Orlovs (there were several brothers, all of them in the Guards) took advantage of the opportunity. Before he had been able to understand what had happened, Peter, who was drunk as usual, was deposed and under

[1] From M. N. Pokrovsky, *A Brief History of Russia* (New York: International Publishers, 1933), vol. 1, pp. 120–24. Reprinted by permission of the publisher.

arrest. His wife became Empress under the name of Catherine II (the first Catherine was the widow of Peter I).

The deposed Tsar was immediately killed in his country-house at Ropsha. But there still remained another inconvenient candidate to the throne, the unfortunate Ivan, who had been deposed by Elizabeth and had grown up in the prison of Schlüsselburg. It was essential to get rid of him, for the example set by the Orlovs might easily find imitators. That the danger was quite real is seen from the fact that even fifteen years later a plain Cossack from the Don, by assuming the name of Peter III, was able to raise half Russia (see below on Pugachev). Mirovich, another officer of the Guards, attempted to become the Orlov of the pretender. But in the course of the attempt Ivan was killed and Mirovich seized and executed. Having stepped to the throne over several corpses—one of them her husband's—Catherine inaugurated a "brilliant" reign. She had more brains and more education than her predecessors. She corresponded with the great scientists and writers of Europe (Voltaire, Diderot), tried to acquire the reputation of a protector of enlightenment and managed to do so rather successfully. But for debauchery she almost beat Elizabeth's record. She used to have several favourites at a time, a head favourite and several assistants. When Potemkin was the head favourite he also selected the assistants. She died at the age of sixty-seven, and had at her side to the last the young officer, Zubov. Before her death she wanted to exclude from the succession her son Paul, whom she hated and who hated her, but she died suddenly before she had taken the step.

Catherine II died enjoying the greatest respect of the gentry and bourgeoisie, and these classes religiously preserved the memory of the "age of Catherine." Names of towns—Ekaterinoslav (now Dnepropetrovsk), Ekaterinodar (now Krasnodar), names of educational establishments (the Ekaterininsky Institute for young ladies), her statues in Leningrad and other towns—which for some unknown reason are still allowed to stand—helped to keep her memory green. How was it that this dissolute and criminal woman acquired such fame? Of course it was not by reading French books and talking with men of letters. The reputation of Tsars was not determined by their personal qualities, but by whether their policy was necessary and useful to the social forces that built up the capitalists' and serfowners' Empire. We have seen that by the conquest of the northern coast of the Black Sea, Catherine opened the way for Russian wheat into Western Europe and gave a great fillip to the prosperity of the landlords of the Black-earth belt. But this was not her only service to Russian merchant capital. By taking part in what is known as the *Partitions of Poland* she also brought within the frontiers of a single empire the whole of the plain of Eastern Europe from the Baltic to the Black Sea.

Years before, in the times of Ivan the Terrible, Poland had been the rival of Muscovy. She ruled over the whole of the Dnieper basin and was able to drive the Muscovite armies from the Baltic seaboard. The Cossack revolution of the seventeenth century was the first blow to her greatness; Muscovy acquired Kiev and established herself on the Dnieper. Peter took Riga, and the Eastern provinces of the kingdom of Poland and Lithuania were thus deprived of another outlet. Henceforward these eastern provinces (Lithuania, White Russia and that part of the Ukraine which had been retained by Poland) become *economically* dependent on Moscow and Petersburg, and no longer on Warsaw. We must keep in mind that this was the age of merchant capitalism when trade routes played a determining part in history.

The establishment of the *political* authority of the successors of Peter over these provinces was now a question of time. The western provinces of Poland were almost as dependent on Prussia as the eastern provinces were on Russia: you will remember that they could communicate with the sea only by way of the foreign ports of Danzig and Königsberg. The former was nominally Polish, but in reality it was a German town, a "free city" (i.e., an independent republic), and gravitated to Prussia rather than to Poland; Königsberg was an integral part of Prussia.

The Polish gentry realized their dependence on these neighbours. The crown of Poland was not hereditary—the king was elected by a "Diet" (Parliament) of the gentry. In order to find support against Prussia the Polish gentry elected the Electors (Princes) of Saxony, who next to the King of Prussia were the most powerful princes in Eastern Germany. After Saxony had been routed by the Prussians in the Seven Years' War, they turned to Russia and elected Stanislas Poniatowski, one of the favourites of Catherine II. But the personal intimacy of the new king with the Russian Empress proved an insufficient safeguard. When Prussia suggested to Catherine that they should divide Poland between them, she readily concurred: it would have been too absurd to miss such an opportunity for uniting all the eastern half of Europe in the hands of Russian commercial capital. The population of the eastern provinces of Poland was Russian; only the landlords and officials were Poles. At first the Russian administration allowed them to retain all their former positions. It only confiscated the estates of those who offered resistance to Russia; these estates were used to provide Catherine's favourites with dowries.

Altogether the partition met with little opposition as far as Russia was concerned; the country gave in almost without a fight. It was different in the west, where the bulk of the population was Polish. There the Prussians and the Russian contingents that had been sent to help them met with fierce resistance. This led to further wars and further partitions, until at last in 1795 (the first partition took place in 1772; so when we speak of Poland *before* the partitions we mean the area within the frontiers of 1772), the Kingdom of Poland ceased to exist as a separate State. In the course of these partitions the Russian army committed many atrocities; in particular the taking by storm of Praga (a suburb of Warsaw on the right bank of the Vistula) was marked by exceptional cruelty. From these times dates the hatred of the Poles for the Russians. But it was Prussia and Austria who gained most from the partitions; Danzig was incorporated in Prussia, and it was Prussia which got the capital, Warsaw, while Austria got Galicia. As for Russia, apart from the Ukrainian and White Russian provinces she only got Courland, which as we have seen she had been coveting for a long time.

If to all these achievements abroad we add that Catherine both extended and intensified the rule of serfdom at home; that she made the power of the serfowners practically unlimited by making it illegal for the authorities to consider the complaints brought by the serfs against their landlords; that she introduced serfdom in the Ukrainian provinces, where the dependence of the peasants on the landlords had hitherto been of a looser nature; and that she crushed the Pugachev rebellion (see below) which threatened the very foundations of serfowning society, we shall easily understand why the gentry and merchants liked her, in spite of all her sins. We shall also be able to understand the fate of her son. Paul could not stand his mother; he resented the love felt for her by the nobility and he detested the nobles and courtiers that surrounded her. His mind was unbalanced. He suffered from a persecution mania; he saw conspiracies and revolutions everywhere. As he had the misfortune to live at the time of the French Revolution, which had struck terror into all the monarchs of Europe, it was natural that those whom he detested should appear to him as conspirators and revolutionaries. He cashiered army officers by the thousand; banished to Siberia hundreds of "suspect" members of the gentry; restored corporal punishment for the gentry, whom Catherine had exempted from it; and even forbade the use of words which in his opinion savoured of revolution. One of the words he could not abide was "representatives," and he once turned out of his carriage a courtier who had the impudence to utter it. It was strictly forbidden to dress after the French fashion, because France was the country of the Revolution. Towards the end of his life he built himself a fortified castle, surrounded by a moat, and lived there as in a besieged fortress.

17

The Soviet View: New Capitalist Relations[1]

The following selections are from a Soviet textbook that attempts to interpret Russia's past for the new generation of Soviet young people. It emphasizes the transition from feudalism to capitalism and a "sharpening of the class struggle."

FEUDAL RUSSIA IN THE LATE EIGHTEENTH CENTURY

The leading European countries completed their transition from the feudal to the capitalist mode of production in the last few decades of the eighteenth century. This was to be seen best of all in England where the industrial revolution had produced the first capitalist factories. In France, Austria, Germany and a number of other countries the capitalist mode of production became dominant in the big manufactories, mostly in the textile trade. There were numerous signs of the onset of a crisis of the feudal system.

The French encyclopaedists, Voltaire and Rousseau, published biting criticisms of the feudal way of life and the Catholic Church. In the Germanic states the democratic wing of the *Sturm und Drang* (Storm and Stress) tendency attacked the lawlessness of the princes and the rule of the militarists.

These conditions helped popularise in France, Prussia, Austria and other European countries the idea of "a union of rulers and philosophers" propounded by the French enlighteners. The sixties, seventies and eighties of the eighteenth century constituted the age of "enlightened absolutism", a period of timid reforms that did not affect the real foundations of feudal absolutism, a period in which governments engaged in liberal flirtations with philosophers and men of letters. But the French bourgeois revolution put an end to this; monarchs immediately abandoned the idea of "enlightened absolutism" and became openly reactionary.

Such was the situation in Europe at the time the government of Catherine II (reg. 1762–96) was in power.

[1] From A. Smirnov, *A Short History of the U.S.S.R.* (Moscow, 1965), pp. 172–87.

In the country's economy commodity relations were gradually becoming capitalist relations and were, furthermore, beginning to supersede the old feudal relations.

Russia was still an agrarian country, but many peasants and even whole villages were no longer engaged in farming; they were occupied in various industrial pursuits and in trade, although they still remained members of the peasant social estate. Ivanovo, Pavlovo and several others were purely industrial villages, where big industrialists such as the Morozovs, Grachovs and Bugrimovs had emerged from among the wealthier peasants. Industrial occupations became more and more separated from agricultural pursuits. The continuing specialisation of agricultural districts promoted the development of commercial relations. The urban population was growing.

New regions entered the sphere of trade—the Middle and Lower Volga, the North Caucasus and the southern steppes. The southern regions of the country were handed out in large parcels to members of the nobility, and peasant serfs were forcibly settled on their estates. Peasants who had fled from the central gubernias, where they paid quit rent to the landowners, were also employed as wage-labourers on the big landed estates and on the estates of foreign colonists. Wage-labour was also employed on the landed estates in the central black-earth region, but to a lesser degree; in this area about 74 per cent of the serfs belonging to landowners performed corvée service. In the non-black-earth regions, however, the reverse proportion was to be observed—55 per cent of the serfs paid quit rent and only 45 per cent did corvée service. In the northern parts of the country the land was held by monasteries and not by private landowners. The huge stretches of Siberia were very scantily populated, the Russians in that area being almost exclusively state-owned peasants.

In the Russian gubernias corvée service for three days a week was the most widespread form, although four-day and even five-day corvée service was sometimes imposed on serfs, mostly in the south.

Quit rent in cash continued to rise, and to pay it peasants hired themselves out for seasonal work on the big landed estates, worked in the manufactories, or engaged in petty industries and in carting. A smaller number of peasants managed to establish their own enterprises. The situation was similar in the non-Russian gubernias, in the Ukraine, Byelorussia and the Baltic provinces.

The new capitalist relations were most clearly defined in industry. As petty commodity production declined, the big capitalist manufactories that grew up developed in a fierce struggle against the privileged manufactories employing serf labour. The capitalist mode of production was most widespread in the cotton industry which, in Russia, began to develop later than in other countries—in the seventies of the eighteenth century; by the nineties the cotton mills employed wage-labour to the extent of 92 per cent.

Capitalist linen mills developed in Moscow, Kostroma, Yaroslavl and a number of other gubernias, i.e., those gubernias in which peasant linen industries had existed for centuries. By the end of the century, 65 per cent of the employees were wage-labourers and the remainder serfs; the silk industry also employed a similar percentage of wage-labourers. Wage-labour also predominated in the metal goods industries of the central gubernias and the Middle Volga. In iron mining and smelting, however, serf labour was still dominant; the Ural Mountains area was the centre of this industry which, at the end of the century, smelted more iron than any other country in the world.

The overall development of industry in the second half of the eighteenth century was considerable; at the beginning of the nineteenth century (1804) there were 1,200 big manufactories in Russia as compared with 663 in 1767. Government policy was forced to recognise these big changes in production; although the policy of strengthening the feudal landed estates continued, the interests of the merchant and manufacturing classes had to be considered.

The feudal landed estates were given support mainly by the transfer of state and royal serfs to the landowners; under Catherine II about 850,000 serfs of both sexes were transferred to landowners. The ukase of May 3, 1783 completed the establishment of serfdom in the Ukraine. In 1764, the government abolished the landed estates of the monasteries to strengthen the land-owning class. Serfs who formerly belonged to the monasteries became a special group known as "economy peasants" and made part of the body of state-owned peasants, a category that approximated that of peasants belonging to the royal family; they constituted some 40 per cent of the peasantry of Russia and usually paid quit rent in cash.

The bonds of serfdom were not only extended but made more harsh as the power of the landowner to deal with the "souls" he owned was increased. The ukase of 1765 granted landowners the right to sentence their serfs to penal servitude. In 1767, serfs were forbidden to make complaints against their owners under penalty of severe punishment. The legal position of the serfs was similar to that of slaves.

Lastly, the government lent its support to the landed estates of the nobility by the granting of loans; in 1786, the new Loan Bank was established, which granted loans to landowners for twenty years at an annual interest of eight per cent; money-lenders in those days took 20 per cent or more for loans. The bank was founded on capital allocated from the state budget. In 1765, the government undertook a general land survey in the course of which the landed estates were rounded off by including within their bounds parts of peasant and state lands.

None of these measures, however, prevented a growth in the indebtedness of the nobility, especially those owning big estates. Government policy of supporting the nobility was inimical to the economic development of the country.

The government also gave some support to the merchant class, which was also the manufacturing class, by extending credits to them. The Manifesto of 1775 gave the right "to each and every person to set up machines and produce all kinds of goods on them". This was a step towards a declaration of the freedom of industrial and commercial activity.

No great changes were made in the state apparatus in the sixties. The nobility was firmly entrenched in all the leading posts in the civil apparatus and in the army. A commission to compile a new Ordinance was convened in 1767; although the elections to it were extended to include the free peasants as well as the nobility and the merchant classes, its purpose was not to extend the political rights of the free classes of the population. It was merely an "enlightened absolutism" manoeuvre by which Catherine II hoped to find out how popular her government was among the nobility and the nascent bourgeoisie. Catherine drew up instructions for the commission which, in their original form, contained some ideas drawn from the philosophy of the eighteenth-century enlighteners; Catherine did her best to demonstrate to her subjects that their Empress was a follower of the enlighteners; she even corresponded with Voltaire, Diderot and others. None of these ideas remained in the instructions in their final form.

The deputies to the commission also brought their mandates with them. The mandates given by the nobility and the merchants were marked by their class limitations. Those of the state peasants reflected the difficult position of that category of the population. The condition of the landowners' serfs, about half the total population of the country, found practically no place in the work of the commission. Using the outbreak of the Russo-Turkish War as an excuse, Catherine called off the commission, never to start it again.

Class interests also determined the foreign policy of the government. With the farms growing greater quantities of produce for the market, it became essential to obtain mastery over the mouth of the River Dnieper as an outlet to the sea through which farm produce could be exported. The annexation of the southern steppe lands was also necessary to make secure the southern frontier of Russia. A victorious war against Turkey, however, required sound relations with the Western Powers. Of these powers, France was conducting a policy obviously hostile to Russia; the French government tried to find support in an alliance with Austria who also saw danger in the advance of Russia towards the mouth of the Dnieper and towards the Slav peoples of the Balkan Peninsula who showed an obvious sympathy for Russia. Austria feared increased Russian influence in Poland even more. Count Panin, who determined the line of Russian diplomacy in the sixties, counterposed to French diplomacy the idea of a Northern Alliance, the nucleus of which was to be an alliance between Russia and Prussia. Panin hoped to be able to draw England, Denmark, Sweden and Poland into his Northern Alliance.

The attempt to organise the Alliance failed. England signed only a trade agreement (1766) and Sweden adopted a wait-and-see position. Panin did, however, succeed in concluding an eight-year treaty of alliance with Prussia (1764). In addition to this a treaty of alliance was concluded with Denmark. Such was the alignment of forces when Turkey, at the instigation of Austria and France, declared war on Russia in September 1768. The peoples of Daghestan, Kabarda, Georgia and the Balkan Peninsula, all under the heel of Turkey, placed their hopes for liberation on the war. The sympathy of these peoples was on the side of the Russian army, and they did whatever they could to help it. This sympathy, the talent of the Russian generals P. Rumyantsev and A. Suvorov and, more than anything else, the heroism of the Russian soldiers, ensured the success of Russian arms in the first year of the war. The successes of 1770 were still greater; at Larga and Kagula Russian troops routed a numerically superior Turkish army, established their positions in Walachia and Moldavia and captured a number of Danube forts. That same year the Russian fleet dealt the Turks crushing defeats in Chesmen Bay and the Strait of Chios. The Russian army occupied the Crimea.

Austria, alarmed by the successes of Russian arms, concluded a defensive alliance with Turkey (1771) and tried to attract Prussia to her side.

It was in this situation that the Russian government, to prevent the Austro-Prussian rapprochement, agreed to the proposal made by Frederick II of Prussia to a partial partition of Poland. The first partition of Poland gave Pomerania and part of Great Poland to Prussia, Galicia to Austria and part of the Ukrainian and Byelorussian lands to Russia. One important result of the partition of Poland was Austria's refusal to ratify the 1771 treaty with Turkey. Lacking Austria's support, Turkey was forced to sign an armistice with Russia, although the subsequent negotiations did not lead to the conclusion of a peace treaty. Russian diplomacy was not successful in getting Turkey to agree to cede the Crimea.

The situation again became serious. There was a growing danger of Sweden again attacking Russia. France threatened to send a strong fleet to the Russian seaboard, and English intrigues supported the French anti-Russia policy. In the autumn of 1773, the peasant war under the leadership of Yemelyan Pugachov broke out.

The government was now in a hurry to end the war with Turkey.

Rumyantsev crossed the Danube; Suvorov routed the Turkish army and Russian troops advanced into the Balkans. Turkey capitulated and a peace treaty was signed at Kutchuk-Kainarji in 1774, under which Russia received Kerch, Yenikale and Kinburn. The Khanate of Crimea was declared independent. The Russian merchant fleet was granted free passage through the straits. Kabarda was annexed to Russia.

The victories of the Russian army and navy concealed the shady side of foreign politics from contemporaries, but Catherine's home policy was sharply criticised. Prince M. Shcherbatov attacked the government for its neglect of the higher aristocracy. Y. Kozelsky criticised the situation in Russia from a different angle; in his *Philosophical Propositions* he condemned the arbitrary acts and indolence of the aristocrats, the laws that were inimical to the people and the ruin of the downtrodden working peasantry. Professor S. Desnitsky of Moscow University appealed for a curtailment of the lawlessness of the landowners and the autocrat by the institution of a representative assembly.

The autocratic feudal system of government was sharply criticised by the Russian enlighteners; Lenin's description of the nineteenth-century Russian enlighteners was equally true for those of the eighteenth century; they possessed three outstanding qualities, he said—hatred of serfdom, hearty defence of education and protection of the interests of the masses. One of the leading enlighteners was Nikolai Novikov; in the magazine *Truten* (The Drone—1769–70) he castigated the usury and trickery of titled officials and made sharp attacks on serfdom. The Empress had no intention of permitting criticism "aimed at individuals", and *Truten* was suppressed. In the spring of 1772, Novikov launched a new magazine *Zhivopisets* (The Painter) which not only exposed the barbarity of serfdom, but attacked the very system itself. In 1773, *The Painter* was also suppressed. Although Novikov's ideas were far from revolutionary, although he put his faith entirely in the all-conquering power of enlightenment, the government regarded those ideas as dangerous.

Increased feudal oppression in the second half of the eighteenth century led to a further sharpening of the class struggle, which reached its peak in the peasant war led by Pugachov. It began in the eastern parts of the Empire, where class contradictions were greatest; here, to the peasants' hatred of the landowners was added the discontent of the serf workers at the mines and iron works and of the local non-Russian peoples, the Tatars, Mordva, Chuvashes and, especially, the Bashkirs who had been robbed of their land. There was also growing unrest among the Cossack poor.

Yemelyan Pugachov, a Don Cossack, lived a hard and stormy life; several times he was arrested but escaped from prison and hid among the Old Believers. After his last escape from the prison in Kazan in

May 1773, Pugachov appeared in the vicinity of Yaik Fort, where he declared himself Emperor Peter III. He was joined by Cossacks and absconding serfs.

From the very outset Pugachov relied on the peasantry for support. All his manifestoes were filled with appeals to the peasants to fight against the "boyars" and the tsarist authorities.

On September 27, 1773, Pugachov seized the fortress of Tatishchevo which opened the way for him to Orenburg, the administrative centre of the region. He did not succeed in taking the town by storm, but cut off all its communications. Villages in the vicinity of Orenburg joined the revolt. Urals workers also joined the ranks of the insurrectionists, handed over to Pugachov the guns in the workshops and manufactured new weapons for his forces. The insurrection took on an organised form. Regiments were made up and Pugachov's most trusted followers were placed in command of them. At the beginning of October Pugachov established an Army Collegiate which took charge of the organisation and supplies of the army.

During November and December the insurrection affected all Orenburg Gubernia and spread to the Perm and Simbrisk gubernias. The non-Russian peoples of the Volgaside began to move; all Bashkiria seethed with revolt. Parties of horsemen were formed in the steppes of Kazakhstan which, against the will of the Khan, attacked frontier fortifications.

The merging of the national liberation movement and the Russian peasant movement constituted a serious danger to the autocratic government. Pugachov, however, was unable to overcome national discord completely; this was one of the weak features of the rebellion. Another weakness was the fragmentation of the insurrectionist forces. In addition to Orenburg there were centres of revolt around Ufa, Ekaterinburg, Kurgan, Krasnoufimsk, Samara and Stavropol (at Ufa the insurgents were led by Chika-Zarubin, a Cossack in whom Pugachov placed great trust); the revolt threatened to spread to Siberia. At the beginning of 1774, however, despite all these successes, the tide of war changed in favour of the government.

On March 22, government forces began their storm of Tatishchevo Fortress where the main body of Pugachov's troops was concentrated. After a battle lasting many hours, during which the flower of Pugachov's army was destroyed, the fortress fell. Almost at the same time (March 24), the insurgent army was defeated at Ufa.

Pugachov retreated to the mining district of the Ural Mountains where he began to form a new army. Bashkirian forces, led by Salavat Yulayev, also fought against government troops. On May 6, 1774, Pugachov captured the fortress of Magnitnaya: on May 19, he captured Troitsk but two days later was again defeated. Pugachov was driven out of the Urals by government troops, and turned westward to the Volgaside gubernias where he could count on the support of the peasantry and the non-Russian peoples who were brutally suppressed by the tsarist regime. He occupied Osa and Izhevsk and moved on Kazan. On June 12, the insurrectionists occupied the town of Kazan with the exception of the Kremlin or citadel, but in a battle with government forces approaching the town they were defeated. Pugachov crossed to the right bank of the Volga and turned south in an effort to reach the Don, where he expected to create a new base for the struggle among his fellow-countrymen, the Don Cossacks.

Never before had the peasant war threatened the nobility as it did in the summer of 1774. By August of that year, there were some 60 peasant guerrila companies active between Nizhny Novgorod and the Don. In July, Pugachov occupied Kurmysh, Alatyr and Saransk, and at the beginning of August, he seized Penza, Saratov and Kamyshin. The Pugachov movement had become a real people's war, and the only real opponent of the movement was the nobility.

Pugachov did not halt anywhere, but continued his advance to the south. However, government troops overtook him at Tsaritsyn and defeated his army.

He fled into the steppes where he was captured by a group of Cossack elders and handed over to the authorities. Pugachov and a number of his supporters were executed in Moscow on January 10, 1775.

The peasant disturbances continued for some time after the execution of Pugachov, but they were easily suppressed by government troops. Pugachov's rebellion failed for the same reasons as the previous peasant rebellions had failed—because the fragmentation of the forces and the absence of sound organisation and a clear-cut programme doomed it to failure. The rebellion, however, was not without its consequences.

Catherine II, in response to the popular rebellion, took immediate measures to give greater power to the autocratic government, especially to local authorities. In 1775, a new "Ordinance on the Government of the Gubernias of the Russian Empire" was published under which the Empire was divided into 50 gubernias and all civil institutions and all troops were placed under the authority of the governor general, the direct representative of the Empress. The new system of government was centralised and bureaucratic in character; the few elective posts it permitted did nothing to change the general nature of the gubernia reform, according to which the police and the bureaucracy dominated all life, since those elected were under the supervision of the local administration.

The government did away with the famous Zaporozhye Sech of the Cossacks (1775) in an effort to "Russify" the borderlands of the Empire. In 1780, the remnants of autonomy in Left-bank Ukraine were also abolished (the division of the territory by Cossack regiments and hundreds) and it was divided into three gubernias with the administrative apparatus common to all Russia. The Cossack elders were granted the same legal rights as the nobility. The reform of 1775 was also extended to include Byelorussia. The reform divided the Baltic area (1783) into two gubernias, Riga and Revel, the administration and the judiciary of which were appointed by the Russian government; former elective posts were abolished. Among the peoples of the north and northeast of Russia the local administration remained in the hands of the tribal aristocracy.

A charter (*zhalovannaya gramota*) granted to the nobility in 1785 legalised all the rights and privileges enjoyed by them at this time; they were, furthermore, permitted to set up uyezd and gubernia associations (assemblies) of the nobility, but these were under the supervision of the governors-general and governors.

Local self-government was introduced into the towns in that same year by the publication of a charter entitled "The Assembly of Urban Society", the right to elect and be elected to which was confined to persons possessing considerable property, although it included all sections of the urban population. All local government bodies were placed under the supervision of the local administration. This new measure, however, was evidence of the growing influence of the urban population in social life.

The charters granted to the nobility and the towns completed the edifice of the eighteenth-century absolute monarchy. This new structure seemed to be more soundly built than any previous monarchy, which enabled Russia to play a greater role in world affairs. In 1779, Russia became the guarantor of the constitution of the German Empire. On February 28, 1780, at the time of the American War of Independence, the Russian government published a "Declaration of Armed Neutrality", which sounded like direct support for the colonies in revolt.

The chief problem in the foreign policy of the eighties was still that of the Crimea. Turkey refused to accept the loss of the Crimea and made a number of attempts in the seventies to regain that province. In 1783, in response to this, Russian troops occupied the Crimea and legalised their position by a treaty with Khan Shagin-Girei.

The friction between Russia and Turkey over the Transcaucasus was no less serious. Georgia was split into three kingdoms—Kakhetia, Kart'hly and Imeretia—and was in the throes of feudal struggles between the princes; under these conditions Georgia was often the object of plunder by her neighbours, Turkey and Persia. In 1762, the eastern kingdoms, Kart'hly and Kakhetia were united into the Kingdom of Kart'hly-Kakhetia, formerly under Persian rule; after the death of Shah Nadir, Persia grew weaker and lost its influence in Georgia. At the same time Turkish pressure was increasing, and the Kingdom of Imeretia (Western Georgia) had to put up a stubborn struggle against Turkish aggression. The more progressive members of the feudal ruling class, headed by King Irakly II of Kart'hly-Kakhetia, realised that the Georgian people could liberate themselves from the yoke of the Persian and Turkish feudals only with the support of their powerful northern neighbour, Russia. Armenia, like Georgia, split into a number of small principalities, also looked towards Russia; in this period Armenia was still divided between Persia and Turkey, and thousands of Armenians fled to Russia to escape the oppression of the Persian and Turkish feudals. The urge to obtain Russian protection was spreading among growing sections of the Armenian and Georgian population. Embassies were frequently sent from Georgia to Russia, always for the purpose of seeking aid. At the same time cultural relations between Russia and Georgia were growing.

Armenian embassies also asked Russia to protect the Armenian people, although close political relations between Russia and Armenia were not established in the eighteenth century. Georgia acted differently; in 1783, the ambassadors of King Irakly II came to the fort of St. George (Northern Caucasus) and announced that Georgia was placing herself under the protection of Russia. Russian troops entered Georgia. The Turkish government refused to recognise the Russo-Georgian Treaty, and in August 1787, a strong Turkish fleet attacked Kinburn. Although the Turkish landing force was numerically superior to the garrison of the town under General Suvorov, the Turks were severely defeated.

Thus began the second Russo-Turkish War, which continued in a complicated international situation. The Triple Alliance of England, Prussia and Holland, formed for the purpose of weakening the Russian position in the Baltic, took final shape in August 1788. England and Prussia instigated the Swedish attack on the forts of Neuschlott and Friedrichsham in Finland, which marked the outbreak of another war with Sweden. The alliance formed between Russia and Austria did not live up to expectations, since Austria despatched an insignificant force to help the Russian army.

Despite all the difficulties the Russian army and navy made themselves famous. In July 1788, a Russian fleet under the command of Admiral Greig dispersed the Swedish squadron at Gogland, and Admiral Ushakov dealt a Turkish fleet a crushing defeat off the island of Fidonisi. On land General Suvorov's outstanding ability as a leader brought further successes to Russian arms. Suvorov was an opponent of the Prussian methods then in vogue; he placed greater confidence on the initiative of his officers and men, and taught them to gain victories "by ability and not by numbers". Suvorov's theory of war brought excellent results. Under his leadership Ochakov was taken by storm on December 6, 1788. In the following year Suvorov was victorious at

Focsani and Rimnic, and the Russian army advanced to the lower reaches of the Danube. That same year Russian forces launched an offensive in Finland.

The victories of 1789 brought about a considerable deterioration in the relations between Russia on the one hand, and England and Prussia, on the other. Under the pressure of these two countries Austria withdrew from the war in July 1790. The English government under William Pitt began making preparations for an attack on Russia but was soon forced to abandon the idea.

The operations of 1790 developed under the following international conditions. In June, a Swedish fleet was routed in Vyborg Bay; in August, despite the protests of England and Prussia, a treaty was concluded in the village of Verele (Finland) that envisaged a return to the *status quo ante bellum,* and Sweden withdrew from the war. This was an important achievement for Russian diplomacy. The Russian army and navy also gained further victories in the war against Turkey. In May and July Ushakov twice defeated the Turks at sea. After a series of minor successes Suvorov stormed and captured the strong fortress of Ismail. The Turks suffered further defeats on land and sea in 1791, but a peace treaty, demarcating the frontier between Russia and Turkey on the River Dniester, was signed in Jassy (Rumania) only in December of that year. Russia obtained Ochakov under the treaty, but was forced to give up Moldavia and Walachia. The question of Georgia was by-passed, and Russian troops were withdrawn from that country. In 1793, the Georgian kings again requested the Russian government to accept Georgia as a Russian protectorate. Russia, however, was unable to legalise Georgia as a subject country in the eighteenth century.

The brilliant achievements in foreign policy in the late eighties and early nineties and the consolidation of the absolute monarchy supported by the propertied classes served to conceal the growing internal contradictions. The government's debts abroad, furthermore, were increasing, and the treasury was empty; this placed a heavy burden on the taxpayers. The disturbances among the peasantry and the manufactory workers continued even after the suppression of the peasant uprisings—there were serious rebellions between 1783 and 1797 in Kazakhstan.

There was growing opposition to the system of serfdom among progressive intellectuals drawn from the nobility and, in part, among those drawn from the middle classes. In the eighties, Nikolai Novikov renewed his publishing activities, founding one magazine after another to defend the freedom of the press and expose the brutality of the landowners and the cupidity of the civil servants. Novikov's newspaper *Moskovskiye Vedomosti* (Moscow Recorder) and the *Prilozheniye* (Supplement) in magazine form in 1783 and 1784 expressed sympathy for the American colonies in their struggle for independence. Novikov also published translations; one translated article on free trade said that free labour must be regarded as the source of progress in industry, agriculture and commerce. These ideas appeared particularly dangerous to the government after the outbreak of the French revolution in 1789. In 1792, Novikov was arrested and confined to Schlüsselburg Fortress and was not released until after Catherine's death; he died in 1818.

From the very outset the Russian government adopted a hostile attitude towards the French revolution and gave generous support to French émigrés. Catherine subsidised the war preparations of Prussia and Austria, and in 1791, concluded an alliance with Sweden for the purpose of joint intervention in France. The allies were joined by England who subsequently became the leader and chief moving spirit of the struggle against the French revolution in the West.

Catherine II, enraged and frightened by the events in France, had to solve the old problem of relations with Poland under these new conditions. In 1788, a four-year Diet had been elected in Poland in which the landed proprietors and bourgeoisie formed a bloc known as the Patriotic Party; it was, however, dominated by the landed proprietors. The Patriotic Party made a big and irrevocable mistake in placing its reliance on Prussia; the latter incited the Diet against Russia, promised Poland support in the struggle for independence but behind the back of the Diet intrigued for a new partition of the country. The greatest mistake made by the party was that of ignoring the interests of the peasantry. The peasantry and the urban poor, especially the Ukrainians and Byelorussians, found themselves in an excessively difficult position. The feudal oppression of these nationalities had added to it national and religious oppression; the peasants responded by revolts.

After passing a series of minor reforms, on May 3, 1791, the Diet adopted the new Polish Constitution. Although the constitution benefited mainly the upper classes, it nevertheless marked a certain progress since it consolidated the supreme authority in the country, curtailed the privileges of the big landed proprietors and extended the rights of the townspeople. The Polish landed proprietors, jointly with the Russian imperial government, opposed the new Polish government. The Patriotic Party's hope for support from Prussia did not materialise. Motivated by the French revolution and the Polish government's liberation movement, Catherine consented to a new partition of Poland, which was effected in 1793; this new dismemberment of Poland was Russia's payment to Prussia for her participation in the anti-French coalition. The constitution was annulled and after the partition Russia obtained Byelorussia and Right-bank Ukraine and Prussia obtained Danzig, Torun and a considerable part of Great Poland.

The people responded to the second partition by an insurrection, the motive forces behind which were the urban poor, the artisans, petty bourgeoisie and intellectuals. The progressive section of the landed nobility also joined the movement. General Tadeusz Kosciuszko, who had taken part in the American War of Independence, took command of the insurrection. On May 7, he issued the Universal Charter which made some improvement in the condition of the peasantry but left them bound to the landed estates that remained in the hands of the nobility; the obligations of the peasants to their masters were retained. Even this limited improvement in the condition of the peasantry was resisted by the nobility. In 1794, the revolt was suppressed and Kosciuszko taken prisoner. The defeat of the revolt led to the third partition of Poland, and the Rzecz Pospolita ceased to exist. Russia obtained Courland, Lithuania, Western Byelorussia and the western part of Volhynia but none of the territory of Poland proper, which was divided between Austria and Prussia.

It had always been the traditional policy of the Russian government, inherited from the fifteenth-century Moscow Grand Dukes, to achieve the reunion of the old Russian, Ukrainian and Byelorussian lands; the policy did not aim at the destruction of Polish statehood. Consent to the partition of Poland was in direct contradiction to this traditional policy and was contrary to the national interests of Russia. The fact that Prussia was the initiator in partitioning Poland does not make the Russian autocracy any the less responsible; the Russian government's diplomatic intrigues at the time of the first partition, and its hatred of the revolutionary and national liberation movement at the time of the second and third partitions, led it to make concessions to Prussia and Austria, and as a consequence this anti-national policy promoted discord between the related Russian and Polish peoples.

The events of the French revolution, the sharp struggle of the peasantry and the national movement in Poland gave further impetus to Russian social thought.

The famous book *A Journey from St. Petersburg to Moscow* by Alexander Radishchev, published in 1790, was an impassioned appeal to struggle against the autocracy and serfdom. Radishchev's sympathies were on the side of the peasants and he developed the idea of the legitimacy of, and necessity for, a peasant revolution. Catherine's indignation knew no bounds. The criminal court sentenced Radishchev to death by quartering and the Senate confirmed the sentence but Catherine, loyal to her "enlightened monarchy" policy, had him banished to Ilim; Radishchev returned from exile only after Catherine's death in 1796.

Progressive social thought in Russia was accompanied by an emancipation trend in Ukrainian writing; one of the leading writers who gave expression to Ukrainian social thought was the philosopher and poet

Grigory Skovoroda (1722–94). Skovoroda was not a revolutionary, but he appealed ardently against the exploitation of the people and exposed the brutality of the authorities and social justice.

Criticism of serfdom also entered into poetry and fiction during the last decades of the eighteenth century. The greatest poet of the period was Gavrila Derzhavin. His odes contained many verses in praise of Catherine II, but also openly criticised the parasitism and harshness of the Russian aristocracy. Derzhavin was one of the founders of realism in Russian poetry, but classicism remained the dominant trend until the end of the century (A. Sumarokov, M. Lomonosov, V. Tredyakovsky). The germs of the new literary trends were, however, making their appearance in the form of sentimentalism, early romanticism and realism. There were marked realistic tendencies in the poetry of M. Kheraskov and V. Kapnist, to be seen chiefly in their bold exposure of the vices of the aristocracy and their protest against increased oppression of the serfs (*Ode to Slavery,* by Kapnist). This protest was also very strong in the works of Denis Fonvizin; his early comedy *Brigadier* (1766–69) and especially his *Hobbledehoy* (1792) were realistic pictures of life on the landed estates of the nobility at the end of the eighteenth century, although Fonvizin himself was far from realising the need for an active struggle against serfdom. The theme of a revolutionary struggle against serfdom in its radical form appeared in Radishchev's poetry (especially his *Ode to Freedom,* 1783) , as well as in his famous *Journey.* The oral folklore of the period was permeated with the appeal for an active struggle against feudal oppression. The aspirations of the people inspired Pugachov's manifestoes.

In the field of science the study of the country's economy, which had been the general trend in the first half of the century, continued. Between 1768 and 1774, five academic expeditions were equipped. The maritime expeditions that studied the northern parts of the Pacific and North-Eastern Siberia made a fine contribution to the geography of Russia. The Economic Society, a non-government body, was founded in 1765; the Transactions of the Society carried very many articles on the conduct of farming. In addition to the leading foreign scientists of the Imperial Academy of Sciences (Leonhard Euler, Peter Simon Pallas and others) the number of talented Russian scholars was considerably greater towards the end of the century than it had been earlier. Among the most outstanding were the naturalists I. Lepyokhin and N. Ozeretskovsky, the astronomer S. Rumovsky, the mineralogist V. Severgin and the mathematician S. Kotelnikov. Another famous name connected with the Academy was that of the Russian engineer I. Kulibin. Far from the Academy, in the distant Urals and the Altai, talented Russian inventors were working—I. Polzunov who designed a steam-engine (1764–65, years before the appearance of J. Watt's engine), and the hydraulic engineer K. Frolov.

Scholarship progressed simultaneously with the natural sciences and engineering. The growing national consciousness of the Russian people engendered a fresh interest in the past history of the country. N. Novikov published a number of important historical documents. The prominent historians M. Shcherbatov and I. Boltin, both members of the nobility, worked in this period. An important feature of Russian historiography was the appearance of the new aristocratic revolutionary trend founded by A. Radishchev.

Social thought, journalism and all literary genres, however, developed on a very narrow social basis, since the vast majority of the population were illiterate. The Commission on the Foundation of Schools, set up in 1782, planned a new school system which gave children from the underprivileged classes certain opportunities in the field of education. The results of the reform, however, were insignificant—in 1786, only 11,000 children attended school, of whom 858 were girls. The children of the nobility were taught at home; Fonvizin's *Hobbledehoy* is a biting criticism of that type of education. Some of the children of the nobility attended privileged private schools. In 1764, the Smolny Institute for the daughters of gentlefolk was founded in St. Petersburg, and similar institutions were opened in other towns.

In 1774, the Department of Mines opened the Mining School which was later expanded into the Mining Institute. Surgeons were trained at the Army and Navy hospitals. In 1757, the Academy of Arts was opened in St. Petersburg. These various institutions made a great contribution to the development of vocational education in Russia.

In the field of the arts, the most noticeable progress was in portrait painting. Courtly portraits were still being produced, but certain realistic qualities had begun to enter into their composition. A. Antropov's portrait of Peter III (1762) is the picture of an ugly, weak-minded tsar, brilliantly dressed and in gaudy court surroundings. I. Argunov's portraits show a thoughtful approach to the depiction of the inner world of the individuals painted. The leading portraitist of the period was F. Rokotov, although D. Levitsky and his pupil V. Borovikovsky were popular painters of their day.

Most of the artists were serfs, and with very few exceptions the portraits they painted were those of the nobility; it was in this period, however, that the first pictures of peasants appeared (I. Yermenov, M. Shibanov).

Some important sculptures were made in Russia in this period; among them are the equestrian statue of Peter the Great by the French sculptor Falconet and the statue of Polycrates by M. Kozlovsky, a chef d'oeuvre of world significance. F. Shubin's sculptured portraits—busts of M. Lomonosov, A. Golitsyn and Paul I—are noteworthy for their realistic tendency and their excellent technique; his sculpture for the tomb of Martos is the epitome of grief expressed in stone.

Architecture also displayed a certain rejection of convention and excessive ornament as the baroque forms were gradually replaced by the severe and simple forms of classicism; the greatest of the classicists of that period of Russian architecture was Vasily Bazhenov (1738–99), whose magnificent plans for the Kremlin Palace still amaze one today by the severity of the lines and the harmony of the treatment. The palace was never built although an excellent model of it has been preserved. Bazhenov met with misfortune in another of his undertakings, the huge palace in Tsaritsyno, near Moscow. The building was almost finished when it was suddenly pulled down by order of Catherine II. One famous building by Bazhenov that still stands today is Pashkov's House, now part of the complex of buildings housing the Lenin Library.

The Moscow architect, Matvei Kazakov, made a profound mark on Russian architecture; many of his buildings have become famous—the Senate in the Moscow Kremlin, Moscow University, the Golitsyn Hospital and the Hall of Columns in the Moscow Assembly Rooms (now Trade Union House). Kazakov's treatment was mainly in the horizontal and his buildings were designed to embrace large, open courtyards; they possess soft lines and an air of calmness that is typical of eighteenth-century Moscow architecture. In St. Petersburg the classical school was represented by I. Starov, builder of the Taurida Palace, an edifice that was given modest external treatment but amazingly luxurious halls and chambers and a wonderful winter garden. Foreign architects also played their part in the design of St. Petersburg's architectural ensembles. Giacomo Quarenghi designed the Academy of Sciences building, the Hermitage Theatre, the English Palace and others. Vallin-Delamoth designed the Old Hermitage, and the Little Winter Palace. A number of buildings in the St. Petersburg suburbs are connected with the name of Charles Cameron.

18

Gershoy: Absolutist to the Core[1]

Professor Leo Gershoy is a distinguished historian of eighteenth-century Europe and the author of the volume on this period in The Rise of Modern Europe *series. The following excerpt cuts through the romantic versions of Catherine's policies and emphasizes her dedication to absolutism.*

In many significant respects Catherine was a true tsarina of the landed aristocracy (*dvorianstvo*). As grand duchess she bathed in the atmosphere of the court; to the elite of the aristocracy in the Palace Guard she owed her throne; and as empress she selected all her leading helpers from that group. In the early years the influence of the Orlovs was predominant: Gregory, the favorite, was the grand master of artillery; Alexis was an admiral of the fleet; and Theodore at one time filled the highly important post of procurator-general. Later, it was another lover, Potemkin, the creator of "New Russia" and the organizer of the Crimea, who gained ascendancy, especially in foreign relations. The scions of the old nobility were entrenched in the diplomatic service: Repnin in Poland; Semen Vorontsov in London; Dmitri Galitsin in Paris. The commanding officers in the army and navy bore the old and distinguished names of Dolgorouki, Roumantsov, Galitsin, Chitchagov, Spiridov. Unconscious class prejudice naturally impelled the empress to favor their interests, while many considerations of policy and all those of personal security confirmed the arrangement. Her reign was therefore to see the completion of the orientation in favor of the nobility begun under Peter the Great's successors: their monopoly of key positions in the administration; the legalization of their status as unpaid governmental agents in the local administration; the extension of their serf rights and the juridic recognition of their privileged position as hereditary serf proprietors exempted from military obligations.

[1] From Leo Gershoy, *From Despotism to Revolution, 1763–1789* (New York, Harper & Row, Inc., 1944), pp. 109–17, 126. Copyright 1944 by Harper & Row, Publishers, Inc. Reprinted by permission of the publisher.

Yet she was more than the tsarina of the *dvorianstvo*. She was an absolutist to the core, a farsighted and capitalist-minded absolutist who worked for the greater glory of the Russian crown. As much as she dared she reverted from the outset to Peter's anti-noble policy and endeavored to make and keep the service nobility in a subordinate position as the civil arm of her authoritarian state. Like the great Peter she was a modern-minded dynast; and she succeeded better because she harnessed the power of large-scale individual enterprise to the chariot of the state. She was more effective too. Peter I had worked almost exclusively through violence and terror, but she divided the opposition and attached her adherents to her cause by the golden chains of self-interest. It was part of her deliberate policy to accelerate capitalist development by associating the rich bourgeois merchants with the great landed aristocrats in a movement that would liberate production and exchange from their old fetters. Grandees like the Orlovs, Viazemski, Potemkin, and Bezborodko, not only pressed for free capitalist enterprise but were the partners and associates in the business ventures of such notable bourgeois entrepreneurs as Schemiakin, Batashev, Vladimirov, Faleev, Jakovlev, and Lazarev. Both groups alike were the sponsors of the aggressive expansionist program which swept Russian arms, prestige, and authority into the Ukraine and the harbors of the Black Sea and ultimately brought their country into military conflict with the Porte.

The empress's tactics against the court groups during the first decade of her rule were primarily a struggle for political control. But they were also the initial phase of a broader effort to win for the crown the direction of Russia's social and economic policy. They reached an early climax in the proceedings of the highly publicized Legislative Commission of 1767–1768. According to conventional interpretations Catherine was at her most liberal in these years, retreating into conservatism after the defeat of her efforts in this assembly. Such interpretations strain reality. The political and so-called constitutional measures that she introduced immediately after her seizure of power bore the germs of the non-liberal and authoritarian administrative changes of 1775 and 1785, even as her social policy in those early years adumbrated what followed in subsequent days. The elaborate paraphernalia of hocus-pocus which deceived so many of the liberals in the west was a classical illustration of Catherine's talent for political maneuvering and her flair for favorable publicity. She was the first Russian ruler fully to appreciate the value of a good press abroad and at home. In Russia she paraded her liberalism in order to upset the plans of the feudal-minded aristocracy. Abroad her paid and unpaid propagandists among the *philosophes* bought her the plaudits of the European intelligentsia. Without being insincere in her admiration for such giants of the French enlightenment as Voltaire and Diderot, Grimm and Alembert, she also had a very nice sense of what they were worth to her. Voltaire, now the venerable Patriarch of Ferney, was a sort of commander in chief of the literary brigade which, for a few *"douceurs"* that the Russian treasury easily spared, wrote commendatory articles concerning her accession, placed inspired stories in the newspapers and periodicals about her devotion to their doctrines, and reinterpreted her Polish and Turkish policy to make good reading in western Europe.

According to her publicity agents, in whose ranks Catherine herself held a high position, her plan was to redraft in a single organic code the bewildering variety of imperial and local legislation which had remained uncodified since 1649. Unlike Justinian she was to accomplish this worthy deed through the medium of a deliberative assembly representative of all the social classes. She issued a *Nakaz* or *Instruction,* supposedly to guide the deputies, and advertised her indebtedness to Montesquieu and Beccaria for the draft of the broad general principles of the proposed code. Liberal Europe melted in admiration over this widely heralded endeavor to legislate parliamentarism into being by one stroke of the pen. But analysis of the various drafts of the *Nakaz* indicates very clearly that Catherine pillaged only what she wanted from Montesquieu. She took over almost nothing of his anti-absolutist political doctrine and little enough of his general social philosophy. Indeed, the very idea of a *Nakaz* was originally conceived as a move to defeat Nikita Panin's project of establishing a small Imperial Council composed of competent advisers from the ranks of the court aristocracy. The earliest draft of the *Nakaz* in 1763 was a counterthrust to Panin's project, which would have effectively limited her real political authority. When she submitted the original version to a small group of advisers, Panin was reported to have exclaimed in horror that it contained "axioms which would batter down walls." What shocked him was not its liberalism, as has been falsely assumed. He was aghast over its absolutism, which thwarted his own design and that of the grandees of keeping the empress in check.

Moreover, the *Nakaz* and the Legislative Commission were not originally joined in her thinking. The idea of convoking that assembly was not fully formulated until 1766, three years after the publication of the first draft of the *Nakaz*. Like the *Instruction,* which had served its purpose at least in part, the supplementary plan was a move in a cunningly conceived campaign. In the words of the French diplomatic agent the plan concealed more elaborative views. This princess realizes only too well her utter dependence upon the grandees. . . . The opinion obtains that in order to shake off the yoke the Empress has assembled the estates so that she may sound out public opinion. In the event that it is favorable to her, she will enact *constitutional* laws which will assure her position and that of her [and Orlov's] son. If not, if public opinion is ill-disposed, she will be satisfied with enacting *civil* legislation from which she will still derive the advantage of being able to subordinate the grandees and their subjects . . . without appearing to subject them.

Hence it mattered little to her that the Commission was poorly organized to fulfill its functions as a lawgiving body. Catherine had stated explicitly in the electoral decree that the deputies were only to provide her with specific information. She never intended and never allowed their suggestions to alter her predetermined ideas. Procurator-General Viazemski rigged the elections in accordance with her views and made the urban deputation, whose loyalty she could count on, the single largest bloc in the assembly. This group consisted of 207 deputies, while the gentry, whose opposition was even more certain than the good will of the town representatives, had only 160. The private serfs, who probably would have opposed her and in any case were uncertain, were not represented by their own delegates. The remaining deputies represented the administration and the other safe social groups.

The sessions were held from midsummer, 1767, to December, 1768, at first in Moscow and later in St. Petersburg. As most of the conscientious but inexperienced deputies were intent upon making themselves heard, the two hundred meetings of the assembly resolved themselves into lengthy and eloquent debates over trivia. The English envoy called them "a farce." When the deputies were not "blinded by outer appearances," they served their own interests "by strewing incense before the idol of the vanity of their Empress." When the outbreak of the war against the Ottoman Empire gave the empress the opportunity to suspend the hearings, the draft of a new law code had not been advanced even by a single paragraph. The task of the Commission was subsequently turned over to subcommittees, some of which held sessions up to 1775.

Catherine's benefits from this "ethnographical rally" cannot be evaluated in terms of its failure to draft a law code. The mandates of the deputies and the rhetorical debates provided her with invaluable information on the state of her realm. Above all, she obtained the sense of security that she wanted and needed. From abroad she received unparalleled acclaim. The measure of her success at home was the assembly's proffer of such appellations as "Great" and "Wise" and her final acceptance of an equally unpretentious title, "Mother of the Country." Her expectations had not been defeated. "By these and other measures," wrote the English envoy, "glittering enough to dazzle the eyes of the Russians, the power of Her Imperial Majesty increases every day, and is already arrived to such a degree that this prudent Princess thinks herself strong enough to humble the Guards, who placed her upon the throne."

The "prudent Princess" proceeded cautiously along the road she had chosen "to humble the Guards, who placed her upon the throne." It is always essential to remember that her admiration for the *"despotisme légal"* of Le Mercier was a much clearer gauge of her constitutional views than her supposed enthusiasm for Montesquieu. She effected no formal reorganization of the central administrative system, but she established her personal rule in the place of the old bureaucratic apparatus. Several of the collegiate boards were abolished, the title of chancellor was allowed to lapse, and the senate, revived in importance by Elizabeth, once again sank into insignificance. Of the officials whose counsel she relied upon, Prince Viazemski, procurator-general from 1764, was one of the most influential. On the other hand, she turned to a comprehensive reform of the provincial administration in the very year of the suppression of the Pugachev rebellion, aghast at the revelation of its disorder and inefficiency.

The basic ordinance concerning the provincial *gubernias* was issued in 1775, and it remained in force for almost a century. The recently issued *Commentaries* of Blackstone may have served Catherine in good stead, as she alleged, but it is more likely that the real model for the reorganization came from the example of her own Baltic provinces. The twenty huge and unwieldy *gubernia* units set up by Peter I and his successors were abolished and, under the supervision of the Balt nobleman, Count Sievers, fifty new *gubernias* were created, each with approximately 300,000 to 400,000 inhabitants. Each new unit, furthermore, was divided into districts (*uyezdi*) so as to give each smaller unit an approximate population of 20,000 to 30,000. In the *gubernia* the presiding official was the governor, a royal appointee endowed with broad discretionary authority. Three collegiate boards were set up to assist him, composed of officials nominated by the central administration: administration and police; finance; and justice. In addition there was an Office of Public Welfare, headed by the governor, to superintend sanitation and hygiene, education and poor relief. Similar boards, except the last, were created in the district administration. There, the personnel was elected locally, save for the presiding officer, who was also an appointee of the state. The reorganized judicial system provided for the separation of civil cases from criminal. Cases of the first instance were excluded from the new provisions, the needs of law and order being upheld in the towns by the district police tribunal under the headship of a local nobleman, the *ispravnik,* and on the manorial estate by the landowner or his bailiff. Each of the three social groups of the nobility, the urban inhabitants, and the crown peasants came under the jurisdiction of its own hierarchy of courts.

Liberal Europe intoned Catherine's praises. The experienced traveler Archdeacon Coxe gave the reform his blessings: "By the new code this enormous power of the lords is reduced to restrictions more consonant to the humane principles which distinguish all the regulations

of the present empress. . . ." Closer scrutiny shows that "self-government" in Russia was still largely an empty phrase. Only the local gentry
were permitted to form assemblies for electoral purposes, so that in the
new local boards their representatives were greatly in the majority and
exercised preponderant influence. The administrative changes did not
in the slightest weaken their control over their serfs, for serf-lord relations were left untouched on the manorial estate. The innovations,
which gave the shadow of authority to the gentry, gave the substance
to the crown. Unable to deprive them of their formal exemption from
state service, Catherine transformed the squirearchy into administrative agents as Peter I had wished to do. The specialized functions once
executed by the abolished collegiate boards of St. Petersburg were now
to be carried out locally, where in fact they belonged. But by one device
or another the royal officials of the *Tchin,* who defended their own
vested interests in the administrative system, restricted the role of the
local officials to carrying out policies that were initiated centrally. The
reform, in brief, was excellent and long overdue, but neither the im-
provements of decentralization nor those of specialization of services
seriously interfered with the progress of Catherine's absolutist rule.

A decade later two edicts, issued simultaneously, gave legal recognition to the corporative existence and organization of the nobility and
the town citizens. The "Letters of Grace to the Nobility" of 1785
largely ratified an already existing state of affairs. This charter ex-
pressly reaffirmed the manifesto of 1762, which exempted noblemen
from military service. They retained their exemption from personal
taxation, corporal punishment, and the billeting of troops. They could
be tried only before their peers. Their peers alone, subject to royal
ratification, could deprive them either of their possessions or of their
position in the Table of Ranks. It gave them what their spokesmen
had asked for in the Commission: the legal recognition that "the estate
of the nobility be separated by its rights and privileges from the rest of
the people of other ranks and status."

The economic privileges threw a significant light upon Catherine's
conception of the new role that the great landowning aristocracy, together with the merchant capitalists, could play in developing industrial enterprise. They could own real estate in towns and cities, dispose
freely of the land which they possessed, and exploit the subsoil. They
were also given the exclusive right to set up factories and sink mines,
but shared the privilege of engaging in wholesale trade with the urban
bourgeoisie. In addition to reaffirming their privileges, the charter also
enumerated their responsibilities: to have their serfs discharge obliga-
tory military service and pay the poll tax. Retention of hereditary nobility and the privileges appertaining to it was made contingent upon
the loyal fulfillment of these auxiliary duties. Exactly like the Prussian
Junkers, the Russian gentry had become unpaid civil agents of the

crown on the manorial estate, rich in prerogatives and privileges and devoid of power to challenge the monarchy. Yet the arrangement was mutually satisfactory.

In the charter for the towns Catherine incorporated as much as she safely could afford of her views concerning the bourgeoisie without unduly antagonizing the gentry. She incorporated town inhabitants possessing the requisite minimum of real, commercial, or industrial property into a separate estate. They were exempted from military service, and they compounded for the poll tax by paying a small percentage of the capital invested in their business. They too obtained an illusory measure of self-government, but it was even less real than that held by the gentry, for the town council to which the propertied citizens elected representatives was narrowly hemmed in by the royal *gubernia* officials in financial matters and by the *ispravnik* in police affairs. By itself the town charter is unimpressive as an earnest of Catherine's policy of organizing and pitting the power of the bourgeoisie against the gentry. Together with measures more purely economic, however, it confirms the impression that she was relying increasingly upon merchant capitalists.

After a stormy and turbulent reign Catherine died peacefully in 1796. Her violent, hysterical outburst against the French Revolution was not the measure of her capacity. Her real greatness consisted in flouting the logic that she admired in the *philosophes,* in combining opposites and uniting contradictions. She concealed her courage transparently under her feminine guile. Her patience was not inferior to her sense of publicity. She did not indiscriminately make her lovers generals or ministers of state. The difficult situation that she inherited, she handled with the realistic flexibility of a masterly and not too scrupulous opportunist. Where administrative decentralization was needed, she relaxed the shadow if not the substance of governmental control. She insidiously transformed the gentry into unpaid governmental civil agents, but kept their loyalty by legalizing their patrimonial privileges. This strategy involved the sacrifice of the peasantry and doubtlessly ran counter to the better side of her nature, but she resigned herself to the sacrifice. Because she had intelligence and historical vision, she favored the growth of the commercial bourgeoisie, whom she linked in interest with the great landed aristocracy, while she pitted them simultaneously against the squirearchy, of whom she was an involuntary dependent. Like Peter I, to whose policy she returned in many essential respects, she made royal absolutism a cement at home, uniting her vast territories and disparate races, but a sword abroad, cutting Russia's way to stronger frontiers and new markets.

Wily and calculating, the tsarina of the nobility was a patriot queen, like Elizabeth of England, brooding over the destinies of her country. She was almost all things to all men, except to the peasantry, who constituted a mere 94 per cent of the population. To them she was a blight and a calamity. She served the old regime, and saved it by making concessions where the exercise of plenary absolutism was impossible. She adjusted the national economy to more modern needs, broke up the rigid social classifications, and made Russia safe for aristocracy for at least another century.

19

Billington: The Dilemma of a Reforming Despot[1]

Professor James H. Billington teaches History at Princeton University, and has been an exchange professor at the University of Moscow. In his brilliant history of Russian culture, The Icon and the Axe, *Professor Billington examines "the conflict between theoretical enlightenment and practical despotism," and evaluates the contributions of Catherine the Great.*

The reign of Catherine illustrates dramatically the conflict between theoretical enlightenment and practical despotism that bothered so many eighteenth-century European monarchs. Few other rulers of her time had such sweeping plans for reform and attracted so much adulation from the *philosophes,* yet few others were so poor in practical accomplishment. In her failure, however, she created the conditions for future change—posing vexing questions for the aristocracy while creating intolerable conditions for the peasantry. As the only articulate ideologist to rule Russia between Ivan IV and Lenin, she changed the terms of reference for Russian thought by linking Russian culture with that of France, and by attempting to base imperial authority on philosophic principles rather than hereditary right or religious sanction.

The attractions of France had, of course, been noticed earlier. Peter had visited the Sorbonne and sent three students to Paris for study in 1717. Kantemir and Tred'iakovsky both spent most of the thirties absorbing French culture in Paris. The former translated Molière and wrote independently in the manner of French satire; the latter, as secretary of the Academy of Sciences and court poet, began the wholesale introduction of Gallicisms into Russian speech. From the beginning, the uneasy aristocracy looked to French thought for philosophic guidance as well as forms of expression; and this philosophic thirst brought them into conflict with the guardians of Orthodoxy in the new state Church. Throughout Elizabeth's reign the Holy Synod made repeated

---

[1] From James H. Billington, *The Icon and the Axe: An Interpretive History of Russian Culture* (New York: Alfred A. Knopf, Inc., 1967), pp. 217–26. Copyright © 1968 by James H. Billington. Reprinted by permission of the publisher.

efforts to suppress Fontenelle's *Discourse on the Plurality of Worlds,* with its popularized image of an infinite universe.

Under Catherine, however, the stream became a flood. Fontenelle was freely published but hardly noticed. New books and ideas flowed in from France and were soon superseded by more daring and fashionable ones. The previous book was discarded before it had been used, like an unworn but suddenly outmoded hat. The first French thinker to enjoy popular vogue under Catherine was "the immortal Fénelon," whose poem *Télémaque* provided an exciting image of a utopian society and whose *Education of Girls* partly inspired Catherine's experiments in educating noble women. Fénelon was succeeded by Montesquieu, and Montesquieu by Voltaire—with each infatuation more intense than the last.

Francomania had an artificial and programmatic quality that did much to determine the character—or lack thereof—of aristocratic culture. Contact with France took place frequently through intermediaries. Catherine herself acquired her own taste for things French during her education in Germany; the first systematic Russian translations of French works were by the German "Normanist" Gerhard Friedrich Miller, in a Russian journal which was an imitation of German imitations of Addison and Steele; Molière reached Russia largely through Baltic intermediaries, and his influence on Russian satire of Catherine's day was mixed in with that of Ludvig Holberg, "the Danish Molière." The Russian word for "French" is derived from German, and the word for "Paris" from Italian.

If French culture often reached Russia through intermediaries, it was nonetheless generally viewed as a single, finished product to be rejected or accepted en block. Even more than in the original confrontation with the Byzantine, Russians sought to transplant French achievement without the critical spirit which had accompanied it. Catherine saw in the French Enlightenment the means of placing her rule on firm philosophic foundations and providing a national guide for the moral leadership of Europe. The Russian aristocracy used French culture to establish a common identity. The French tongue set them off from both the Russian- or Ukrainian-speaking peasantry and the German-, Swedish-, or Yiddish-speaking mercantile elements of the empire. Chateaux, parks, and theatrical productions provided a congenial and elegant place for leisured gatherings and communal functions and a relief from the austerities of long years of warfare.

Catherine described the purpose of her reign in one of her many philosophical parables: "the thornless rose that does not sting." The rose represents virtue which can be attained only by following the guide, reason, and avoiding the irrational temptations that try to impede this secular pilgrim's progress. Catherine saw no element of pain or unhappiness in true virtue which must naturally lead to "the heavenly city of the eighteenth century philosophers": the rule of justice and right reason.

Her self-confident optimism helped her to create, and forced her to confront, the dilemma of the reforming despot. This dilemma was also to haunt her grandson Alexander I and his grandson Alexander II, while his grandson Nicholas II was to flee in terror from even facing it. How can one retain absolute power and a hierarchical social system while at the same time introducing reforms and encouraging education? How can an absolute ruler hold out hope for improvement without confronting a "revolution of rising expectations"? The two Alexanders, like Catherine, were to find it necessary to check the liberality of their earlier years with despotic measures later. Each of them was to be succeeded by a despot who would seek to block all reform. But the Prussian methods of these successors—Paul, Nicholas I, and Alexander III—could not solve essential problems of state, and thus rendered the need for reform even more imperative. By frustrating moderate reformers, moreover, Paul, Nicholas I, and Alexander III strengthened the hand of extremists in the reformist camp and saddled their imperial successors with artificially pent-up and exaggerated expectations.

The scent of violence hovered about all these imperial reformers. Catherine and Alexander I had each come to power by encouraging the assassination of their predecessors and next of kin; Alexander II, whose reforms were the most far-reaching of all, was rewarded not with gratitude but assassination.

It was almost certainly fear which drove Catherine first to confront the dilemma of reforming despotism. Her position on the throne was initially little more secure than that of her recently murdered husband, Peter III. Threatened in particular by the plan of Nikita Panin to limit severely imperial authority by an aristocratic Imperial Council, Catherine turned in 1763 to the drawing up of a comprehensive defense of absolute monarchy. After three separate drafts, she submitted it to a specially convened legislative commission of 1766–7 which had a majority of non-aristocratic elements subject to her bidding. The commission unanimously awarded Catherine the title "Catherine the Great, Wise, Mother of the Fatherland" and arranged for the publication in Russian, German, French, and Latin of the final draft of her flowery philosophic defense of monarchy, generally known as the Instruction, or *Nakaz*.

Catherine and her successors paid a severe price, however, for this curious method of legitimizing usurpation. By undercutting the Panin proposals for bringing the aristocracy into the business of government, Catherine added to the already substantial sense of rootlessness which beset this class. The fact that she subsequently granted the aristocracy vast compensatory economic authority over their serfs and exemptions from government service only increased their capacity for idleness without increasing their sense of participation in affairs of state.

Even more important was the unsettling effect of justifying one's right to power on the totally new grounds of natural philosophy. Though the legislative commission did not in fact codify any laws, its detailed discussion and formal approval of Catherine's treatise helped put a large number of new and potentially subversive political ideas in circulation. According to the *Nakaz*, Russia was a European state, its subjects "citizens," and its proper laws those of the rational, natural order rather than the traditional historical one. Although the *Nakaz* was not widely distributed within Russia, the legislative commission was broad enough in its representation to carry its ideas to every social group in Russia except the bonded peasantry. With four out of 18 million Russians represented by the 564 deputies, the commission was the first crude attempt at a genuinely national assembly since the *zemsky sobors* of the early seventeenth century; but it was strikingly different from all previous assemblies ever held on Russian soil in that it was totally secular. There was one deputy from the Synod, but none at all from the clerical estate.

Catherine's basic idea of the "good" and "natural" encouraged scepticism not only toward revealed religion but toward traditional natural philosophy as well. Her "Instruction" directed men's thinking not to ultimate truths or ideal prototypes but to a new relativistic and utilitarian perspective. It seems altogether appropriate that Jeremy Bentham, the father of English utilitarianism, was one of the most honored of foreign visitors to Catherine's Russia; and that translated books of and about Bentham in Russia soon began to outsell the original editions in England.

Like a true utilitarian, Catherine defined legislation as "the Art of conducting People to the greatest Good," which is "whatever may be useful to mankind" in a given tradition and environment. Autocracy must rule through intermediary powers and clear laws, which require that the individual "be fully convinced that it was his Interest, as well as Duty, to preserve those Laws inviolable." The French monarchy rightly appraised the subversive implications of such an approach to the justification of authority, confiscating some two thousand copies en route to France in 1771, and preventing any of the twenty-four foreign versions of the work from being printed there.

Catherine admired not only Bentham but his adversary, Blackstone, whose *Commentaries* she carefully studied and had translated in three volumes. She was widely admired not only in England but also in Italy, where a vast treatise was dedicated to her in 1778, celebrating the victorious alliance of power and reason in the eighteenth century. Nearly one sixth of the articles in Catherine's *Nakaz* were taken directly from the work of another Italian, Beccaria's *On Crimes and Punishment*, which armed Catherine with her conviction that crime comes from ignorance and poor laws, and punishment should be precise and pedagogic rather than arbitrary and vindictive.

But it was always with the French that Catherine felt the greatest kinship. Commenting on the new alliance with France in 1756 just after it was concluded and well before her own accession to the throne, Catherine wrote that "if the gain is not great in commerce, we shall compensate ourselves with bales of intelligence."

The bales had already begun to arrive with the first appearance of a French-language journal on Russian soil in 1755, and with the unprecedented sale of three thousand copies of Voltaire's *Philosophy of History* in St. Petersburg alone within a few days of its appearance in 1756.

Voltaire soon became the official historian of the Russian Empire and a kind of patron saint for the secular aristocracy. The many-sided French Enlightenment was thought to be all of a piece, with Voltaire at its center. Friend and foe alike spoke of *Vol'ter'ianstvo* ("Voltairianism") as the ruling force in Western culture, just as they had spoken of *Latinstvo* ("Latinism") in the fifteenth century. With Catherine's active encouragement, much of the Russian aristocracy became enamored with Voltairianism, which had the general meaning of rationalism, scepticism, and a vague passion for reform. In the first year of her reign, at the age of 34, she opened a correspondence with Voltaire, who was nearly 70. Almost all of the sixty-odd separate works of Voltaire translated into Russian in the last third of the eighteenth century appeared during Catherine's reign. At least 140 printed translations of Voltaire's works were published in the course of the aristocratic century; numerous abstracts and handwritten copies were made; and no aristocratic library was thought complete if it did not contain a substantial collection of his works in the original French. The name of Voltaire was enthroned literally as well as figuratively; for the new high-backed, thin-armed easy chair in which Russian aristocrats seated themselves for after-dinner conversation was modeled on that on which Voltaire was often depicted sitting, and is known even today as a *Vol'terovskoe kreslo* or "Voltaire chair."

If Voltaire was the symbol, the Gallicized German Friedrich Grimm was the major source of information for Catherine's court. He supplemented his famed literary newsletter on the intellectual life of the salons with a voluminous correspondence with the Empress, who showered him with many favors, including eventual appointment as her minister in Hamburg. Grimm became a kind of public relations man for Catherine, and was probably only partly jesting when he rephrased the Lord's prayer to read "Our mother, who art in Russia . . ."; changed the Creed into "I believe in one Catherine . . .";

and set a "Te Catherinam Laudamus" to the music of Paisiello. Voltaire avoided distinctively Christian terminology, addressing Catherine as "a priest in your temple," confessing that "there is no God but Allah, and Catherine is the prophet of Allah." Only a more systematic materialist like Helvetius was able to refrain from theistic references altogether, dedicating his last great work, *On Man, His Intellectual Faculties and His Education*, to her as a "bulwark against 'Asiatic despotism,' worthy by her intelligence of judging old nations as she is worthy of governing her own."

On this all-important question of government, Catherine was most indebted to Montesquieu. His mighty *Spirit of the Laws* was both the final product of a lifetime of urbane reflection and the opening salvo in the "war of ideas" against the old order in France. Within eighteen months of its first appearance in 1748, Montesquieu's work had gone through twenty-two editions, and infected previously untouched segments of society with its ranging curiosity about politics, its descriptive and comparative approach, and its underlying determination to prevent arbitrary and despotic rule.

All these features of Montesquieu's work appealed to the young empress as she sought to fortify herself for combat against the political chaos and religious mystique of Old Russia. Her attitude upon assuming power was that of one of her generals, who satirically remarked that the government of Russia must indeed be directed "by God himself— otherwise it is impossible to explain how it is even able to exist." Her *Nakaz* sought to introduce rational order into the political life of the Empire, and Montesquieu was her major source of inspiration. She set aside three hours each day for reading the master, referred to his *Spirit of the Laws* as her "prayer book," and derived nearly half of the articles in the *Nakaz* from his works.

To be sure, Catherine's entire effort went against Montesquieu's own assumption that Russia was foredoomed by its size and heritage to despotic rule; and she distorted or neglected some of his most celebrated ideas. Montesquieu's aristocratic "intermediary bodies" between the monarch and his subjects served not, in Catherine's proposal, to separate power between executive, legislative, and judicial functions but rather to consolidate government functions and create new lines of transmission for imperial authority.

Nevertheless, Catherine was closer to the spirit of Montesquieu's politics than many who followed him more literally on specific points. Her effort to make monarchy unlimited yet fully rational; her sense of adjusting political forms to environmental necessities; her increasing recognition of the need for active aristocratic support so that the spirit of honor could be enlisted to support the rule of reason—all of this was clearly in the spirit of the man who did so much to turn men's eyes away from the letter to the spirit of law.

If the *Spirit of the Laws* provided Catherine with the image of rationally ordered politics, the *Encyclopedia* of Diderot and D'Alembert, which began to appear three years later in 1751, provided the image of rationally ordered knowledge. Her enthusiasm for this work soon rivaled her passion for Montesquieu. D'Alembert declined Catherine's invitation to serve as tutor to her son; but Diderot considered transferring the editorial side of his work to Riga, and eventually sold his library to Catherine and came to St. Petersburg. Three volumes of the *Encyclopedia* had been translated almost immediately into Russian under the supervision of the director of Moscow University. A private translation was concurrently being made by the future historian Ivan Boltin, and many articles and sections were translated individually.

For the rational ordering of economic life, Catherine turned first (at Diderot's suggestion) to the French physiocrat, Lemercier de la Rivière; then, following his unhappy visit to Russia, she sent two professors from Moscow to study under Adam Smith in Glasgow. Her most original approach was the founding in 1765 of a Free Economic Society for the Encouragement in Russia of Agriculture and Household Management: a kind of extra-governmental advisory body. Two years later she offered one thousand gold pieces for the best set of recommendations on how to organize an agricultural economy "for the common good." The society received 164 entries in this remarkable Europe-wide contest, with the greatest response and the prize-winning essay coming from France.

In practice, however, there was no reorganization of agriculture, just as there was no new law code or synthesis of knowledge. The shock caused by the Pugachev uprising put an end to the languishing legislative commission and to the various efforts to make the *Encyclopedia* the basis for widespread public enlightenment. Boltin's translation died at the letter "K"—the first of the host of uncompleted reference books with which Russian history is so tragically full.

Yet even while Catherine was preparing Pugachev for quartering, she continued to correspond with the Corsican revolutionary Paoli (and another restless Corsican, the then obscure Napoleon Bonaparte considered entering her service).

Only after the French Revolution did Catherine's thoughts turn away from reform altogether to a final assertion of unleavened despotism. Even then she bequeathed the dilemma to Alexander I by assigning to him the Swiss republican La Harpe as a tutor and by surrounding him with an aristocratic entourage of Anglophile liberals. Alexander I in turn infected Alexander II with the same dangerous taste for partial reform by appointing a friend from his own liberal days, Michael Speransky, as one of the tutors of the future "tsar-liberator."

At the end of her long trail of literary and literal seductions, Catherine left aristocratic Russia stimulated, but in no way satisfied. By sending most of the aristocratic elite abroad for education, she imparted a vague sense of possibility, a determination to "overtake and surpass," the Enlightenment of the West. Yet the actual reforms accomplished in her reign were too meager even to provide clear guidance toward this goal. From Catherine, aristocratic thinkers received only their inclination to look Westward for answers. They learned to think in terms of sweeping reforms on abstract, rationalistic grounds rather than piecemeal changes rooted in concrete conditions and traditions.

Particularly popular under Catherine was the vague idea that newly conquered regions to the south could provide virgin soil on which to raise out of nothing a new civilization. Voltaire told Catherine that he would come to Russia if Kiev were made the capital rather than St. Petersburg. Herder's earliest dream of earthly glory was to be "a new Luther and Solon" for the Ukraine: to make this unspoiled and fertile region into "a new Greece." Bernardin de Saint-Pierre believed that an egalitarian agricultural community, possibly even a new Pennsylvania, might be created in the region around the Aral Sea. Catherine herself dreamed of making her new city below Kiev on the Dnieper, Ekaterino-slav ("Praise Catherine"), a monumental center for world culture and her newly conquered port on the Black Sea, Kherson, a new St. Petersburg.

Rather than come to grips with the concrete problems of her realm, Catherine became infatuated in her declining years with her "grand design" for taking Constantinople and dividing the Balkans with the Hapsburg emperor. She named her second grandson Constantine, placed the image of the Santa Sophia on her coins, and wrote a dramatic extravaganza, *The First Government of Oleg*, which ends with this early Russian conqueror-prince leaving his shield behind in Constantinople for future generations to reclaim.

Having subdued at last the entire northern coast of the Black Sea, Catherine adorned it with a string of new cities—often on the site of old Greek settlements—Azov, Taganrog, Nikolaev, Odessa, and Sevastopol. The latter, built as a fortress on the southwest corner of the Crimean peninsula, was given the Greek version of the Roman imperial title *Augusta*. Built by an English naval engineer, Samuel Bentham, the "august city" (*sevastē polis*) inspired nothing original except for the eerie plan of Samuel's famous brother Jeremy for a panopticon: a prison in which a central observer could peer into all cells. Sevastopol is remembered not for the awe it inspired but for the humiliation it brought to Russia when captured by British and French invaders during the Crimean War. More than any other single event, the fall of the "august city" in 1855 dispelled illusion and forced Russia to turn from external glory to internal reform.

But external glory preoccupied Catherine during the latter part of her reign. Her world of illusion is symbolized by the famed legend that portable "Potemkin villages" were devised by her most famous courtier to camouflage the misery of the people from her eyes during triumphal tours. She spent her last years (and almost her last rubles) building pretentious palaces for her favorites, foreign advisers and relatives: Tauride in St. Petersburg and nearby Gatchina and Tsarskoe Selo (which she intended to name Constantingorod). The costumes and sets were more impressive than the actual plays in Catherine's theater. She expressed a preference for extended *divertissements,* and insisted that serious operas be cut from three acts to two. It seems strangely appropriate that four different versions of the Pygmalion story were staged during the reign of Catherine. This minor German princess had been transformed into a northern goddess by the sages of the eighteenth century; but in this case the reality was less impressive than the figure on the pedestal. Even today the monument to her in front of the former imperial (now Saltykov-Shchedrin) library in Leningrad still is usually seen rising up from a sea of mud. Her every movement was surrounded with cosmetic camouflage and rococo frills. In an age when cutout silhouettes and surface flourishes were in vogue throughout Europe, Catherine brought the silhouette without the substance of reform to Russia. As a final monument to her vanity, she left behind five feast days consecrated to her alone on the church calendar: her birthday, day of succession to the throne, day of coronation, name day, and the day of her smallpox vaccination, November 21.

Catherine's turn from inner reform to external aggrandizement is dramatically illustrated by the three-sided and three-staged dismemberment of Poland. Having helped place her youthful friend and lover, Stanislaw Poniatowski, on the Polish throne in 1764, Catherine participated in the first partition of Poland in 1772; then took the lead in the last two, which followed Stanislaw's adoption in 1791 of a reform constitution not dissimilar to those which Catherine had considered in earlier days. The absorption of Poland had, however, the ironic effect of helping to perpetuate the very tradition that Catherine was rejecting. For Stanislaw promptly moved to St. Petersburg along with his relatives, the Czartoryski family, and many other reform-minded survivors of the old Polish republic.

Catherine's first grandson, Alexander, resembled less the Macedonian conqueror for whom he was named than the Polish visionaries whom he met in his youth. Her second grandson, Constantine, became the rallying point for the reformist elements in the guards regiments who assembled in Senate Square in St. Petersburg on December 14, 1825, after Alexander's death. But these "Decembrists" related the name Constantine not to Constantinople but to constitution—some of their illiterate followers even believing that the Russian word *konstitutsiia* was the name of his wife. The Decembrists were calling not for an imperial commander but for a man who had become the governor of

Poland and was thought to provide some kind of link with its more moderate reformist traditions. To understand why these moderate constitutionalists were crushed, and the dilemma of the reforming despot firmly resolved in favor of despotism under Nicholas I, one must turn from symbols and omens to the crucial substantive changes which were effected in the direction of Russian thought under Catherine.

Bibliographical Note

Those interested in pursuing an examination of the life and times of Catherine the Great will be impressed by the multitude of volumes on her life and depressed by the value of most. Older biographies include Kasimir Waliszewski, *The Romance of an Empress* (New York, 1905), and William Tooke, *Life of Catherine II, Empress of All the Russias* (London, 1802). More recent works are K. S. Anthony, *Catherine the Great* (Garden City, N. Y., 1925); E. A. B. Hodgetts, *Life of Catherine the Great of Russia* (New York, 1941); Gina Kaus, *Catherine, Portrait of an Empress* (New York, 1935); Ian Grey, *Catherine the Great* (New York, 1962); Gladys S. Thompson, *Catherine the Great and the Expansion of Russia* (New York, 1950), and Zoé Oldenburg, *Catherine the Great* (New York, 1965). Catherine's early years in Russia can be followed in R. N. Bain, *Daughter of Peter the Great* (New York, 1900), and R. N. Bain, *Peter III: Emperor of Russia* (New York, 1902). Biographies in Russian include the twelve volume work of Bilbasov, *Istoria Ekaterina Vtoroi* (Saint Petersburg, 1885); and the five volume study of A. Bruckner, *Istoriia Ekaterina Vtoroi* (Saint Petersburg, 1885).

It is relatively easy to obtain materials produced by the Empress herself. Her *Memoirs* are available in the original French, as well as a wealth of other materials, in A. N. Pypin, ed., *Sochineniia Imperatritsy Ekateriny II* (Saint Petersburg, 1906, Volume 12); the *Memoirs* are available in English, edited by Alexander Herzen (London, 1859), K. S. Anthony (New York, 1927), and Dominique Maroger (New York, 1955). Also available are W. F. Reddaway, ed., *Documents of Catherine the Great* (New York, 1931), and *Correspondence of Catherine the Great While Grand Duchess with Sir Charles Hanbury-Williams* (London, 1928). Catherine's correspondence with the great names of the Enlightenment is readily available in editions of the collected works of Voltaire, Diderot, Grimm, etc. A fine selection of Catherine's own literary attempts are provided in Volume II of Harold B. Segel, ed., *The Literature of Eighteenth Century Russia: A History and an Anthology* (New York, 1967). Official decrees are contained in G. N. Shmelev, ed., *Tsarstvovaniia Ekateriny II* (Saint Petersburg, 1907).

Specialized studies include biographies of Catherine's marshals, favorites and enemies, such as W. L. Blease, *Suvorov* (London, 1920); L. M. P. de Laverne, *The Life of Field Marshal Suvorof* (Baltimore, Md., 1814); Frank A. Golder, *John Paul Jones in Russia* (Garden City, N.Y., 1927); Philip Longworth, *The Art of Victory: The Life and Achievements of Field Marshal Suvorov, 1729–1800* (New York, 1965); George Soloveytchik, *Potemkin* (New York, 1947); A. McConnell, *A Russian Radical: Alexander Radishchev* (The Hague, 1964); D. M. Lang, *The First Russian Radical, Alexander Radishchev, 1749–1802* (London, 1959).

Cultural and intellectual developments can be followed in Hans Rogger, *National Consciousness in Eighteenth Century Russia* (Cambridge, Mass., 1960); S. R. Tompkins, *The Russian Mind From Peter the Great Through the Enlightenment* (Norman, Oklahoma, 1953); Alexander Vucinich, *Science in Russian Culture* (Stamford, 1963); Marc Raeff, *The Origins of the Russian Intelligentsia* (New York, 1966); Marc Raeff, ed., *Russian Intellectual History: An Anthology* (New York, 1966); S. V. Utechin, *Russian Political Thought* (New York, 1964); N. Hans, *History of Russian Educational Policy, 1701–1917* (London, 1931); Anatole Mazour, *Modern Russian Historiography* (Princeton, 1958); Dmitri von Mohrenschildt, *Russia in the Intellectual Life of Eighteenth Century France* (New York, 1936); M. S. Anderson, *Britain's Discovery of Russia, 1553–1815* (London, 1958); and Paul Miliukov, *Outlines of Russian Culture* (New York, 1960), with volumes on literature, religion and art. There is also an annotated bibliography of English language accounts by travellers since the ninth century in Harry W. Nerhood, *To Russia and Return* (Columbus, Ohio, 1968).

Economic problems can be examined in Jerome Blum, *Lord and Peasant in Russia From the Ninth to the Nineteenth Century* (Princeton, N.J., 1961); Clifford M. Foust, *Muscovite and Mandarin* (Chapel Hiill, N.C., 1969); Walther Kirchner, *Commercial Relations Between Russia and Europe, 1400–1800* (Bloomington, Indiana, 1966); P. I. Lyashchenko, *History of the National Economy of the USSR to the 1917 Revolution* (New York, 1949); and John Letiche, ed. and trans., *A History of Russian Economic Thought* (Berkeley, 1964).

Political developments are covered in Alan W. Fisher, *The Russian Annexation of the Crimea, 1772–1783* (Cambridge, Eng., 1970); Isabel de Madariaga, *Britain, Russia and the Armed Neutrality of 1780* (London, 1962); Herbert H. Kaplan, *The First Partition of Poland* (New York, 1962); Herbert H. Kaplan, *Russia and the Outbreak of the Seven Years' War* (Berkeley, 1968); L. Jay Oliva, *Misalliance: A Study of French Policy in Russia During the Seven Years' War* (New York, 1964); John T. Alexander, *Autocratic Politics in a National Crisis: The Imperial Russian Government and Pugachev's Revolt, 1773–1775* (Bloomington, Indiana, 1969); R. H. Lord, *The Second Partition of Poland* (Cambridge, Mass., 1915); Albert Sorel, *The Eastern Question in the Eighteenth Century* (New York, 1969, reprint).

Recent periodical literature includes Arcadius Kahan, "The Costs of Westernization in Russia: The Gentry and the Economy in the Eighteenth Century," *Slavic Review* (March 1966), pp. 40–65; Alan Fisher, "Enlightened Despotism and Islam Under Catherine II," *Slavic Review,* (December 1968), pp. 542–53; David M. Griffiths, "Nikita Panin, Russian Diplomacy, and the American Revolution," *Slavic Review* (March 1969), pp. 1–24; and Marc Raeff, "The Domestic Policies of Peter III and His Overthrow," *American Historical Review* (June 1970), pp. 1289–1310. The Fall 1970, issue of *Canadian Slavic Studies* will be devoted to Catherine's reign.

There are a number of collections of articles and original materials now available, including Ivo Lederer, ed., *Russian Foreign Policy* (New

Haven, 1962); Sidney Harcave, *Readings in Russian History*, Volume I (New York, 1962); Marthe Blinoff, ed., *Life and Thought in Old Russia* (University Park, Pa., 1961); Basil Dmytryshyn, ed., *Modern Russia: A Source Book* (New York, 1967); L. Jay Oliva, ed., *Russia and the West From Peter to Khrushchev* (Boston, 1965); Warren B. Walsh, ed., *Readings in Russian History* (Syracuse, 1963); Alfred F. Senn, ed., *Readings in Russian Political and Diplomatic History* (Homewood, Ill., 1966); Hans Kohn, ed., *The Mind of Modern Russia* (New York, 1962); George Alexander Lensen, ed., *Russia's Eastward Expansion* (Englewood Cliffs, N.J., 1964).

Index